Uganda's Katikiro in England
by Ham Mukasa

MANCHESTER
UNIVERSITY PRESS

Exploring Travel

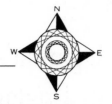

Series editors   Sara Mills and Jill LeBihan

Exploring Travel is a publishing initiative which makes accessible travel writing which may be out of print or difficult to obtain. Travel literature currently has enormous popular appeal, and there is widespread academic interest from a number of fields, including anthropology, colonial and post-colonial discourse theory, literary theory, history, geography and women's studies.

The series has two main aims. The first is to make available a number of key, edited texts, which will be invaluable to both the academic and general reader. The texts will be edited by scholars from a range of disciplines, and a full introduction to each edition will aim to set it within its socio-cultural context, and explain its literary and historical importance. The second aim of the series is to make available monographs and collections of critical essays on the analysis of travel writing. In this way, the *Exploring Travel* series aims to broaden perspectives on travel writing and the theoretical models used for its analysis.

Already published:

Tracey Jean Boisseau *Sultan to sultan: adventures among the Masai and other tribes of East Africa, by M. French-Sheldon, 'Bébé Bwana'*
Neil L. Whitehead *The discoverie of the large, rich and bewtiful empyre of Guiana, by Sir Walter Ralegh*

Forthcoming titles:

Amanda Gilroy *Ramantic geographies: discourses of travel, 1775–1844*
Sara Mills and Shirley Foster *Women's travel writing: an anthology*
Sara Mills and Indira Ghose *Wanderings of a pilgrim in search of the picturesque, by Fanny Parks*

Uganda's Katikiro in England

by Ham Mukasa

With notes and an introduction by

Simon Gikandi

Manchester University Press

Manchester and New York

distributed exclusively in the USA by St. Martin's Press

Published by Manchester University Press
Oxford Road, Manchester M13 9NR, UK
and Room 400, 175 Fifth Avenue, New York, NY 10010, USA

Distributed exclusively in the USA by
St. Martin's Press, Inc., 175 Fifth Avenue, New York,
NY 10010, USA

Distributed exclusively in Canada by
UBC Press, University of British Columbia, 6344 Memorial Road,
Vancouver, BC, Canada V6T 1Z2

British Library Cataloguing-in-Publication Data
A catalogue record for this book is available from the British Library

Library of Congress Cataloging-in-Publication Data applied for

ISBN 0 7190 4898 2 *hardback*
　　　0 7190 5437 0 *paperback*

First published 1998

05 04 03 02 01 00 99 98 10 9 8 7 6 5 4 3 2 1

Typeset in 10 on 12pt Adobe Garamond
by Best-set Typesetter Ltd., Hong Kong
Printed in Great Britain
by Bell & Bain Ltd, Glasgow

Contents

Illustrations

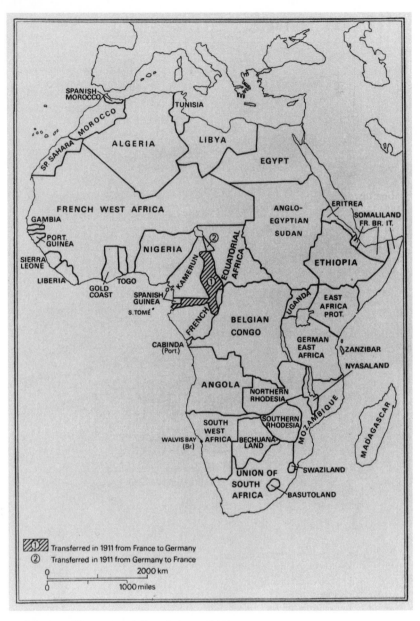

Map 1 *Africa in 1914 (from Roberts, 1990).*

Key within image:

Transferred in 1911 from France to Germany
Transferred in 1911 from Germany to France

0   2000 km
0   1000 miles

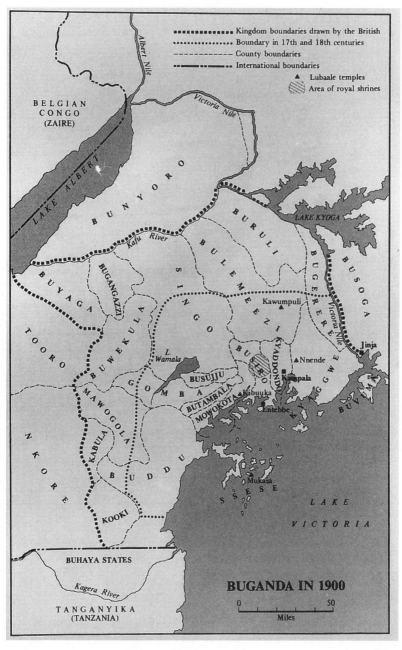

Map 2 *Buganda in 1900. The kingdom's boundaries were expanded considerably under British colonial rule (from Ray, 1991).*

Chronology of [B]Uganda

This chronology is adapted from Pirouet (1995). A comprehensive historical background can be found in the works by Kiwanuka (1971), Low (1971), Ray (1991) and Twaddle (1993).

The principal events of Sir Apolo Kagwa's and Ham Mukasa's lives are in bold.

1200–1500	The kingdom of Buganda is established.
1840s	Swahili-speaking Muslim traders from the East African coast reach Buganda.
1850s	Swahili traders establish a base in the Bugandan court.
1862	John Hanning Speke is received in Kabaka Mutesa's court and 'discovers' the source of the Nile.
1865	**Apolo Kagwa is born in a household of chiefs.**
1871	**Ham Mukasa is born in a chief's household.**
1875	Henry Morton Stanley is received in Mutesa's court and sends a letter to the *Daily Telegraph* appealing for British missionaries to be sent to Uganda.
1876	Mutesa orders the massacre of Bugandan Muslims.
1877	Missionaries of the (Anglican) Church Missionary Society (CMS) arrive in Buganda.
1879	French (Roman) Catholic White Fathers arrive in Buganda from North Africa.
1884	Mutesa I dies and is succeeded by his son, Mwanga. **Apolo Kagwa is baptised by CMS missionaries.**
1885	Mwanga orders the murder of Bishop Hannington (CMS); the first Bugandan Christians are also killed. **Ham Mukasa is converted to Christianity by the CMS.**

1886   Killing of Christian converts continues.

1887   **Apolo Kagwa is appointed keeper of Royal Stores. He becomes head of Protestant converts in the Bugandan court. He is also made a chief.**

1888   The struggle for power in Buganda begins. Mwanga is forced into exile after a coup by Muslims in his court. He is replaced by Kiwewa who is in turn replaced by Kalema. **Apolo Kagwa is exiled to Ankole.**

1889   Mwanga is reinstated as Kabaka by a faction of Christian chiefs, led by Apolo Kagwa, but with restricted power and functions. **Apolo Kagwa is appointed Katikiro (chief minister) of Buganda.**

1890   Captain Frederick Lugard of the Imperial British East Africa Company (IBEAC) arrives in Uganda.

1892   Fighting occurs between Protestant and Catholic factions around Mengo. Protestant forces (again led by Apolo Kagwa) triumph with support from Lugard.

1894   Uganda is declared a British Protectorate.

1897   Mwanga rebels against British rule, but is defeated by an alliance of Christian chiefs and pages.

1899   Mwanga is captured and exiled to the Seychelles. His infant son, Daudi Chwa, is installed as Kabaka under the regency of three senior chiefs. **Apolo Kagwa becomes chief regent.**

1900   The [B]Uganda Agreement is concluded. Sir Apolo Kagwa is the major signatory on behalf of Buganda. **Apolo Kagwa publishes *Basekabaka be Buganda* (The Kings of the Buganda). Ham Mukasa publishes a commentary on the Gospel According to St Matthew in Luganda.**

1901   The Uganda Railway (from Mombasa) reaches Kisumu (Port Florence).

1902   **Apolo Kagwa and Ham Mukasa travel to England to attend the coronation of Edward VII. Kagwa is knighted by the king.**

1903   Coffee is first exported.

1904	Cotton is introduced. **Ham Mukasa's *Uganda's Katikiro in England* is published by Hutchinson and Co.**
1905	**Ham Mukasa becomes a Saza (county) chief.**
1906	Three major educational institutions are established in Buganda: King's College, Budo, Gayaza High School and St Mary's College, Kisubi.
1913	**Ham Mukasa accompanies Kabaka Daudi Chwa on a visit to Britain.**
1914	Outbreak of World War I. Ugandans are recruited to fight the Germans in Tanganyika. Kabaka Daudi Chwa comes of age. **Sir Apolo Kagwa loses many of the powers previously invested in him as regent.**
1918	World War I ends.
1925	**Sir Apolo Kagwa is forced to resign as Katikiro of Buganda.**
1926	**Sir Apolo Kagwa dies.**
1931	The Uganda Railway reaches Kampala.
1939	Outbreak of World War II.
1944	Africans begin to demand greater representation in the Legislative Council.
1945	World War II ends in Europe.
1948	Uganda Electricity Board is established.
1950	Makerere College is established as a University College affiliated with the University of London.
1953	Sir Edward Mutesa II, Kabaka of Buganda, is exiled for refusing to cooperate with the colonial government.
1955	Mutesa II returns to Buganda.
1956	**Ham Mukasa dies.**
1960	Buganda declares itself independent from the British Protectorate, outside Uganda. The declaration is ignored by the Protectorate Government.
1961	Buganda boycotts national elections.

1962   Uganda becomes independent.

1963   Kabaka Mutesa II becomes president of the whole of Uganda.

1966   The independence constitution is suspended; a new national constitution denies Buganda special privileges. Following the battle at Mengo between Bugandan and Ugandan forces, a state of emergency is declared in Buganda. Kabaka Mutesa II escapes to Britain.

1967   Kingdoms are abolished in Uganda.

1969   Kabaka Mutesa II dies in exile in Britain.

Acknowledgements

In preparing this work I have incurred many intellectual and personal debts and I would like to acknowledge them here. My understanding of the history of Buganda and the lifes and times of Sir Apolo Kagwa and Ham Mukasa could have been limited without the works of four great historians of Buganda: M.S.M. Kiwanuka, D.A. Low, Benjamin Ray, and Michael Twaddle. David William Cohen's works (and our occasional conversations) have made me aware of the problems of temporality and colonialism in the history and anthropology of East Africa. I owe a great debt to Taban Lo Liyong who was the first to recognise the intellectual influence of Ham Mukasa and Sir Apolo, and to my colleague Lemuel Johnson for challenging me to rethink what it means to be an African in the West. Many conversations with Abiola Irele have left their imprint on my understanding of colonial culture and the African problematic. Sara Mills provided insightful comments on the introduction and provided general editorial support, as did the staff at Manchester University Press, namely, Matthew Frost, Stephanie Sloan, Gemma Marren, and Rachel Armstrong. Finally, I could not have undertaken this project without the support of Tim Youngs. He was the first scholar of travel narratives to recognise the significance of this work in the corpus of colonial literature and I thank him for his initiative in getting this project commissioned. As always, my wife and children have provided the necessary distraction from things abstract.

Part 1

Introduction

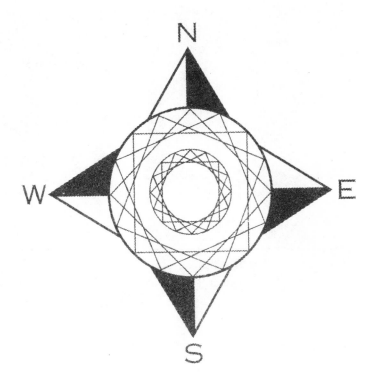

Plate 1 *Ham Mukasa and Sir Apolo Kagwa during their 1902 visit to England. This photograph was taken in a Bond Street studio.*

African subjects and the colonial project

I

In 1902, Sir Apolo Kagwa, the Katikiro (chief minister) and Principal Regent of the kingdom of Buganda, arrived in England for the coronation of Edward VII. The coronation of Edward VII may have been a familiar regal event for British subjects, but for many members of the colonised elite, such as Sir Apolo, this event was a turning point in the transformation of colonial relationships. It marked the end of the long reign of Queen Victoria – the powerful symbol of British imperialism – and the beginning of an era of uncertainty and crisis in the culture of colonialism. Sir Apolo was accompanied on the journey by two men who were influential in the mapping of Britain's relationship with Buganda within a colonial arrangement in which the latter was protected by the former: the Reverend Ernest Millar, an Anglican clergyman based in Uganda, who was to act as guide and translator, and Ham Mukasa, the Katikiro's secretary, who was charged with taking notes and eventually writing *Uganda's Katikiro in England* (1904). Although they did not know it, the Africans were travelling in a country that was increasingly being defined by a sense of cultural decline and moral crisis. The Edwardian era, whose inauguration they had gone to witness, was not the new beginning it pretended to be; the monarch who was taking over was old and sickly, an appropriate symbol of the state of the imperial domain he had inherited from his mother. But for the colonised elite, the encounter with Britain was nothing less than a moment of cultural apotheosis, of their arrival on the scene of the modernity which colonialism had promised them when, in their youth, they had converted to Christianity and embraced the culture of Englishness.

To read *Uganda's Katikiro in England* from the vantage point of the success and failure of the colonial project, then, is to confront a series of questions that are central to understanding the nature of colonialism and postcolonial studies. How was Britain represented in the writings of its colonial subjects? What was the role of colonial subjects, especially those who posited themselves as translators of the metropolitan 'centre' to the colonial 'periphery', in the shaping of the culture of colonialism? Did narratives of travel into the heart of the colonising culture follow the same conventions as the dominant writings of European missionaries, explorers and conquerors? Can we have a complete history of the colonial project without the inclusion of the writings and subject positions of minor colonial writers such as Ham Mukasa and Sir Apolo Kagwa?[1] (See Pratt, 1992: 7; Adorno, 1996: 33.)

For Sir Apolo and Mukasa, the journey to Britain was an important form of discovery, but not exactly in the terms we have come to expect from the imperial travellers – most notably Richard Burton, John Huntington Speke and Henry Morton Stanley – whose arrival in the kingdom of Buganda and 'discovery' of the source of the Nile has provided many scholars with the paradigms that define the nature of travel narratives in the colonial economy of representation.[2] Imperial travellers, as Mary Louis Pratt has observed, produced narratives whose epistemological authority was derived from their association 'with European forms and relations of power', an authority which found its form, as it were, in the heroic dimension implicit in the act of discovery (Pratt, 1992: 203). Imperial travel writing could hence be considered the process by which difficult and dangerous ordeals could be transformed into what Pratt calls 'heroic narratives' (Pratt, 1992: 204). It was in their performance of the heroic that European travellers would inscribe their masculinist conquest and containment of the colonial space (Dawson, 1994; Phillips, 1997).

One might assume that because he was a colonial subject, Mukasa could not position himself as a conqueror or adventurer in Britain; and since he had not read the narratives of travel, he could not possibly have appropriated their conventions. But the question of his position in the colonial economy of representation and his relationship to imperial texts is more complicated. Mukasa was familiar with heroic imperial narratives, narratives of conquest and the overcoming of difficulty, not simply because of the British colonial influence in his country, but also because Buganda was itself an imperial force in Eastern Africa, trying to expand its powers even as it was being drawn into the orbit of British colonialism (Kiwanuka, 1971: 154–88). Mukasa did not write a narrative to master Britain in the same way Richard Burton and John Huntington Speke had set out to master Buganda, but he was familiar with narratives of conquest and rule from his own tradition. Given his own subject position in the colonial project, Mukasa could not conceivably see his work as an instrument of Bugandan power over Britain, but he understood the significance of narratives and discourses in the colonial relationship and their capacity to consolidate modes of domination (Mill, 1994: 29–51; Richards, 1994). At the same time, however, colonial subjects like Mukasa could not produce a narrative of power without an awareness of their precarious identity in the imperial space.

For this reason, it is important to read Mukasa's narrative as a work conceived – perhaps unconsciously – as a measured attempt, by a colonised subject and his mentor, to emplace themselves within the cultural and political economy of Englishness and to turn their colonisation into a source of moral, cultural and political authority. Thus, while traditional (imperial) travel narratives often valorised racial and cultural difference as the condition of possibility of a European identity, Mukasa and Sir Apolo strove to establish connections with the British polis even in the face of obvious racial and cultural difficulties. As even a cursory reading of Mukasa's book will show, the African travellers sought to present both their colonial and Bugandan heritages as sources of cultural authority, one derived from Christianity and literacy, the other from custom and tradition. They went out of their way to abrogate any cultural capital they might derive from their racial difference or the exoticism which the British people who flocked to see them expected.

Mukasa's narrative would thus seem to call into question many of the ideological and discursive conventions which we have come to expect from the literature of travel in the culture of colonialism. It does not seem to want to produce a knowledge of Britain as the radical other. As we shall see in detail below, Britain is conceived as different from Buganda, but this difference is presented as transient, one which the African subject will overcome through education and modernisation. Britain is presented as the depository of modern knowledge, but this knowledge is one that incorporates colonial spaces and thus makes colonial subjects entitled to its authority and dissemination. Mukasa marvels at Britain, but he does not seek to inscribe an unbridgeable temporal distance between Africa and Europe. Indeed, his major claim in his book is that overcoming difference is the inevitable condition of establishing a modern African identity.

Mukasa's text seems oblivious to the imperial travel narratives of its time in another important respect: it is totally uninterested in natural history and topography; it even effaces the presence of the writing subject in order to foreground the material objects and conditions which constitute modern Englishness. And yet, in many ways, we cannot read Mukasa's text without sensing how it occupies – and even contests – the same cultural space as imperial texts such as Richard Burton's *Lake Regions of Central Africa* (1860), John Speke's *Journal of the Discovery of the Source of the Nile* (1864) and Henry Morton Stanley's *In Darkest Africa* (1890). Indeed, I want to argue that the historical and cultural significance of Mukasa's text is to be found in its ambiguous location inside and outside the literature of travel in the Western tradition.

There is no better way of making this point than by comparing the climactic moment in Mukasa's text (the meeting with King Edward VII) with a similar – and perhaps precursory – moment in Speke's journal, his encounter with Kabaka Mutesa of Buganda, surely one of the most famous scenes in colonial travel narratives. Let us start with Speke's representation of his arrival in the Bugandan Court in 1862:

> A more theatrical sight I never saw. The king, a good-looking, well-figured, tall young man of twenty-five, was sitting on a red blanket spread upon a square platform of royal grass, encased in tiger-grass reeds, scrupulously well dressed in a new mbugu. The hair of his head was cut short, excepting on the top, where it was combed up into a high ridge, running from stem to stern like a cockscomb. On his neck was a very neat ornament – a large ring, of beautifully-worked small beads, forming elegant patterns by their various colours. On one arm was another bead ornament, prettily devised; and on the other a wooden charm, tied by a string covered with snake-skin. On every finger and every toe he had alternate brass and copper rings; and above the ankles, halfway up to the calf, a stocking of very pretty beads. Everything was light, neat, and elegant in its way; not a fault could be found with the taste of his 'getting up'. For a handkerchief he held a well-folded piece of bark, and a piece of gold-embroidered silk, which he constantly employed to hide his large mouth when laughing, or to wipe it after a drink of plantain-wine, of which he took constant and copious draughts from neat little gourd-cups, administered by his ladies-in-waiting, who were at once his sisters and wives. A white dog, spear, shield, and woman – the Uganda cognisance – were by his side, as also a knot of staff officers, with whom he kept up a brisk conversation on one side; and on the other was a band of Wichwezi, or lady-sorcerers, such as I have already described. (Speke, 1864: 290–1)

Having already prepared his readers for what he aptly describes as 'a novel spectacle', Speke moves quickly to visualise the Bugandan court in the most dramatic terms possible. The theatrical, however, is not a neutral term of representation, for by emphasising the performative nature of the court – and of one of Africa's most important monarchs in the nineteenth century – the English author deprives both of any aura they might have; the king is conceived in his most corporeal nature (with emphasis on his figure and youth), not his regal authority. The most lasting image of the young Mutesa, as Stanley was to observe in a critique of Speke's narrative, was his vanity and heartlessness (Stanley, 1890: 192). In addition, native insignias of power and divine aura – the cockscomb, the beaded ornaments and charms – are presented to the audience as fetishes, signs of African heathenism and primitivism. Finally, although Speke has only been in Buganda for a few days when he witnesses the above scene, his description exudes immense knowledge of the kingdom; everything fits into a clear taxonomy and is represented with an authority which does not allow for the simple fact that the author's representation of the court is ultimately his personal 'first' impression. We have to remember, of course, that Speke's view of Buganda is a reflection of his 'aesthetic disappointment' which is, in turn, connected to his 'public Oedipean battle with Burton' over the sources of the Nile (Pratt, 1992: 208).

Let us now turn to Mukasa's representation of his long-awaited encounter with Edward VII as it is represented in *Uganda's Katikiro in England*:

> There was a very large door, which was covered with gold; – the whole palace was very magnificent, all the walls being covered with gold and mirrors, the space not filled by a mirror being covered with gold, except in the rooms which we had first entered – the inner rooms were wonderfully fine. On one side of this great door was a looking-glass about 10 ft. high and 5 ft. wide, and we passed through it, Lord Lansdowne going first, and then the Katikiro and myself, and then Captain Hobart. When we passed through the door we saw the 'Father of the nation' sitting upon his throne, dressed in magnificent kingly raiment; he bowed his head three times, and we did the same and bowed three times, and he then told the Katikiro to sit down, and he sat down on a golden chair, while I and Captain Hobart stood up. (p. 157)

There are certainly many instances when Mukasa represents Britain as a novel spectacle, but when he describes the institutions of British civilisation, he does so with deference; he accepts the fact that British social practices and rituals are different from his own, but he goes out of his way to emphasise their (relative) value. In the above description, then, what the author foregrounds (and he has his Bugandan readers very much in mind here) is the splendour of the English court, its capacity for aesthetic satisfaction. He has come face to face with an unfamiliar spectacle of power, but what he wants to inscribe is not performance for its own sake, but its ritualistic authority. Gold and mirrors are the most obvious symbols of the use-value of political rituals.

But if Speke and Mukasa approach their subjects from different directions and cultural positions, the above passages, dissimilar as they appear to be, are actually connected in subtle ideological and discursive ways. And it is by examining at least three instances of conjuncture in the colonial relationship, as it was played out in Buganda in the second half of the nineteenth century, that we can begin to understand the significance of *Uganda's Katikiro in England* as a work of cultural translation. These instances are the historical moment in which Buganda, in the process of expanding its influence in the Lake Region of East Africa, encountered Britain at the height of its imperial power; the invention of a Bugandan culture as a collective enterprise in which both agents of British colonial rule – beginning with Speke and his contemporaries – and members of a new, Christianised elite – represented here by Sir Apolo and Mukasa – were deeply involved; and African attempts to redefine the terms of the colonial encounter.

II

By the 1880s, Buganda had become a pawn in the European scramble for Africa and an important stage on which various external factions could perform their political and cultural desires. One of the great ironies of the history of Buganda in the middle of the nineteenth century was that just as it was trying to expand its power over other East African kingdoms, such as Toro and Bunyoro, it had to deal with British, French, German and Egyptian interests trying to establish control over the source of the Nile. If one were to visit the Bugandan court during the 1880s, or even the two previous decades, one would expect to encounter an assortment of European and Muslim agents jostling for influence in the kingdom, trying to convert monarchs, princes and pages to their own particular brand of Christianity or Islam (Kiwanuka, 1971: 192–212). That Buganda was a favourite stage for performing European rivalries has not been surprising to commentators on African politics: the kingdom was unique, at least in an East African context, for its centralised bureaucratic institutions, its elaborate monarchical rituals and its openness 'to new ideas and ways of doing things' (Wrigley, 1996: 1). The most memorable thing about Mutesa I, Buganda's reigning monarch in the middle of the nineteenth century, was his eagerness to make his kingdom a major player in the politics of the modern world. Even before the arrival of the first Europeans in Uganda, Mutesa had developed close political, economic and cultural ties with Arab traders from the East African coast. He had learnt to write in the Arabic

Plate 2   *The presentation of Mutesa's envoys to Queen Victoria (1879).*

script and had assimilated many Muslim practices (Kiwanuka, 1971: 155–73).

But Mutesa's conversion to Islam was incomplete and ambivalent: he was more interested in the function of the religion as a conduit to the emerging global economy than as a substitute for his ancestral beliefs. Mathias Kalemba, a convert to Christianity from this period, has provided us with an intriguing description of Mutesa's – and the Baganda's – paradoxical relationship with the Arabs:

> Mutesa himself, anxious to please the Sultan of Zanzibar, of whose power and wealth he had been given an exaggerated account, declared that he also wanted to become a Muslim. Orders were given to build mosques in all the counties. For a short time, it looked as if the whole country was going to embrace the religion of the false prophet, but Mutesa had an extreme repugnance to circumcision. Consequently, changing his mind all of a sudden, he gave orders to exterminate all who had become Muslims. A good many perished in the massacre, two or three hundred managed to escape and, with Arab caravans, made their way to the Island of Zanzibar. I succeeded with a few others in concealing the fact of

9

my conversion, and continued to pass for a friend of our own gods, though in secret I remained faithful to the practices of Islam.

That was how things stood when the Protestants arrived. Mutesa received them very well; he had their book read in public audience, and seemed to incline to their religion, which he declared to be much superior to that of the Arabs. I asked myself whether I had not made a mistake, and whether, perhaps, the newcomers were not the true messengers of God. I often went to visit them and attended their instructions. It seemed to me that their teaching was an improvement on that of my first masters. I therefore abandoned Islam, without however asking for baptism. (quoted in Low, 1971: 8)

The fortunes of Christians and Muslims in the Bugandan court would change often during the nineteenth century, but it would be a mistake to explain these changes in terms of the temperaments of the reigning monarchs or their courtiers. A more useful way is to see Bugandan kings and their subjects as increasingly, and often, compelled by external and internal pressures to walk a tightrope between their desire to maintain the autonomy and integrity of their kingdom and to come to terms with an unprecedented – and extremely volatile – political reality, that is, the presence of Europeans who had been attracted to the kingdom because of its location at the source of the Nile. This paradox – the desire to maintain autonomy while coming to terms with the political and moral economy of colonialism – will help us understand Mukasa's ideological agenda in *Uganda's Katikiro in England*. It is a paradox which also lies at the very foundation of Buganda as a modern polis. For as Stanley was to note when he met the African monarch in 1875, the kingdom of Buganda and its leaders appeared eager to adopt new ideas and to serve as agents of 'the light that shall lighten the darkness of this benighted region'; Mutesa seemed to be 'a prince well worthy of the most hearty sympathies that Europe can give him' (Stanley, 1890: 193). But the Bugandan court was also stubbornly attached to its history and traditions.

One of the roles played by the elite in the Bugandan court was the balancing of these paradoxical demands; in the process many of them came to accept and celebrate their colonisation as the only guarantee of Bugandan autonomy in the new order. Was this enthusiasm for the colonial order symptomatic of a desire for modernity or was it a political tactic? That many young Bugandan men were eager to embrace colonial modernity and its religions has never been in doubt: it is apparent in the rapidness with which many of them, including pages in the royal court, adopted Islam or

Christianity and their level of devotion to the new faiths. When Mutesa turned against the Muslims in 1876, or when his son Mwanga massacred Christians in 1886, many adherents to the new faiths were willing to die for beliefs unheard of until recently. This devotion to the new faiths appears puzzling especially within the context of Buganda's volatile politics in the colonial age.[3] For as we can see from the chronology at the beginning of the book, there was clear evidence that the Bugandan monarch's adoption or valorisation of a particular religion did not secure that faith's objectives or authority; to become a convert, especially during Mwanga's reign, was to court martyrdom since one was never sure which way the ecclesiastical winds would blow. What, then, was the attraction of the new religions and civilisations? Why were thousands of young Bugandan men, including Ham Mukasa and Apolo Kagwa, willing to die in the name of Christianity or Anglicanism?

The most common response to this question begins by locating the ambitions and identities of the Christianised Africans within the culture of colonial modernity. In this version of events, the young Bugandans were ready to die for their new faith because, as Mutesa himself had told his European interlocutors, they perceived Christianity – and sometimes Islam – as the source of the instruction and knowledge that would make Buganda the centre of civilisation in East Africa (Low, 1971: 3). Like Mutesa before them, Mukasa and Kagwa could be expected to conceive the superiority of Britain primarily in terms of industrial achievement. At the same time, however, the desire for a modern economy could not justify conversion if it was not underwritten by a new epistemology. As their testimonies reveal, many Bugandan converts saw their journey through the landscape of foreign religions and sects as part of a continuous quest for what they called 'the truth' or 'true understanding'. And since many of the converts came from the elite classes, they assumed that this quest for 'true understanding' through European religions, cultures and texts was a prerequisite for sustaining the integrity of their own kingdom and its ancient traditions. The Bugandan aristocracy, always proud of its genealogy and cultural heritage, its continuous dynastic history and centralised political institutions, considered itself to be the equal of its European counterparts.[4] As an ally of the colonisers, and through the instruments of European knowledge, Buganda could pursue its own cultural and political objectives (Twaddle, 1993: 1–32).

By the middle of the nineteenth century, Buganda had become, by all accounts, an important imperial power in its own right. With the kingdom's imperial ambitions curtailed by the arrival of the European powers, the challenge for its elite was how to sustain the moral and cultural authority of their kingdom in the absence of an imperium in the age of imperialism. Every political and cultural initiative undertaken by the Bugandan elite – including wars, agreements and even the writing of books such as *Uganda's Katikiro in England* – was, therefore, intended to ensure the survival of their kingdom as an autonomous cultural and political entity. Sir Apolo Kagwa was the main architect of this policy, a policy whose apotheosis was the signing of the [B]Uganda Agreement of 1900, a policy which was to continue until the kingdom of Buganda was abolished by the postcolonial Ugandan government in 1969.[5]

A second point to consider is the strange convergence of Bugandan and imperial interests in the invention of the colonial entity that came to be known as Uganda. Why did the Bugandan aristocracy assume that their interests were identical with those of Christian missionaries and colonial administrators? We can begin to address this question by noting that while Christian conversion in many parts of Africa could rarely be undertaken until colonial conquest and rule had been accomplished, Bugandan Christianity predated the formal institution of colonial rule by almost forty years. This point is important to keep in mind if we are to understand why writers such as Mukasa could easily abstract what they considered to be the universal message of Christianity from the mechanics of colonial power politics. From our vantage point, the religious wars that broke out in Buganda in 1886 cannot be understood outside the political rivalry between various European and Arabic interests; it is easy to conclude, in these circumstances, that religion provided a convenient ideological mask for imperial ambitions. But this is not how the situation appeared to Bugandan Christians, either in moments of adversity when they were involved in the slaughter of each other, or in their triumphant disposal of Kabaka Mwanga. On the contrary, even before the establishment of colonial rule, Christian chiefs and pages in the Bugandan court saw themselves as involved in a crusade which was as much about the future of their new faith as it was about the destiny of their polis and its established, that is, traditional, structures.[6]

Now, students of colonial culture, especially those who might be seduced into reading the colonial relationship within the paradigm of collaboration and resistance, might be surprised to discover that Bugandan Christians posited their alliance with colonialism as a strategic (oppositional) gesture.[7] And yet, if there is one unifying theme in numerous letters sent to agents of British expansion by Mutesa (to General Gordon), Mwanga (to F. J. Jackson) and Apolo Kagwa (to the British Consul General in Zanzibar), to cite just a few examples, it is that Buganda's interests could only be served under British protection (Low, 1971: 5–7, 24–6). In his letter to the British Consul dated 25 April 1890, Apolo Kagwa, then Katikiro under Mwanga, began by observing that although the Bugandans had become Christian, they were divided into two factions: one faction was 'Katoliki' (Catholic) under French patronage; the other was made up of 'the people of the religion of the book' (Protestants) who had placed themselves under British tutelage. He concluded by observing that Mwanga had already placed Buganda 'under English protection' in an arrangement which he considered irrevocable (Low, 1971: 25–6). Clearly, Britishness and Protestantism had endowed the Bugandan elite with some cultural and political capital. Under British protection, Buganda could perhaps propagate its own imperial designs.

But the Bugandan elite's desire for the protection of a European power needs to be contextualised in two ways: first, by foregrounding the complex situation in which the new Christian elite found itself, in a court where they held a lot of sway but one in which they could not, because of their new faith, derive their legitimacy from traditional institutions and rituals. Mutesa had been able to balance the demands of the new religion and the ritual structures he had inherited because his policy had always been to master the new religion and its culture without accepting full conversion. Thus by being half Muslim (he had refused to be circumcised) or half Christian (he had resisted baptism), he had maintained a critical space in which he could turn to the rituals of his ancestors when his authority was threatened, something he did in his massacre of the Muslims in 1876. In this instance, a political strategy (the containment of Muslim influence) could be explained as an act of *kiwendo*, 'the random slaughter carried out from time to time to ensure the health of king and kingdom' (Wrigley, 1996: 4). But when Mutesa died in 1884 and was succeeded by his son Mwanga, balancing the demands of imperial powers and domestic factions proved difficult. The young Kabaka's task was made even more difficult by the fact that, unlike his father, he could neither appeal to traditionalists (they had been increasingly marginalised by the Christian and Muslim chiefs and pages in the court) nor appeal to the new religions for legitimacy. Mwanga had converted to Christianity and had been baptised – his Christian name was Leon – but this gesture was not enough in itself.

In 1885, unsure of his own authority in the court, Mwanga ordered the killing of the Anglican Bishop Hannington and several young Christians and demanded the recantation of Christianity, under the threat of death, from the ones who survived. In 1888, Christian pages joined hands with their Muslim counterparts and rose in revolt against Mwanga, thereby initiating what have come to be known as the Religious Wars in Buganda. Between 1888 and 1892, war would be waged not only between forces loyal to Mwanga and an alliance of Christian and Muslim factions, but also

13

Plate 3   *King Daudi Chwa of Buganda (1897–1933). Sir Apolo Kagwa was the chief regent of Buganda until the young king came of age in 1906.*

between Protestants and Catholics, Christians and Muslims. Eventually, with the help of the British colonial authority, Mwanga was exiled to the Seychelles in 1899, and his infant son, Daudi Chwa, was installed as Kabaka with an oligarchy of three Protestant chiefs, led by Apolo Kagwa, serving as regents. In 1900, the new oligarchy signed an agreement with the British imperial authorities.

The [B]Uganda Agreement of 1900 was an intriguing document because – on the surface, at least – it was the consensual product of an arrangement between the coloniser and colonised, a sign of mutual respect and common interests (Low, 1971: 37–41). In practical terms, of course, the Christian oligarchy had facilitated the colonisation of their country and invested the act of conquest with the fiction of free agency. Nonetheless, many of them would die believing that what made Uganda different from a real colony (like Kenya) was that it controlled its own affairs under British 'protection'.

But what is of particular interest to readers of *Uganda's Katikiro in England* – and this is the second way of contextualising the mythology of a Bugandan protectorate – is the culture that emerged out of this fiction of free agency. The issue here is not the obvious fact that Mukasa and Sir Apolo travelled through Britain without any awareness of their inferior status in the colonial relationship, but the even more remarkable fact that it was under the mask of protection that they embarked on a unique cultural project – the invention of Buganda as a modern polis. *Uganda's Katikiro in England* is manifestly about the colonised subjects' view of the imperial centre, but underneath the author's concern with Britain is a latent, but systematic, attempt to project Buganda's modern identity and probe the meaning of the culture that Mukasa and his peers sought to construct, a culture which, as I have argued elsewhere, was both inside and outside the symbolic economy of Englishness (Gikandi, 1996: 23–41). The book appears to be mostly about Britain, but underneath the elaborate descriptions of life in the metropolis lurk the figures of two Africans trying to understand their role in the making of colonial culture. In the end, though, *Uganda's Katikiro in England* is as much about Buganda as it is about Britain, as much a narrative of personal identity as it is about collective entities.

III

It is easy, of course, for us to read Mukasa's book without any sense of the persona behind the narrative. Indeed, the subjectivity of the African travellers in Britain is so carefully effaced, or taken for granted, that readers might be forgiven for not paying much attention to the people who travel or the person who writes *Uganda's Katikiro in England*. This effacement of the writer's and travellers' personae is, however, deceptive and serves two closely related functions: on one hand, the itinerary that the travellers follow, the people they meet, the institutions they visit and the scenes they valorise are over-determined by their ideological interests and subjective desires; on the other hand, the effacement of the writing self is symptomatic of a certain cultural dislocation. Another way of presenting this argument is to note that while the African travellers stride into Britain confident and sure of their own (hybrid) identity – as both Bugandans and British subjects – they are less sure about the terms which define this mode of being. And thus, it is in our reading of the masking of the self, as it were, that we can best glimpse how the political demands which this text serves are connected intractably to the biographies of its principal subjects.

I have included the main events of the two subjects' lives in the chronology at the beginning of this book, but I would like to underscore three instances in which the nature of the text and its meaning and function are determined by biography. First, as the sons of prominent Bugandan chiefs, both Sir Apolo and Mukasa were associated, quite early in their lives, with the Royal Court: their service to the Kabaka pre-dated their Christian conversion, and much of the authority they were to hold in Buganda in the twentieth century, an authority which survived numerous changes in political and religious affiliations, could be explained by this connection. Sir Apolo entered the Kabaka's service early in his life: beginning his royal duties as the Caretaker of the King's Mosque, he rose through the ranks to become the Keeper of the Royal Stores, a chief, and eventually Katikiro and Senior Regent. Mukasa, too, was brought up as a page in Mutesa's court where he learnt Arabic and made his reputation as a scribe, eventually becoming the official secretary and confidant to the Katikiro.

Second, for both Sir Apolo and Mukasa, this affiliation with the traditional Bugandan court was reinforced by their early conversion to Christianity which was as much an act of faith as it was the acquisition of what we may call the authority of modernity. Both men had exhibited their commitment to the new faith during the second massacre of Christians by Mwanga (in 1888) when they barely escaped with their lives; they had gone on to fight in the Religious Wars, suffering exile (in the case of Sir Apolo) and serious injury (in the case of Mukasa). It was in the name of Protestantism, more accurately Anglicanism, that Sir Apolo had led the triumphant Christian forces to power; it was from his position as the Protestant Katikiro that he was to oversee the modernisation of Buganda under the tutelage of colonial rule. What is important for us here, then, are the implications of this Christian connection: what did it mean for the destiny of Buganda that its shepherd was an Anglican? What effect did Anglicanism have on Sir Apolo's identity as a Bugandan and an African?

Questions of faith aside, there is no doubt that the value of Anglicanism lay in two cultural areas – its function as a conduit to the highest circles of the British establishment and as an instrument of literacy. Being an Anglican, even a colonised one, meant that one had access to institutions of British political power and cultural influence; there was a powerful line connecting Namirembe Cathedral (the centre of Bugandan Anglicanism) and St Paul's Cathedral in London, Cambridge University and Canterbury. More significantly, the cultural capital of Protestantism lay not so much in its doctrines, but in its close association with British colonialism and its investment in literacy and textuality: Christian converts in Buganda, as elsewhere in Africa, were known as readers not only because they were marked from their contemporaries by their ability to read, but also because literacy had a cognitive value, it denoted a certain way of looking at the world and a discernible moral economy. As the Reverend H. W. Lang was to observe in 1888, when the Christian readers came to power in Buganda, their primary demands were not religious but cultural, and culture spoke to them in the form of the scriptural:

> It must be borne in mind that during all this time the king was merely the tool of his advisers and counselors, namely the chiefs of the Readers both Christian and Mohammedan who had seated him upon the throne. These chiefs began to regulate and set in order many matters of law and order needing important attention. As an indication of the commencement of a milder rule, the executioners or court policemen were forbidden to attend court armed as formerly with ropes. They were now ordered to arm themselves with sticks. It was even said that the king was to be deprived of the power of passing the sentence of capital punishment for many offenders before criminal, and punishable only by death. Another manifest change must not be omitted. It was most interesting with respect to ourselves as Christian teachers. The Promises regarding Freedom of thought and liberty to be taught the white man's religion spread far and wide. These promises doubtless brought gladness to many who had secretly been reading the Arabs Religion. For those Baganda who were Christian Readers, and who had for a long time been in hiding, the news was most acceptable and welcome. Many who had been for a long time hidden and were thought to be lost or fled the country now boldly came forward without fear. (quoted in Low, 1971: 19)

Plate 4 *Interior of the Anglican church at Mityana, Buganda. While the materials used in the construction of the church were local, its architecture was very British.*

Indigenous Christian readers presented themselves as agents of order and civility, of rights and due process, and in this presentation they were also making the claim that they could be better agents of civilisation in the colonial domain than foreign missionaries. Indeed, one of the primary demands of the Christian readers in the [B]Uganda Agreement of 1900 was that because Buganda was different from other colonised spaces, it could only be ruled indirectly, through the traditional institutions – such as the Lukiko (council of elders) – which the Christianised elite now controlled. In these circumstances, Mukasa and Sir Apolo were to travel to Britain in 1902 both as representatives of the kingdom of Buganda and as mediators between the coloniser and colonised. One of the primary functions of their travel narrative – and indeed of their other works – was to translate Buganda to the British and the British to the Baganda.[8]

But there is a third reason why the effacement of the writing self in *Uganda's Katikiro in England* is germane to our understanding of the cultural context of the text: in repressing their own unique individuality, the writer and his companion could transform themselves into the collective voices of their culture. It is true that Mukasa and Sir Apolo were not ordinary colonial subjects; indeed they were the first generation of Africans who cultivated what we may now call bourgeois manners. And yet, instead of producing a narrative that would call attention to their unique individuality within their culture – their modernity, as it were – the two men saw themselves as cultural representatives, voices of a new order which encompassed the desires of the whole kingdom. In this respect, the act of writing was closely connected to the imagination of a new modern polity. More than Christian readers, the two men were writers, and it was in their writings (ranging from Mukasa's commentary on the Gospel According to St Matthew to Sir Apolo's numerous ethnographic works on the Baganda) that they sought to determine the shape of the invented colonial community. If the colonising European powers valued Buganda because of its strategic location in the political economy of colonialism, the colonised Bugandans valued the Europeans for granting them what they saw as the gift and power of literacy. That is why the day when the Christian forces deposed Mwanga came to be represented as the day when literacy triumphed, as Reverend Lang recounted:

> Many Christians now emerged from their places of concealment and flocked to the king's court and began to enter into his service as pages and messengers. Thus released Christians and seekers after the Truth began to come about our Mission station in crowds on Sundays and in great numbers on all the days of the week. Very

many indeed were wanting alphabet sheets. Many more were asking for first syllables, then others were demanding more advanced papers and printed portions while a large number were imploring for prayer-books and New Testament gospels and single Epistles. (quoted in Low, 1971: 19)

Christian soldiers now fought their wars with pens as much as guns.

IV

What are the theoretical and scholarly implications of texts such as *Uganda's Katikiro in England* in the ongoing debates on the culture of colonialism and postcoloniality? The above quotation – the representation of the culture of colonialism as a textual event – can help us open up a whole line of inquiry. It can show us, for a start, that from the very beginning, the colonised understood one of the important lessons we have learnt from contemporary colonial studies – that 'culture was what colonialism was all about', and that 'If colonialism can be seen as a cultural formation, so also culture is a colonial formation' (Dirks, 1992: 3).

To say that culture was the key term in the colonial event is not to denigrate the horrible experiences associated with conquest and rule; rather, it is to call attention to the mediatory, or paradigmatic, function of culture. In its very existence, a book by the colonised served as their mode of entry into the culture of colonialism; it was clear evidence of the 'others'' attempt to transform the terms of representation at a time when colonial authorities were turning traditional cosmologies and institutions upside-down (see Bhabha, 1994: 66–84 and Sinha, 1995: 1–32). For this reason, the texts produced by colonised subjects like Sir Apolo and Mutesa, even when written in European languages and/or conventions, were already contesting the colonial terrain. This contest was not necessarily in the form of a polemic or counter-discourse (this was to come later); rather, it was oppositional in the sense in which the term has been used by Ross Chambers – in appropriating the means available to them, the colonised were making 'the shifts in desire that produce change' (Chambers, 1991: xiii). Chambers's crucial distinction between opposition and resistance is important for my argument here: while resistance is driven by the need to challenge 'the legitimacy of a given power-system' by the deployment of a counterforce, opposition works within the structures of the dominant and is dependent on its capacity to use the existing system towards its own ends or modes of desire (Chambers, 1991: xiv–xv). My contention here is that it would be a conceptual mistake to see Sir Apolo and Mukasa simply as collaborators with the colonial system; rather, their works were oppositional to the extent that they strove to shift modes of British colonial desire towards what they would consider to be Bugandan ends. This shift in desire was evident in the books they read and the ones they wrote; it was in such modes of reading and writing that the colonised would become instrumental in changing the nature of what has come to be known as the colonial library (Mudimbe, 1988).

Indeed, to the extent that the colonial library had become the depository of modern knowledge, colonial subjects were scrambling to become major contributors to this body of culture and enlightenment. If the superiority of Englishness depended on its mastery of the written word, as colonial subjects were often made to believe, then the colonised had, by infiltrating this form, claimed its authority. This is how Mukasa and Sir Apolo saw the situation when they stood outside the University Library at Cambridge in 1902:

> After this we went to see the building in which they keep every book of every kind, one copy of each (University Library). Of every book that is printed they take one copy, and put it in this building as a remembrance. We saw there a great many books some fourteen to seventeen hundred years of age, and they told us there were about half a million books in the library. Is this not amazing? If you count the number of books in the Bible from Genesis to Malachi, how many would you find? then, again, how many are there from Matthew to Revelation? Well, this is the way they count their books; one book of every kind is stored up, just as Apolo Katikiro wrote *Basekabaka Bebuganda* ('Kings of Uganda'), and they took one copy and kept it; in this way the number of five hundred thousand books is made up. (p. 116)

Several conclusions can be drawn from this description. First, the University Library was positioned at the centre of a nexus of colonial relationships by which the African visitors were connected, through Anglicanism, to Cambridge University, which had produced many of the missionaries who had educated them. Second, while Cambridge was perhaps a metaphor of Englishness in its ideality, the two Africans did not see themselves as marginal to it; on the contrary, they perceived themselves as partners, with English ethnographers such as Sir James Frazer and John Roscoe, in the making of a modern (colonial) culture; consequently, the Katikiro's own book was foregrounded as a major body of knowledge in the colonial library. Third, the representation of the colonial library was mediated by the Bible, which both Sir Apolo and Mukasa considered to be the universal metatext – the measure of all modes of knowledge and cognition.

The privileging of textuality discussed above, nevertheless, presents some conceptual problems to students of colonial culture. The most obvious problem is this: as products of a culture that was primarily oral, Mukasa and Sir Apolo would appear to have subordinated their inherited modes of knowledge to colonial scripturalism. This charge is important because, as Michel de Certeau has argued, Western hegemony is inextricable from the practice of writing, a practice whose power and identity depends on its differentiation from orality: 'The "oral" is that which does not contribute to progress; reciprocally, the "scriptural" is that which separates itself from the magical world of voices and traditions' (de Certeau, 1984: 134). In Mukasa's and Sir Apolo's case, however, colonialism had complicated and even reversed this logic. Their education and experiences had convinced them that far from being the mode in which traditional values and cultural forms were negated, or even being the instrument that suppressed precolonial voices, writing was the form in which cultural vectors which had hitherto relied on orality and memory could be preserved and authorised; instead of sidelining the oral as atemporal, writing would bestow a telos on it. This was what Sir Apolo's primary ethnographic texts had set out to do; it is not accidental that they all revolved around questions of genealogy, progress and teleology. Writing was seen as the transportation of knowledge from the oral to the scriptural.

From our vantage point, however, this transportation of the oral into a scriptural register raises a corollary problem: could the voices of tradition maintain their cultural authority in the language of the coloniser, or were they condemned to be subordinated to the dominant? This is a question which Mukasa foregrounds in *Uganda's Katikiro in England* every time he uses the Bible as his primary referent or the prism through which quotidian and moral practices are to be judged. It is the question raised by Sir Apolo's books, most notably *Ekitabo kye Empisa Za Baganda* (The Book of the Traditions and Customs of the Baganda), where the very notion of *Ekitabo* (the book) invokes the authority of the Bible and where the general tone is canonical. We will return to this problem later. For now, let us note that in preserving Bugandan voices and traditions through writing, Mukasa and Sir Apolo did not intend to affirm their authenticity (as a Christian, Sir Apolo abhorred many of the practices he wrote about); rather, they saw the production of knowledge about the past as one way of constructing a new order within the culture of colonialism. The two writers, then, belonged to a tradition which simply would not be contained by postcolonial notions of cultural hybridity or colonial insurgency. Their works bear interesting parallels to the works of early colonial writers in Latin America examined by Rolena Adorno (1996); indeed if we substitute the precolonial African for the pre-Columbian, the following formulation could apply as well to writers of Mukasa's generation:

> Produced in the colonial period, most often with reference to the pre-Columbian, and created by individuals who preserved and communicated their native traditions through recourse to the foreign, the traditions under consideration here bring together diverse cultural formulations and symbolizing activities both oral and written. Diverse systems of thought and expression come together in these cultural productions yet the resulting reformulations of native experience tend not so much to resolve tension or conflict between the donor cultures as to create new cultural syntheses whose hallmark is the uneasy coexistence of their diverse and sometimes contradictory components. (Adorno, 1996: 35)

In their prolific writings, the new Christian elite in Buganda, led by Sir Apolo Kagwa as both Katikiro and Regent, could simultaneously display its mastery of colonial modernity and perform its new (modern) identity. The new Africans could use their writings to bring together what appeared to be conflicting systems of thought, but far from being a synthesis, this bringing together of the traditional and the modern (as it came to be called in ethnographical literature) could only hope to sustain the tension between them. Readers of Mukasa's text may marvel at what appears to be his unproblematic synthesis of the self and the other – Buganda and Britain seem to exist in a state of cultural equilibrium – but beneath the fiction of syncretism lurks a tense cultural struggle over the meaning and implication of cultural formulations and symbols. Above all, Mukasa's invocation of synthesis cannot be explained by the model of colonial hybridity which, according to Homi Bhabha, 'intervenes in the exercise of authority not merely to indicate the impossibility of its identity but to represent the unpredictability of its presence' (Bhabha, 1994: 114). Mukasa and Sir Apolo are not interested in the production of difference, nor the devalorisation of the colonial presence; on the contrary, they seek to establish their identity within the authority of colonial rule.

This acceptance of the colonial presence is, nevertheless, predicated on the belief that colonial culture emerges out of a multilateral exchange between the coloniser and the colonised. Thus, Mukasa and Sir Apolo see their work as closely aligned to that of Anglican missionaries such as Ernest Millar (their guide through the British landscape and the translator of their book) and John Roscoe (the author of the first British ethnographic texts on the Buganda).[9] They see their cultural project as a continuation of colonial ethnography. The clearest evidence of this mutuality is that Sir Apolo was the 'native informant' in Roscoe's ethnographic project on the Baganda, a project which was to culminate in *The Baganda* (1911), still considered to be the most authoritative study of the culture of the kingdom. In addition, Anglican missionaries such as Millar were to serve as the conduit through which knowledge about the African kingdom was presented to the outside world.

What this mutuality concealed, however, was that there was a struggle going on – between the missionaries and their disciples – over the nature of tradition and culture. As Terence Ranger has noted, the period in which Mukasa and Sir Apolo wrote their books 'was the time of a great flowering of European invented tradition – ecclesiastical, educational, military, republican, monarchical' (Ranger, 1983: 211). Native informants were busy trying to produce their own version of the invented tradition. That the new Africans saw themselves as the best interpreters of such traditions and the ideals they were supposed to secure is not surprising; colonialism had, after all, privileged those African communities, like the Baganda, who appeared to fulfil a certain British desire for ecclesiastical and monarchical rituals and institutions. In these circumstances, men like Mukasa and Sir Apolo perceived their cultural work as essentially that of inventing traditions which the colonised themselves could use as points of entry into the culture of colonial modernity. But this culture – and the subjects it was producing – could only be understood in relation to the traditions and customs which the new Africans had abandoned when they had converted to Christianity. This is how tradition came to have a dual status in the culture of colonialism: it was both what the native informants were inventing and what they thought they had transcended.

Clearly, *Uganda's Katikiro in England* is a travel narrative that is obsessed with the dual status of tradition: it valorises the language of customs and manners, both British and Bugandan, as the key to a stable political and civic order; it pays close attention to antiquity as it is manifested in museums and libraries; and it privileges the customary law, be it secular or biblical, as the precondition for a civilised society. It does all these things because its author assumes that tradition is what gives a community a cultural history and also secures its destiny. What came to be referred to as the mind of Buganda was ultimately the desire, among Buganda's elite, to secure 'the cultural destiny' of their society in the language of colonial modernity (Low, 1971: xv). The invention of tradition – and the written text – was one way of securing this destiny. The written text would guarantee that the invented tradition outlived its authors. And it did. Over fifty years after it was written, *Ekitabo kye Empisa Za Baganda*, Sir Apolo Kagwa's book on the kings of Buganda, was one of the primary texts driving the economy of debate in Uganda: 'By the 1950s there were copies of Kaggwa's [*sic*] book in most villages, and it would have been hard for an outsider to go beyond it' (Wrigley, 1996: 8). It was the basis for educating a new generation of Bugandans on their history, it was the foundation of a set of rules and regulations for governing the kingdom, and it was the basis of the traditional law that was practised in the courts side by side with British common law.

In considering the theoretical implications of this writing of Buganda's identity in the narratives of the coloniser, we should not forget another issue which Mukasa's text asks us to consider: the relation between the colonial 'periphery' and the metropolitan 'centre'. One of the most important issues we have learnt from contemporary theoretical work on travel writing is the way in which representations of the other, or rather notions of cultural alterity, are ultimately about the identity of a self (see Abeele, 1992, Lowe, 1991, Mills, 1991 and Pratt, 1992). It is interesting, however, to see what happens when the trajectory is reversed, when the movement is from the 'periphery' to the 'centre'. I put these two categories in quotation marks because in writing *Uganda's Katikiro in England*, Mukasa did not consider Buganda (the colony) to be peripheral to Britain (the metropolis). As is evident in his constant use of analogy and similitude, Mukasa assumed that for him and his readers, Buganda could function as the 'transcendental point of reference', the axiom that would 'organize and domesticate a given area by defining all other parts in relation to it' (Abeele, 1992: xviii).

But could a colonised space have the same transcendental status as an imperial one? Could Buganda really be the vantage point from which British wonders could be observed and contained? Two factors militated against the privileging of the colony as a transcendental space. First, while Buganda could function discursively as the familiar terrain against which the wonders of Englishness could be judged, it could not acquire the status of what Abeele has called 'the absolute origin and absolute end of all movement' (Abeele, 1992: xviii). Indeed, while Buganda was not construed as marginal to Britain in Mukasa's text, there is no doubt that the African travellers did not consider it the source and centre of civilisation in the same terms Britain was considered to be the centre of values and culture by imperial travellers. Unable to make Britain either the centre of his world or its radical other, Mukasa seems to have come up with an intriguing compromise: he would represent the metropolis, in eschatological terms, as a sign of where Buganda would be when it had fully mastered modern civilisation.

25

In a remarkable reversal of imperial tropes, then, the author and his companion assumed that they were travelling in Britain in order to confirm that the 'mother' country was the true place of enlightenment; while imperial writers often travelled to Africa to confirm its darkness and savagery, Mukasa was in Britain to confirm the 'the cleverness of the English' (p. 71).

One point that needs to be underscored in this consistent admiration of British 'cleverness' is the specificity with which it was delineated and presented.[10] In other words, Mukasa did not assume that Britain was superior to Buganda in total (he had in fact found some of the practices of the English, such as the sight of men and women dancing close together in public, quite shameful (p. 72); what he admired and celebrated were the specific moments in which Britain appeared to be the model of civility (or what he considered to be the customary) and modernity. In fact Mukasa and Sir Apolo were following an itinerary which would take them through depositories of the customary (libraries and museums) and institutions of modern industrial civilisation (mostly factories). Defined as a culture without the institutions of civility and modernity, Buganda could not be the origin and end of being.

The second point to consider, however, is that Britain could not be assigned the transcendental function either: it could not be the absolute point of origin because, in spite of the authority it held in the colonial imagination, it was not the Africans' 'natural home'. Beneath his adulation of Englishness, then, Mukasa was eager to mark his difference from it; he was never in doubt that what he called the 'fashions' of the British were different from his own, that their ancestors were not his, that while they had been conjoined by a recent history, the colonised and the coloniser did not share a common genealogy or even destiny. Buganda's duty was to learn from Britain and then move on alone. Mukasa was ostensibly writing his book to establish the common identity he shared with his colonisers, and he often went out of his way to valorise this common Christian identity, but he was also writing with a clear sense of his identity in the alterity of Englishness. In examining the discursive structure of this book, then, readers will notice how the author inscribes his identity in what has come to be known as the discourse of wonder.

V

Like many travellers in foreign lands, Mukasa assumed that the British landscape was going to challenge all the known conventions of language. He, in fact, began his narrative by reminding his readers that what they were about to witness in their reading of his book – the 'wonders' of Britain –

defied representation: 'My friends, I cannot tell you about all the beautiful and wonderful things the English have in their boats, because it is impossible to explain them in a book' (p. 60). As an experienced writer, he would try to meet the challenge of representing British difference through analogy – 'These English factories are as large as the space in front of the king's enclosure in Uganda' (p. 126). But he would eventually come to recognise that the experiences he was encountering in Britain were 'not explainable in Luganda', his native language (p. 138). If the author had begun his journey by assuming that the act of writing could contain the unfamiliar (this is the traditional justification for writing a travel narrative), he had, at the end of his journey, come to derive some measure of authority from the difficulties of representing the wonders of Englishness. ('See how hard it is to tell of the wonders of the English!' (p. 199) was the signature gesture.)

It is when we consider the authority Mukasa derives from talking about the impossibility of representing British marvels that we realise the extent to which his constant invocation of wonder is more ambivalent than it initially seemed to be – an expression of admiration for Britain and Englishness. The expression of wonder is, first and foremost, the recognition that the 'truth' the author seeks to represent exceeds the concepts and categories he has mastered; since it cannot be adduced from such categories, truth is only available to certain readers or listeners (see Greenblatt, 1991: 20). This is the moment of wonder which Mukasa relishes at the end of his journey:

> I went out into the courtyard and sat on a chair, and they all sat looking at me, and I told them about all the wonders of England and what the country was like, and what a fine land it was . . . I also told them how great was the population of England, and how they tamed elephants and all kinds of animals. Some of my hearers thought I was merely telling stories when I told them how an elephant fired a gun, and beat a drum, and lit a candle, and how a hippopotamus was called, and came just like a dog in other lands that they knew of. They were very much astonished to hear of a hippopotamus leaving the water when it was called, and going back again when it was told. Some did not understand that I was speaking the truth, while others, who knew that we would not tell them what was false, did not hesitate to believe it. I sat there from half-past six in the evening until one o'clock in the morning. (p. 202)

At the beginning of the book, Mukasa constantly tried to contain British experiences through analogy; he indeed relishes 'telling stories' and is not worried that some of his readers will not believe him; indeed, the audience's scepticism reinforces the authority of the story teller who is now represented as a master of the different and unusual. Wonder marks the separation between the narrator and his interlocutors.

On another level, however, wonder is a recognition of the author's ambivalence towards the object of admiration – in this case, Britain. As Greenblatt has noted in a different context, 'When we wonder, we do not know if we love or hate the object at which we are marveling; we do not know if we should embrace it or flee from it' (Greenblatt, 1991: 20). In this respect, it is possible to argue that Mukasa writes his text as a way of simultaneously embracing Britain and fleeing from it: he embraces Britain by retracing the journey made by imperial travellers and, in the process, places his people on a circuit of cultural formations and narratives in which the experiences of the coloniser are confronted with alternative perspectives. Mukasa's journey to Britain may not have been deliberately fashioned after the journeys of the imperial travellers who had come to Buganda fifty or so years earlier, but as I suggested at the beginning of this introduction, the two narratives – the imperial and the African – insist on being read in relation to one another. Indeed, these narratives would not exist if the historical event that brought the British to Buganda – and thus the Baganda to Britain – had not taken place. Mukasa must embrace Britain in order to come to terms with his imbrication in the colonial project begun by Speke and Stanley.

What of his flight from Britain? This is perhaps the most difficult part of the narrative to make a case for simply because *Uganda's Katikiro in England* is a book which strenuously refuses to provide a critique of Englishness. And yet, there are subtle ways in which Mukasa wonders at Englishness in order to differentiate himself from it. This is the kind of differentiation we find in a remarkable passage at the end of the book:

> Well, my friends, you should read this book very carefully and attentively, that you may understand what other and wiser lands are like; and though we call these lands wise, you should remember that wisdom does not come to a lazy and weak man, but to one who works hard and thinks daily about his work. Thought and perseverance thus increase a man's wisdom every year and every month. 'He who goes slowly goes far'; 'a crackling sound is not a fire,' and a great city is not built in one year. Let us then go ahead slowly and surely; perhaps our grandchildren will be much wiser than we are, but we should encourage our children daily to learn all they can, that they may teach their children after we have gone, and so they may go on increasing in wisdom both in the mind and in handicrafts. (p. 204)

Although this would appear to be a passage haunted by the idea of lack – Mukasa's awareness of the gap that exists between his culture and the civilisation it desires and of a wisdom whose totality has eluded his own generation – it is ultimately a valedictorian's speech: it is an acknowledgement of the triumph of the act of translation which both marks the author's identification with colonial Englishness and his difference from it. For if Mukasa set out to write a book in which Britain could be translated to the Baganda, the necessity of translation is the ultimate acknowledgement of the gap that separates metropole from colony. A valedictory, after all, is intended to be a gesture of parting or separation.

We can perhaps understand the complexity of Mukasa's differentiation from Britain if we recall the important role accorded translation by both coloniser and colonised. As Vincente L. Rafael has noted, translation is predicated on a double movement – the discernment of differences 'between and within social codes' – and is concomitant with the translator's recognition or acceptance of the limits of 'a linguistic and social order' (Rafael, 1993: 210). Translation can only take place within a context of expectation – 'that in return for one's submission, one gets back the other's acknowledgement of the value of one's words and behavior. In this way, one finds for oneself a place on the social map' (Rafael, 1993: 210). Mukasa's conclusion, above, does not blur the difference between Buganda and Britain; but to the extent that the wisdom he seeks is European (or Christian), we can conclude that he has submitted to the coloniser's linguistic and social order. This act of submission is not, however, without its rewards: by giving in to the culture of Englishness, Mukasa is recognised as both a native informant and an indispensable presence in the shaping of colonial culture. Rather than seeing himself as either an incomplete Bugandan or British person, Mukasa has used his intermediary role to create a new space for himself in the culture of colonialism. He wants his children to master British wisdom, but not to become British; he wants them to value the culture of their Bugandan ancestors, but not to revert to a precolonial identity. The culture he will help construct in Buganda will not be imprisoned by the marvels he has seen during his travels – he will appropriate some of them and discard others. This is the essence of his work.

VI

It has taken us a long time to recognise the cultural project in which colonised subjects such as Mukasa, subjects who seemed to identify with colonial authority, were engaged: the textual history of *Uganda's Katikiro in England* – and its very scant reception – reflects a certain misunderstanding about the role of colonial subjects who saw themselves as intermediaries between the coloniser and the colonised. At the beginning of the colonial period in Africa, these subjects occupied positions of incredible power and authority, and their writings – committed to the invention of traditions and usable pasts – were the sources of many ethnographic texts by missionaries and colonial administrators. These writings were, in turn, indispensable in the system of indirect rule, providing the philosophical basis for court systems and other regulatory practices. By the 1920s, however, there was a rupture in the terms of the colonial relationship, a break which changed the way these texts were received and the explicit role they played in the colonial project. Simply put, works by people like Mukasa and Sir Apolo were superseded by a new tradition of pan-African writing, a tradition which was more militant both in its representation of the nature and place of the precolonial past in the culture of modernity and in its critique of the colonial contract enshrined in documents such as the [B]Uganda Agreement of 1900.

By the time Uganda became independent in 1962, Mukasa and Sir Apolo were associated with reactionary politics. What had appeared (in their writings) as the defence of Bugandan histories and traditions came to be dismissed as an attempt to subordinate these histories and traditions to colonial authority. People like Mukasa and Sir Apolo were now considered collaborators with British imperialism. From the vantage point of decolonisation, there was clearly no sympathy for texts or authors which saw their role as mediating the delicate relationship between coloniser and colonised. Mukasa's 'sons' had acquired 'wisdom' and had come to power, but their agenda was different from his: while the father had sought to understand the colonial event that had radically changed the world of his youth, the sons were seeking to rewrite and transcend the culture of colonialism. The theoretical assumption now was that colonialism and decolonisation were paradigmatically opposed.

In looking at the textual history of *Uganda's Katikiro in England*, however, we can read the anxiety that accompanied the moment of both colonial conquest and decolonisation as the perhaps intangible factor that connected them. It is amazing to note that while Mukasa wrote his book on his travels to Britain in his native tongue, Luganda, there is no evidence that this original text was ever published. It is equally amazing that the Reverend Millar's translation of Mukasa's manuscript was printed by a prestigious London publisher (Hutchinson) barely two years after the visit to Britain. What this means, among other things, is that while Mukasa had written his text with a Luganda-reading public in mind, his book was condemned to be

Plate 5   *Ham Mukasa with his father, wife and children.*

read only by foreigners (mostly missionaries and anthropologists) and by
the tiny group of Ugandans who could read English. This ironic situation
was compounded by another factor: literacy in English became widespread
in Uganda at precisely that time (between World War II and the
postcolonial period) when Mukasa's book was considered irrelevant. A
heavily abridged version of the book was published by Heinemann in 1975
under the editorship of Taban Lo Liyong, the Sudanese/Ugandan writer,
but this text did not fare much better and the book quickly went out of
print. The politics of the time were clearly not in favour of the intermediary
position Mukasa had taken in the book.

Lo Liyong had concluded his introduction to the abridged edition with
a salutation to Mukasa and Sir Apolo: 'These are people who accepted the
challenges of their times, rose above them and everybody else. They had
their vices, but these fade when compared with their lofty virtues and
achievements' (Lo Liyong, 1975: xv). Lo Liyong, too, was ahead of his time,
for it was hard, even in the midst of Idi Amin's dictatorship in Uganda in
the 1970s, to convince intellectuals that what was being destroyed around
them – modern institutions such as universities and a liberal culture – had
been founded by people such as Mukasa and Sir Apolo. Now, as Africans in
Uganda and elsewhere try to reconstruct such institutions and ideals, and
try to figure new ways of adjusting to a world that sometimes threatens to
leave them behind, they can perhaps learn useful lessons from *Uganda's*

Katikiro in England. For in the end, our postcolonial condition is perhaps the dystopian (or utopian) fulfilment of the colonial event which Ham Mukasa and Apolo Kagwa had witnessed in their childhood and youth, the colonial event they had tried to transform into an African occasion.

Notes

1 A systematic study of the political function of 'minor' literature is provided by Deleuze and Guattari in their famous reading of Kafka and any attempt to rehabilitate the 'minor' colonial text should keep in mind the claim they make here: 'A minor literature doesn't come from a minor language; it is rather that which a minority constructs with a major language' (Deleuze and Guattari, 1986: 16).

2 In addition to Pratt, I have in mind here works by Lowe (1991), Melman (1992), Mills (1991) and Youngs (1994).

3 The question of Bugandan acceptance of Islam is particularly germane here, for the Arabs who brought the new faith to the kingdom were also heavily involved in the African slave trade.

4 As the Bugandan regents reminded Sir Harry Johnston, the British Commissioner, in a memorandum sent on 16 January 1900, they had always considered their colonial status as consensual: 'We invited Europeans in this country of our own free will so that we may receive help at their hands; we did not do so because we had been conquered by force' (quoted in Low, 1971: 34).

5 The kingdom of Buganda was restored in 1993 by the government of Yoweri Museveni, but without any of its previous political power.

6 Just before the special status of Buganda was enshrined in the [B]Uganda Agreement, the governing elite responded to what they saw as their demotion in a memorandum which spoke of the honour of their king and kingdom in the familiar language of ethnocentrism: 'We would . . . enquire the reason which has prompted the Queen to degrade her faithful and loyal subjects by placing us on the same level as the Kavirondo, Masai and others' (Low, 1991: 35).

7 This claim depends on the validity of the distinction made, most notably by Ross Chambers, between resistance and oppositionality. Chambers argues that unlike resistance, which challenges the legitimacy of the dominant, opposition 'works within the structure of power' (Chambers, 1991: xv). My whole argument in this introduction is indebted to another of Chambers's claims: 'The fact of mediation is the key to oppositionality, which is therefore necessarily situated *within* the (mediated) structure of the discourse of power itself' (Chambers, 1991: xiv).

8 For a comprehensive understanding of the role of the colonised elite as mediators of complex relationships, India provides some of the best lessons (see Guha and Spivak, 1988 and Sinha, 1995).

9 Millar was more than a translator for the duo; he was also their official chaperon through the arcane culture of official Englishness; as the most prominent scholar on Buganda, Roscoe provided important connections to Cambridge and Whitehall.

10 As I have noted in *Maps of Englishness*, the colonised assumed that England and Britain were the same. Mutesa's itinerary includes Scotland, but the title of his book is *Uganda's Katikiro in England* (Gikandi, 1996: 34).

Part 2

Uganda's Katikiro in England

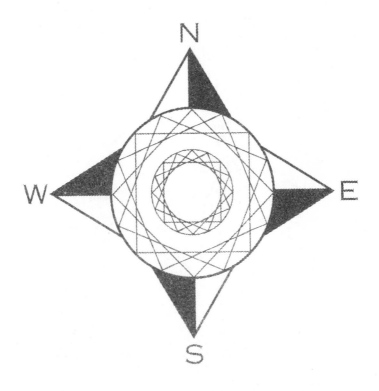

UGANDA'S KATIKIRO
IN ENGLAND

BEING THE OFFICIAL ACCOUNT OF HIS VISIT TO THE CORONATION OF HIS MAJESTY KING EDWARD VII.

BY HIS SECRETARY
HAM MUKASA
AUTHOR OF 'A LUGANDA COMMENTARY ON THE GOSPEL OF ST. MATTHEW'

Translated and Edited by
THE REV. ERNEST MILLAR, M.A., F.Z.S.
OFFICIAL INTERPRETER TO THE KATIKIRO DURING HIS VISIT,
AND MISSIONARY OF THE CHURCH MISSIONARY SOCIETY IN UGANDA

With an Introduction by
SIR H. H. JOHNSTON, K.C.B.

London: **HUTCHINSON & CO.**
Paternoster Row 1904

Preface

This book has been translated into English at the request of some of those who, having met the Katikiro of Uganda during his visit to England in 1902, wished to know what impressions he had gained during that visit.

It was written in Luganda by Ham Mukasa (the Katikiro's secretary during the visit) after his return to Africa, and was based on copious notes taken at the time, the whole book being written in collaboration with the Katikiro himself, so that it may be regarded as their joint production. It was written for the natives of Uganda, as a description of the journey and what was seen on it, and everything is described from an entirely native point of view, and not with the idea of any translation into English.

The book simply shows what impressions the visitors gained during their visit; some of the impressions are obviously false ones, and many of the numbers given are quite unreliable; sometimes similar events occurring in different places have been confused – but I have not attempted to rectify such things, as I think they add to the charm of the book.

In translating it, I have tried to keep as closely as possible to the native idiom, and if at times I have adhered to it too closely, I must ask my reader's pardon. There is in the original a good deal of repetition, and of long explanations which would have been wearisome to an English reader, and these parts have therefore been omitted. I have also omitted a few remarks that might have caused pain to some, or that were of too personal a nature; and have added where necessary a few explanatory notes, which as a convenience to the reader have usually been put in brackets and inserted in the text, though where a longer note has been necessary it has been put at the foot of the page.

I myself had never read the book through until, when once again in England, I began the work of translation, and I therefore wish to disclaim all responsibility for the various statements made in it, even though they have sometimes apparently been made on my authority.

The author frequently states how impossible he finds it to explain in his own language many of the things which he saw in England, and I similarly sometimes found it quite impossible to make the Katikiro and the author fully understand many of our English customs and methods of government.

As an explanatory note, I may add that from Uganda to England the party was in the official charge of Mr. H. Prendergast, an officer of the Uganda Administration, and during the stay in England was in the charge of Captain C. V. C. Hobart, of the Grenadier Guards, who obtained his D.S.O. for services in Uganda.

In the text of the book I have used the generally accepted method of calling the country itself Uganda, a single native Muganda (plural, Baganda), and the language Luganda.

In conclusion, I wish to express my thanks to all those who have kindly assisted me in the preparation of this book, to Sir H. H. Johnston for his Introduction, to Mr. Herbert Samuel, M.P., for his kind advice and suggestions, and to Mr. C. W. Hattersley for kindly allowing me to reproduce some of his photographs.

ERNEST MILLAR.

July 22nd, 1904.

Introduction

To see ourselves as others see us is, or should be, an ever fresh source of interest to the British peoples of these two islands who have taken their turn in the cycle of the world's history as an Imperial race. Motives first of honest commerce, secondly of greed for gain, then of sheer philanthropy, and lastly a lust for power over the destinies of other peoples, have sent the adventurers of Great Britain and Ireland over America, Asia, and Africa during the last five centuries, seeking first to found colonies, then empires, and latterly to educate backward races, the commission or gain on the last-named enterprise being the securing of fair fields for our commerce and the satisfaction of implanting our religious beliefs, laws, language, and customs in many waste places of the earth, and among many people of widely differing racial origins.

In order that our Empire may continue and flourish, and include within its limits not only those who are descended from Celts and Anglo-Saxons (and who have made new Englands, Scotlands, Waleses, and Irelands in the western or the southern hemispheres), but also Maltese, Greeks, Indians, Arabs, Persians, Chinese, Egyptians, Malays, American Indians, and Negroes of every shade, from olive-yellow to sooty black, it is becoming absolutely necessary that Force shall not be the only element by which our sway is maintained. We have had in the past to use the force which is derived from individual courage, strongly marked individuality, knowledge applied to such practical purposes as the manufacture of superior arms or superior ship-building in the conquest of the many subject races which now own our sway. All things considered, our crimes and our mistakes have been few, and our honest dealing a thing to be proud of and thankful for. But the very thoroughness with which we have carried out our mission as empire-builders has weakened the force with which at present we impose our rule. We have striven to educate all our subject races to think and act for themselves. We have concealed from them none of the tricks of our trade. Negroes and natives of India have been taught to shoot as well as – sometimes better than – the soldiers of our own race. Kru-boys from the West African coast are nearly as smart naval seamen as the British bluejacket. We have raised up great lawyers in India, clever casuists in Malta, and Negro Attorneys-General in Sierra Leone who have been justly knighted for their attainments. It is time, therefore, that we sought to lay the foundation of our most diversified Empire on lines of affection and mutual trust, as well as on respect for that force emanating from the forty millions of these two little islands, who are enormously out-numbered by our alien fellow-subjects in mere masses, and who are within measurable distance of being equalled in intelligence, aptitude, and bravery by the black, brown, yellow, and foreign-white associates of the Empire. In plain words, it is our business as an Imperial race to show all those people who are British subjects or British-protected persons, and who dwell outside the limits of the white man's lands, that it is to their interest and advantage to remain of their own free will a part of that British Empire which should develop as time goes on into a vast league of peace and good will, unhampered commerce, tolerant beliefs, and unbounded knowledge. In dealing with the non-British elements in our Empire we have often to mend our manners, enlarge our sympathies, and rid ourselves as a nation of a tendency to believe – a tendency still subsisting – that the only perfect human being absolutely acceptable in God's sight is he or she of pink-and-white complexion, who plays all or a selection of the pastimes in vogue in the United Kingdom, and wears the exact costumes ordained by London or Cheltenham, and can quote faultlessly the Mayfair shibboleths of the moment. Nothing in my conception is so vulgar and saddening as the typical up-to-date Indian rajah, who, in the belief that he is thereby getting into closest sympathy with his Anglo-Saxon over-lords, abandons his native costume for ours, and introduces to an Indian climate and tropical surroundings modes of killing time and wasting money which are only tolerable in association with English scenery, Scotch mists, or Irish meadows.

We are constantly publishing the impressions made on our own pioneers, or on our people at home, by the exotic subjects of the Empire. Much less numerous are the recorded impressions which we make on the minds of those visitors to our shores. The book, therefore, which follows these remarks should be of interest and advantage. I desire to state that I disclaim all responsibility for the opinions and impressions of the Katikiro Apolo and his interpreter and friend, Ham Mukasa. The same, I believe, might be said by the Rev. Ernest Millar, who has translated the work from Luganda into English. Very few excisions, I understand, have been made in this literal translation. Here and there a somewhat too personal remark has been omitted, lest it should give offence. Mr. Millar has added a few explanatory notes.

The points on which I should like to set right the Negro author of this book are as follow. He has expressed a belief in one passage that, in reviewing the peoples of the Uganda Protectorate in my recent book, I described his own nation, the Baganda, as being a short people. In this he is quite mistaken, as any one who is interested in this question of stature can ascertain for himself by consulting the pages of *The Uganda Protectorate*. He refers to much the same matter in retailing a conversation with Lord Rosebery. This mistake seems to have arisen from the fact that he was asked questions about the Pygmies, who either reach to the borders of Uganda on the west, or who crop up as exceptional human types in the Uganda county of Kiagwe.

Ham Mukasa is very severe on the dancing of Europeans, speaking in terms of reprobation of the waltz, or of the custom of men and women dancing together. Curiously enough, this impression of indecency is often made on the minds of Arabs and Indians when they see the men and women of Europe swaying to the waltz; yet we who know the inner side of things realise the falseness of this accusation. There may be much vulgar buffoonery in the Kitchen Lancers, while of course in many European lands deliberately indecent dances are of old date or recent invention; but what might be styled the official dance of the Europeans is, as Mr. W. G. Gilbert would phrase it, 'blameless'. The same kindly adjective cannot certainly be applied to the majority of dances in Uganda itself – at any rate, such as were still in vogue at the beginning of the twentieth century. Even though the indecent suggestions may be of old date and historic interest, they left no doubt as to their meaning; and wisely tolerant as all the Christian missionaries in Uganda have shown themselves in reference to native customs which did not impinge on actual immorality, I think they will agree with me in deprecating any praise being given to either the elegance or propriety of the established native dances. So that, my friend Ham, we might both glance at the parable of the beam and the mote in this respect.

In another direction I cannot associate myself with the author's opinions, at any rate in every particular; and this is in regard to the Germans and their attitude towards the Negroes, either on board ship or on land. Some harshness, no doubt, has characterised the gradual extension of German power over East Africa, including the lands which border the southern half of the Victoria Nyanza. Having no direct personal knowledge of what has taken place in these lands, I shall here neither condemn nor approve; but judging merely from what I have heard in epitomised native opinion, I do not think the German rule in the lands south of Uganda is so harsh as it has been depicted by the writer of this book. I much regret to note the way in which he and the Katikiro seem to have been treated on one particular German steamer; yet I remember, in reference to this very line of steamers, some years ago sending detachments of Indians and Negroes by these German vessels in preference to other lines plying on the East Coast, because of the kindly care given to their wants and prejudices on board; and I have also been impressed myself with the courtesy which the German officials on those steamers showed to Portuguese coloured subjects from Goa or Moçambique whose means enabled them to travel first class, and whose manners were to the full as good as those of other passengers of lighter complexion. Is it not actually the case that in parts of East and West Africa the Germans have snapped up a good deal of passenger traffic from British and French lines, on account of their unusual consideration for the feelings of coloured passengers who conducted themselves in a proper manner, and who were sensitive to the aloofness with which on other steamships they were regarded by both ship's officers and fellow-passengers of British or French extraction?

These prefatory remarks might be concluded by a brief biography of the two principal Uganda personages mentioned in this book – the actual author, Ham Mukasa, and the personage whom he accompanied as secretary, the Katikiro (Prime Minister) of Uganda, Apolo Kagwa.

Ham Mukasa, like all natives of the kingdom of Uganda, belongs to a specific clan or totem. In his case it is the clan or tribe of the *Mamba*. *Mamba* is the name in Luganda for the *Protopterus*, or lung-fish, a description of which is given in my book on the Uganda Protectorate. Ham is about thirty-six years old. His father was a small chief of the name of Sensalire. This Sensalire is the man whom the Katikiro in his letters compares in stateliness of bearing to His Majesty King Edward VII. Ham Mukasa began his working life as a page to the King Mutesa. He became converted to Christianity about seventeen years ago. He was severely wounded in the knee during the first great war between the Christians and Muhammadans, and is still lame in consequence. After the war he was given the chieftainship of Kiyoza, which he has held ever since, at any rate in a titular way. He surrendered some of the functions of his chieftainship in 1893 to become a teacher and a licensed lay reader of the Uganda Anglican Church, into which offices he was inducted by Bishop Tucker. The estates which he administered had already become the property of the Church by gift from King Mwanga.

Mukasa now helps the Uganda Admiral (Gabunga) in his special work dealing with natives, canoes, daus, etc. As his own personal property he possesses the island of Lujabwa, which was given to him by King Mwanga. He was one of the first amongst the Baganda to learn English, which language he writes and speaks fairly well. He has written in the Luganda language a commentary on the Gospel of St. Matthew which has had a good sale. He is much esteemed and liked by all Europeans in Uganda, and by his fellow-countrymen. He is a man of extremely kind disposition, and has been appointed by the chiefs one of the guardians of the little King Daudi Chwa. In spite of his lame leg he is an ardent bicyclist.

Apolo Kagwa, the Katikiro or Prime Minister, who visited England on the occasion recorded in this book as the Uganda representative at His Majesty's coronation, is aged about forty. He is a very tall and muscular man, about 6 ft. 3 in. in height, and of absolutely unmixed Negro race; whereas Ham Mukasa is somewhat lighter in colour, and has about him a slight element of the aristocratic caste in Uganda, known as the Bayima or Bahima. (The Bahima were originally of Gala origin, and in their purest types of the present day are a light reddish-yellow in complexion, with absolutely European features, though they have the curly hair of the Negro.) Apolo is the grandson of Bunya, the Kangawo or chief of the Uganda county of Bulemezi. Bunya ruled over this once semi-independent principality in the time of Semakokiro, a monarch of the Uganda Empire, who was the great-great-great-grandfather of the present boy-King. Apolo Kagwa belongs to the tribe or clan of the 'Nsenene', or Grasshoppers. To this tribe belonged many great chiefs of the Baganda nation, and many kings' wives. It is a clan the history of which goes back very far in the legends of Uganda.

Apolo Kagwa was brought up at the king's court, and was one of the first pages who learnt to read. He was baptised nearly twenty years ago. He became chief store-keeper to King Mwanga. He narrowly escaped death at the hands of that monarch on various occasions, partly because he refused to associate himself with the revolting orgies which disgraced Mwanga's court, and partly because he sent word to the British missionaries at Mwanga's court of the murder of Bishop Hannington. When Mwanga was expelled by Christians and Muhammadans united, in 1888, Apolo became Mukwenda, or chief of the county of Singo; but when the Muhammadans turned on the Christians and expelled them, Apolo became the General of the Christian forces, and played a great part in the eventual expulsion of the Muhammadans. When Mwanga became converted to Christianity and returned to Uganda, he singled out Apolo for his bravery and made him Prime Minister. It was Apolo who took the lead of the English or Anglican party among the Baganda Christians, and invited the representatives of the Imperial British East Africa Company to enter Uganda. His influence has always been exerted in favour of a British Protectorate, and he has taken the lead in most great reforms. He commanded Uganda armies in the long struggle against the recalcitrant King of Unyoro, Kabarega. I might add that he was of all others the man who did most to help me to the settlement of

Uganda affairs during my special commission in 1899, 1900, and 1901. Apolo built the first two-storied house erected by any native in the country of Uganda, and also the first house made of burnt bricks. In his newest residence he has introduced many European ideas, such as drain-pipes, bathrooms, electric bells. He was perhaps the first native of his country to learn to ride a horse and to master a bicycle. He was likewise the first to construct a wheeled carriage or to use a typewriter, with which last instrument he has long been a proficient. He made up his mind as far back as 1899 to visit England. The visit was postponed on account of the arrival of the Special Commissioner to effect a settlement in the administration of the Uganda Protectorate. It was further postponed in order that it might coincide with the coronation of King Edward. In the opinion of all who have conversed with him since he returned from England, his disposition has been wholly unspoilt by the attention he received during his stay in this country. He has come back with a great many practical and sensible notions as to the development of Uganda.

The Katikiro has eight children – four boys and four girls. His eldest son is now at a small preparatory school near Cambridge, getting an English education. Like all natives of Uganda, he is intensely patriotic, as proud of his country and its past history (which has been a wonderful one in Africa) as any Englishman could be. He is humble-minded in his desire to learn from our teaching the best elements of our civilisation, but, if I may judge from the conversations I have held with him, his great ideal is to make his fellow-countrymen the best of black men, and not servile imitations of Europeans.

As to the names of these two men, Apolo is the Luganda rendering of Apollos, the first Gentile convert to Christianity. This name was given by the missionary who baptised Kagwa, Kagwa being the Luganda name. Ham Mukasa derives his first name from the son of Noah, who has been associated in tradition with the dark-coloured races, and whose name – curiously enough – has been applied by derivation in the form 'Hamitic' to a very important section of the Caucasian race in North-East Africa – a section to which the ancient Egyptians, the modern Somalis and Galas, and, more than this, the Bahima aristocracy of Uganda, belong. Mukasa is, I believe, not only a well known name in Uganda, but was the title of one of the principal divinities of its old religion.

H. H. JOHNSTON.[1]

---

[1] Sir H. H. Johnston was the Special Commissioner for Uganda in the critical period between 1899 and 1902. He negotiated the [B]Uganda Agreement of 1900 and initiated tenure reform in the colony.

Chapter I

The start – Crossing the lake – Kisumu – First impressions of the train –
First experience of cold on Mau escarpment – Arrival at Mombasa

On May 6th, 1902, at 10 a.m., we started from Mengo.[1] A great many
people came to see us off; chiefs of counties[2] and other chiefs, both great and
small, boys and peasants, all came and escorted us as far as the River
Nalokolongo, and there turned back, and there remained only those who
were going – namely, Apolo Kagwa Katikiro, Yakobo Kago, Andereya
Kimbugwe, Batolomayo Musoke, and those of our people who were going
with us. We reached Kitala, the Mugema's country seat, and found Yosuwa,
the Mugema, waiting for us; he had pitched tents for us to sleep in, and had
got soda-water and a large quantity of biscuits ready for us.

The next morning we reached Entebbe[3] at 8 a.m., and found Mr. J.
Martin and Saulo Sebugwawo awaiting our arrival at the house that had
been prepared for our reception. They made us very welcome, and brought
us twenty water-pots full of water to wash our feet, and also plenty of
biscuits and sweet fruits, and we had a nice meal.

At one o'clock we went to the Commissioner's house, and found there

[1] In precolonial times, the capital of Buganda was moved from place to place at the discretion
of the reigning monarch, but by the time British rule was consolidated in the early 1890s,
Mengo had become established as the capital of the kingdom and thus a symbol of its
centralised authority.
[2] The constant reference to chiefs in the text calls attention to their cultural and political
authority in the Bugandan political establishment. Both Ham Mukasa and Sir Apolo Kagwa
were the sons of prominent chiefs and, as noted in my introduction, they held various
positions in a political system in which chieftaindom defined one's relationship to both
traditional and colonial centres of power.
[3] During the colonial period, Entebbe, a small town on the shores of Lake Victoria, was the
seat of the Protectorate – i.e. British colonial – Government of Uganda. Mengo and Entebbe
can be read in the text as signs of the ambivalent relationship between Bugandan traditional
institutions (represented here by Sir Apolo) and the British colonial government: for unlike
many other countries under colonial rule, Buganda was under the 'protection' of Whitehall
rather than its direct control. The fiction of a protectorate was one that served both sides
well: the colonial authorities could rule without appearing to do so, and the Baganda could
find this rule palatable because it was masked by the mythology of autonomy.

47

the Rev. E. Millar and Mr. J. Martin, and after stopping for about twenty minutes went to see what the steamer was like. The Katikiro showed us all over it, as on another occasion he had had it all explained to him; and after seeing it we went to see Mr. de Boltz, the Government printer, who showed us the wonderful new printing-press, a very ingenious one.

At night we received a hundred and fourteen baskets of food from various friends, and at half-past eight went to the Commissioner's house. He met us at the door, and welcomed us and made us sit down, while they got ready for us a very clever table, which they made larger by putting other boards into it; on the top they put a net, and fastened it with irons at each side, and brought a round ball about the size of a quail's egg; and the Commissioner and Mr. Prendergast, our escort, first began striking it to show how it was done, and then they let the Katikiro and me (Ham Mukasa) play, and then the others. The Commissioner told us that this game was very hard to learn, and was called 'Pongpon'. After we had had some soda-water we went home at 9.30 p.m.

The next morning at nine o'clock we went to embark on the steamer, but before we had reached the lakeshore Mr. Cunningham kept us in order to photograph us with our people, and we then went on to the pier, and found there a very large number of Europeans, including the Commissioner, who had come to bid us farewell. After we had said good-bye they released the cables that fastened the steamer, and we started off at 9.30 a.m.

When we started there were two canoes about half a mile ahead of us, but we passed them at once. We then went to the front of the steamer to see where our servants were travelling, and then came back to the stern, where they had put our chairs, and there sat, each one reading his book. The sea was quite calm and we had no trouble at first. From Entebbe to Mbiru we took fifty-seven minutes – our canoes would have taken about two hours and twenty minutes – and there we began to feel the vibration of the steamer, which resembled the vibration of an earthquake, owing to the screw which drove it, and the strength of the engines and the water which it churned up; this caused the great vibration, which stopped when the steamer left off going and the engines were quiet, and there only remained the rolling motion. After we had passed Mbiru a slight breeze got up, and they put up the sail to make the steamer travel faster, being driven both by the wind and by the screw.

We reached Bugaya at one o'clock – a journey of two and a half or three days by canoe – and there waited half an hour to take on firewood. Muzito and Bisogolo, the chiefs of the island, came off to see the Katikiro; the former brought us an ox as a present, but we refused it as we had nowhere to put it on the steamer. After they had finished taking in wood, we left

Bugaya at half-past four to go to Dolwe Island, which we reached at 9 p.m. After we had had some meat and biscuits we went to bed, and were given the cabin of the steamer to sleep in; all the Europeans slept on deck, where we had sat during the day.

We left at half-past five the next morning, at the time Captain Fowler had arranged. When the Katikiro heard them getting ready to start, he asked how he was going to be ill, if he had nothing in his inside; and Mr. Millar said to him, 'When you think you are going to be sea-sick, you had better eat a piece of dry biscuit', and I called our boys and they brought us some biscuits, and we all ate a few.

Batolomayo Musoke and Yakobo Kago were the first to be unhappy over the motion of the screw, and at first we thought we would do better in the cabin than sitting on deck, but afterwards Andereya and I went on deck; he sat on the afterpart of the deck, and I went to watch the engines working with the power of the fires, and then Mr. Millar fetched up the Katikiro and the others, because it is not customary on a steamer to sit in the cabin, but to go on deck, where every one sits.

At eleven o'clock Mr. Millar called us to have lunch, and I was amazed at his kindness, as he waited on us like a servant, and gave us too much honour, as all our servants could not wait on us – they were constantly sea-sick, and others of them did not know how to wait at table; and therefore he took pity on us because he knew how to walk about on a steamer. We and all our servants were like invalids on the steamer, and he asked each of us, 'What would you like to eat or drink? and I will tell some one to bring it.' And he kept asking us how we were getting on; just as a father and mother look after their children under all circumstances, thus did Mr. Millar to us. We have a proverb, 'He who travels with his father has no sorrow', because he helps him in every thing, and Mr. Millar looked after us like this.

Three of us, Andereya Kimbugwe, Yakobo Kago, and I, Ham Mukasa, had lunch first, and then the Katikiro and Batolomayo Musoke. The Katikiro at first would not eat, as he felt ill. Batolomayo had lunch with him in order that he might eat more cheerfully, not being alone at the table.

After lunch I showed them the hills of Kisumu, and the Katikiro and I went forward to look at the place through our glasses, and we saw the corrugated iron houses by the railway line. At four o'clock they blew the whistle of the steamer to tell the people on shore that we had arrived, and at a quarter past four we reached our stopping-place, and were very much amazed at the cleverness of the Europeans making such a short journey of what used to be such a long one. From Dolwe the canoes take four days, and we took eleven hours and seventeen minutes.

The Europeans went ashore in the small boat which they carry hung up on the steamer. They then took off all our goods, and we went ashore ourselves; and when we had landed, we all congratulated one another on our safe arrival.

We met there a Swahili named Makangala, whom we knew, as he had been in Uganda in the time of Mutesa;[4] and he asked us, 'Where is the Katikiro going, and why has he left Uganda?' I told him, 'He is going to see what other countries are like'; and he said, 'It is very wrong of the Katikiro to leave Uganda and go to visit other countries; it is not right – he will find the country upset when he returns; if I had known he was going to leave Uganda, I would not have brought my goods up to sell'; and I asked him 'Why?' and he said, 'The Katikiro and you people are my friends, and if you are not in Uganda, I do not care for the place; when the Katikiro is away the country is no longer nice, and we traders are now afraid of it'; and I said, 'Don't be afraid, all the chiefs have not left the country – only a very few have come'; but he refused to listen to me, though I told him this.[5]

We then went up to the fort, though really there was not any fort, but only some houses; but it is called the fort because the Europeans and the soldiers live there, but there is no fort as in other places.

When we arrived there Mr. Millar went into the house, and presently they called the Katikiro and gave him a seat on the verandah, and some 'soda-water', which is water with gas in it.

Paulo Kawawulo (the chief of the Baganda at Kisumu) then came to see

---

[4] The phrase Mukasa uses here – 'the time of Mutesa' – is important because of its double meaning and epochal connotation. Mutesa I was the last Bugandan king before the imposition of colonial rule (1857–84) and was thus associated with a past of autonomy and self-assertion. He was remembered from a vivid encounter with the British travellers Grant and Speke in 1862 and his later meeting with Stanley in 1875. Caught between the competing interests of Muslim traders from the East African coast, British travellers and Turkish/Egyptian hegemony in the north, Mutesa became famous for his ability to manoeuvre between these interests while governing his people with ruthless efficiency. He half-converted to Islam when Arab traders held sway in his court, but turned against Bugandan Muslims in the 1870s when he welcomed members of the Church Missionary Society to his kingdom in 1877. As devout Anglicans, Mukasa and Sir Apolo conceive Mutesa both as a symbol of precolonial terror and as a pioneer of modernity and Christianity.

[5] The association of the Katikiro with the maintenance of order is a subtle reference to the precarious state of the kingdom the travellers were leaving behind. Beneath the posture of authority taken by the travellers – and the confidence of Mukasa's prose – Buganda in 1902 was a kingdom which had yet to recover from the cataclysmic events associated with colonial conquest and rule. As senior Regent, Sir Apolo was the centre of authority and order in Buganda. He was leaving behind a kingdom that had lost most of its power to the British colonial authorities and one in which insignias of tradition were vested in a six-year-old boy.

us, and we asked him what had prevented him from coming before; he told us that he had only just heard of our arrival.

We then heard that Mr. Hobley (Sub-Commissioner) had returned, and we told Kawawulo to go and give him our compliments. Soon after this he himself arrived, and asked who was taking us to England, and we told him Mr. Prendergast, who used to be in charge of the station in Budu. He said to us, 'There is no house you can use, so you must sleep in a tent outside'; and then we were very unhappy indeed and very much annoyed, as Kisumu is a very unhealthy place, and the cold at night is bad and makes many people ill.[6] We waited a long time, as the Soudanese and Swahilis could not get the tent pitched; we were there Andereya, Batolomayo, and I, Ham Mukasa, our friends the Katikiro and Kago having gone with Mr. Millar.

After a short time they came back, Mr. Millar himself saying, 'Come along, we have found a nice house to sleep in; pick up your things'; and we all picked up our things and went along, and reached the house they had given us to sleep in; it was one of the rooms of the hospital, and there were in it four beds belonging to the hospital, and we had a fifth of our own, and so we five slept there. The Katikiro had a very bad cold that day, and they got some medicine from the doctor for him. I myself got a bad attack of fever there because I stayed up late writing, and when I went to sleep about 2 a.m. I was very cold indeed, as I had been sitting outside.

Paulo Kawawulo gave us fifty rupees[7] as a parting gift, to be divided thus: Katikiro, 20; Yakobo Kago, 8; Andereya Kimbugwe, 8; Batolomayo Musoke, 7; Ham Mukasa, 7; and we thanked him very much for such a large present. Nkolo, one of the Katikiro's men, brought us a bundle of flour and one rupee, and the Katikiro refused the flour, saying, 'It is hard to get food in this country; keep it for yourself and give me the rupee only'; and this he did, and we thanked him for it, and he thanked us for taking pity on him in the scarcity of food. Our boys killed one of the goats we had brought with us, and sat up till about 1 a.m. eating it.

The next morning, May 10th, the Katikiro woke us up, and after we had had prayers together, he went off with the chief of the servants of the Queen-mother, a boy named Enoka, who took him round the place to show him what it was like, and to see the market, etc. He was away a long time, looking at the Bakavirondo and observing their habits, – neither the men

---

[6] Until 1925, the Ugandan territory included the Eastern Coast of Lake Victoria. The description of the port of Kisumu as 'a very unhealthy place' is telling here, for this was the archetypal frontier associated with disorder, lawlessness and the lack of civility.

[7] In the early part of the twentieth century, British territories in East Africa shared the same currency as the Raj; the rupee was an important signifier of Indian involvement in the economy and culture of the East African empire.

nor the women wear any clothes; they walk about naked, and do not wash themselves at all, – and the Katikiro was looking at them until the time came for us to leave. On this day also we cleaned out the cages of the animals we were taking to England; I had an ape, and Mr. Millar had two servaline cats, which were a great trouble to him, as he kept having to feed them and clean out their cages.

A great many Baganda women also came to see the Katikiro, who had left Uganda with Swahilis, and he asked them, 'Why have you left the country of your birth and come into this country which is not yours, and which is so very unpleasant?' and they said, 'We came with our husbands who brought us.' He asked them if they still had any religion, and some said they had, and others said, 'We are Muhammadans.'

At half-past four we went to the place from which the train started off. They put me on to an ox-waggon, as all my joints were paining me, and so they had pity on me because I could not walk. I was afraid that I was going to have small-pox, but it was only bad fever. A very large number of Baganda women went with us and said, 'They are going to have the case between themselves and Mwanga tried; if they are in the wrong, they will be put in prison', although this was not a fact.[8]

When we got to the train they gave us our places, each one his proper place, and those things which we did not wish to take with us we left in the charge of Paulo Kawawulo. We slept in the train that night, and they told us it was to start at five o'clock in the morning. I could not sleep at first, as there were some Swahilis in the 'room', and they were drunk, but I got changed to another 'room'.[9]

Mr. Millar asked, 'If I put you in a room by yourself, will you mind it?' and I told him I should like it very much, and he took me by the hand and helped me along to another 'room' that had no one in it, and I slept well, having escaped the noise of the drunkards, and I was very pleased with his kindness; all the way he looked after me, coming in and asking how I was, and giving me such food as suited an invalid, until I got well. I was ill three days, and got better on the fourth.

[8] 'They are going to have the case between themselves and Mwanga tried'. This phrase appears ambiguous in its representation and translation, but it calls attention to the sensitive politics (see note 5) which the text occludes. The women had perhaps witnessed Mwanga on his way to exile in the Seychelles in 1899, and seeing Sir Apolo – the king's nemesis – on the same route, they had assumed that he was on the way to have their political conflict adjudicated.

[9] The image of drunk Swahilis is an example of the author's ethnocentrism. But it is also important to remember that the term Swahili had by now become, in an East African context, both a reference to a particular ethnic or linguistic group and a general term for cosmopolitan individuals, people not bound by traditional rules of conduct.

Well, at 5.30 a.m. on May 11th the train blew its whistle to tell people we were going to start, and those who were standing about got into their places: for if you are not quick in getting back to your place after the whistle sounds, you find the train has gone, and has left you behind; a great many people are constantly being left behind like this. The train started off quickly, and we were amazed at the way they had made the line, and how they had filled up the hollows, and bridged the rivers with bridges that made one giddy to look down from.

The first thing to astonish us was seeing what the train was like, and how it went, and I remembered the proverb of our forefathers, which they used to sing, 'You who stagger about under your burdens, those who come after you will be filled with amazement.' The meaning is, 'You are still bothered with your burdens and wonder at what you see, but we men have seen very little; our grandchildren will see more than the things we wonder at now.' Well, see how we who have come after them have seen wonders; as our grandfathers used to sing this proverb, now it is fulfilled in all the things we see made by the cleverness of the Europeans, and what our ancestors did not see, we, their children, see – things that one would not think were made by mere men, such wonders!

When we reached the hill of Mnara, which is in the Nandi country, we first saw the Nandi; in appearance they are like the Lendu. Here they took off the 'head' of our train, which had brought us from Kisumu, and gave us a new one to take us on to Lumbwa, where we met Mr. F. J. Jackson, who had come from Nairobi, the largest inland town, to look round the territory he rules over.

At Lumbwa or Fort Ternan they make the railway climb up in a very clever manner; they go round the hills, and the road goes backwards and forwards, and the train goes up thus until it gets to the top of the hill, and if you are not looking out, you do not know what it is doing; it goes backwards and forwards as if it were going back to the place it came from, and when it has gone backwards and forwards three or four times it reaches the top of the hill; or if the hill be very large, it may go five, six, or seven times, or even more.

We went on through passages they had cut through the rocks, and over rivers and huge valleys which they had bridged. When you see a new piece of work done by the Europeans, you become like a little child in thinking about their work, it is so wonderful.

After leaving Lumbwa, where we waited some time and saw Mr. Jackson, we reached Molo and stopped there the night, as we arrived at 8 p.m., and it was raining very heavily.

It is terribly cold on Mau escarpment; the cold is like that of Europe, because it stiffens all the hands and body, and makes the nose run.

We left Molo at 6.30 a.m., having got a new head to the train, and went across a huge plain at the bottom of the Mau escarpment. In the plain there is a long tube that sucks the water up and carries it a distance of sixteen miles or more to the town of Nakuru; there is a fairly large lake about the size of the lake at Mityana, but the water of it is undrinkable, being salt, and therefore they make the pipe run to a river a long way off to where there is good water.

When we reached Nakuru, all the passengers showed their tickets, which allowed them to travel from place to place, and after they had all done this; the overseer who orders the train to go on blew his whistle to tell us to go on, and all those passengers who were scattered about came back to get into the train, and the engine-driver blew the whistle of the engine itself, and we went off very fast, because the road from Nakuru onwards is very good, and so the train goes quickly, and the embankments do not give way as they do in other places.

This is the place where we saw how fast a train goes; every minute it went a whole mile – that is to say, from Mengo to Entebbe it would only take twenty minutes, but in other places the train goes slowly, and takes a minute and a half or two minutes to go each mile.

We reached Nairobi at 6.30 p.m. on May 13th, and saw how it was built; the houses are all of corrugated iron, and there are a hundred, or a hundred and twenty of them, on a fine wide plain. We left there at 7.30 p.m., and the train went very fast; I can compare it to nothing but to a swallow, because it went so very fast. When anything travels very fast, we Baganda say it goes like a swallow, because a swallow flies so rapidly, and there is nothing else on earth to which I can compare the rate at which a train travels.

Daybreak found us at Mtoto Andei, and we then saw Mount Kilimanjaro, which is on the Anglo-German boundary, a very large mountain indeed, which has much snow on the top, and is very high; we also saw giraffe and many kinds of animals, zebra and antelope, ostriches, jackals, etc., like herds of goats in numbers.

On that day – May 14th – we also went round the hill called Ras Kedong, where there are very high bridges, as high as the Namirembe Cathedral;[10] the bridges are made of iron, the supports are iron, and the parapets of iron and of very strong timber. We afterwards entered the desert of Maungu, and

[10] Namirembe Cathedral is one of the most prominent symbols of the culture that emerged when the Baganda converted to Christianity and its aura here and elsewhere in the book derives from its function not simply as the headquarters of the Anglican Church in Uganda, but as the centre of a new civilisation.

after that reached a place called Mazeras, from which we first saw the sea at Mombasa, and went on and saw for the first time cocoa-nuts which the Swahilis had planted, and of which their gardens consist, as ours do of plantains in Uganda. When you look at their gardens from a distance they look like a forest of palm-trees.

We then arrived at the sea and crossed the bridge from Changamwe to Kilindini – the height of it is about the height of Silasi Mugwanya's house (the second regent) from the ridge-pole to the ground – and reached Mombasa station at 5.26 p.m. We waited some time in the train, while they were arranging about where we should stay, and were getting out our luggage. We met there some people we had seen before in Uganda, as well as the official who had come to meet us.

He was a very kind man indeed – it was of course right for him to welcome us, but he was far kinder in his welcome than many others had been; he made the Katikiro and myself travel up to our house on his trolley, the others walking beside us. They had set apart two houses for us in case we were too many for one; however, we found one house large enough for our needs. The house we slept in was that in which Kings Mwanga and Kabarega had slept, when they were deported from Uganda.[11]

---

[11] See note 8. After the failure of his uprising against the British in 1897, Mwanga had sought refuge with Kabarega, the king of Bunyoro, who had resisted British rule for many years. Captured in 1899 the two were exiled to the Seychelles. It is ironic that Mukasa and Sir Apolo follow the same route on their way to visit Britain, the country in whose name they had helped defeat Mwanga and Kabarega.

Chapter II

Mombasa – What a ship is like – Lamu – The wonderful English – Aden – Truth stranger than fiction

The next morning we went at 9 a.m. to see the chief man of the town, and with him we found the Liwali or chief of the Arabs of Mombasa, a very old man, perhaps seventy or eighty years old, and they both welcomed us to Mombasa. The Liwali said he would call for us at 4 p.m. to show us the chief sights of the town.[12] The others then went home as it was raining heavily, but the Katikiro, Mr. Millar, and I went to the house where they store rupees, which is called the 'Bank', to arrange about our journey.

At four o'clock the Liwali came, and we received him with great honour, on account of his age and position, and he put the Katikiro and Yakobo Kago and Andereya on his trolley and gave them a guide to show them round, while he himself went home. The guide showed them where the kerosine oil is stored, in a thing as big as the Katikiro's dining-room; from this tank they draw oil for lighting purposes and for selling.

While the Katikiro was seeing this the rest of us went round the town with Mr. Millar, and saw the fine houses, some of them very old, the English and Indian shops, the mosques of the Arabs, and the wells from which they draw their water. They dig them very deep indeed, and draw water from them with a rope, as in the well you read about in St. John's Gospel, about which the Samaritan woman spoke to our Lord, 'The well is deep and I have nothing with which to draw water'; perhaps if we too had asked the people near the well the same question, they would have given the same answer.[13]

The next day we went to visit the mission station of Kisauni (Frere

---

[12] A Liwali is 'a headman, usually an Arab, appointed by the government to deal with the affairs of the Muhammadan community' (*Standard Swahili–English Dictionary*, 1939). Muslim communities on the East African coast had a limited degree of autonomy under British colonialism and the Liwali was considered their nominal (secular) leader.

[13] The Bible – and the New Testament in particular – constitutes an important point of reference for Mukasa. He was an avid reader of the Gospels and Letters and he had already written a Luganda commentary on the Gospel According to St Matthew.

Town);[14] we went in small boats rowed by Swahilis; they row in the same way in which large boats are rowed, turning their backs in the direction in which they are going, and do not paddle like we do with our faces in the direction in which we are going.

We saw the chief man of the place, Mr. Binns, who came there twenty-seven years ago, and the lady missionaries, and also went over the beautiful church which they have, and the schools where the elder children were learning English and the younger ones were learning to read books. The seats in the church are like the desks Mr. Hattersley has made at Mengo, and in the schools they have a custom when any honoured visitor comes in – all the children stand up straight and say together Ja-a-a-ambo Bwa-a-a-na (Good mor-r-r-ning, Si-r-r-r), just like people say Amen in church, and when one goes out they say Kwaheri Bwa-a-a-na (Good-bye, Si-r-r-r). We thought this a very good custom.

After we had been round the place we went to the ladies' house, and they received us very nicely and had made tea for us, which we enjoyed very much; they also offered us ripe bananas, thinking that we would like them as they knew the Baganda were accustomed to eat mashed plantains – you all know how kind ladies are, and how they welcome every one as if he were their own countryman. After this we saw the Rev. Ishmael Semler, the father-in-law of Mika Sematimba, and then came home in the rain.

After a short rest we went to see the wife of the Bishop of Mombasa, and a great many ladies came there to welcome us for her sake; there were about eleven of them and six men; I should like to have known all their names, but I did not like to ask them. After tea we went all over the house, which was a very fine one, quite like an English house, and saw also the English church, which had one hundred and twenty-nine seats in it, sixty-five on one side and sixty-four on the other. The bishop himself was away visiting some of the distant mission stations, and so we did not see him.

The next day, May 17th, we heard that our steamer had arrived, and so fastened up our belongings and separated those which we were going to take from those which were to be left behind, and those which were to go were put into a trolley and taken down to the pier. The rest of the things we left with Mr. Bailey, the store-keeper of the mission at Mombasa, and at 2 p.m. we started off.

We first arranged with Mr. Bailey about the Kago and those of our

[14] Frere Town had special significance for Anglican communities in East Africa for two reasons: first it was the site of the first mission by the Church Missionary Society (CMS); second, as a town established for Africans rescued from Arab slave traders by British forces, it was seen as a symbol of a benevolent Englishness.

friends who were going to Zanzibar, and about our attendants who were going back to Uganda, and he said he would look after them, and help them as Mr. Millar had been doing. He agreed to all this because he is a very kind man, and talks nicely to every one and jokes with them; you never see him angry; there are few like him.

After saying good-bye to him, we went down to the sea, all our friends and attendants coming with us, and there we saw our ship, and how wonderfully large it was; but the Europeans did not call it large, but small.

Let me tell you about it. Its height is twice as great as that of Silasi Mugwanya's house – that is, from the sea-level to the deck; the whole height is about two and a half times the height of Mugwanya's house, because the ship has seven stories. Well, what can I compare it to? what do you think of it? with what can you compare a seven-storied ship? It is as wide as Ham Mukasa's brick house, including the verandahs; the masts are as big round as the Katikiro's drum 'Basengeja'; the length is one and a half times as great as that of Namirembe Cathedral; the great tube out of which the smoke comes is as large or larger than the largest drum in Namirembe Cathedral. In the ship there are pens for all kinds of animals – cows, goats, fowls, every kind of animal you find on land is there on the ship; I did not actually see cows myself, but I saw goats and fowls, and these we ate every day on the journey. There is also a place where they stow things, very large and very deep; when you stand above and look down, you are afraid to go too near to the edge. This ship will take twenty thousand loads, is not that a wonder? but there are others larger. The chains that draw goods out of the ship are as large as a man's arm, or in some cases as large as the calf of a big man's leg. The poles to which these are fastened are as large as the head of a small drum. This is what our ship was like, and there are others larger in every respect than it was.

Half an hour after we got on board, they told those who had come with us to go back to the shore after they had seen over the ship; and we said good-bye to our friends, both European and Baganda. Yakobo Kago and Andereya Kimbugwe were so sorry at Apolo Katikiro going away that they refused to come on board, and remained on the pier near the machines that unload the goods from vessels.

The anchor was then pulled up, and we started off; the darkness came on, and the vibration caused by the screw was like the vibration of an earthquake, and we went on our way wondering at the cleverness of the Europeans. When you are on a ship you would not think that the waves could break it, because you are like people on dry land, and can visit one another like those in a town; there are roads in a ship like the roads in a town, and there are bath-rooms. There are lights all over it, and rooms for the rich and for the poor; those of the rich are very fine. Each room has two or three bedsteads in it, and arrangements for washing the face, and drinking-water in bottles. A ship is exactly like a man; it has a life like the life of a man; its life is the machinery that drives it; its food is fire and oil and water – if they do not feed it with these things it dies from want of food. It has arteries like a man; these are the pipes that carry water all over it for drinking purposes and for doing all the work that has to be done, just like a man's blood goes through all the arteries of his body. Just as a man would die if he had no blood, so would a ship without water. I therefore compare it to the life of a man; although it is a lifeless thing, yet it is like a man in these ways.

The next morning we found ourselves at daybreak near a place called Lamu, a three days' journey for our Uganda canoes, but it only took our boat sixteen hours. We saw Lamu at 9 a.m., and at first thought it was an island, though it was really the mainland to which we were going. We arrived at about 11 a.m., and found thirty-five native boats waiting for us in order to take off the cargo which we had brought, and which consisted of three thousand sacks of rice for the troops. After the anchor had been thrown into the sea the ship came to rest, and I saw how clever the natives were in managing their boats and in trying to get the best place for themselves, each man wanting to get some of the cargo to take ashore in order that he might get payment for so doing, and so they all tied their boats to the ship.

The ship had ropes on it, and an iron fence all round to prevent people falling overboard; there were also large iron standards to which the boats were fastened which were carried along by the ship, in order to take people ashore or to save the passengers in case the ship itself came to grief. Some of the boatmen fastened their boats on to these things which I have mentioned, so that they should not be carried away by the waves, and others were looking after the boats themselves, so that their places should not be taken by later comers. They ran up the ship's side and up the ropes like monkeys, in order to make their boats fast, and we were very surprised to see how little afraid of the sea these men were. They themselves were like Arabs, not black men, but red, and spoke a language which differed a good deal from Swahili; they also rowed very well.

The sea there has a sandy beach and all the shore was merely sand hills, and there was no grass at the landing-place; it cannot grow because the sea is salt, and you know how grass will not grow well on sandy soil; well, when to the sand is added the saltness of the sea, the grass cannot grow at all.

After we had landed all our cargo, we stayed the night and paid visits to one another on the boat, and Kabo* (Mr. Prendergast), with whom we were travelling, when we were talking together, and I said, 'This is a large boat', replied, 'No, it is very small; you will see others two or three times as large and much longer.' I fully understood this, because I had already seen the *William Mackinnon*, which I had thought very large indeed, though others despise it for its small size; and when I saw the steamer that took us from Mombasa, I myself no longer thought anything of the size of the *Mackinnon*, and so I believed Mr. Prendergast when he said, 'In our country you will see much larger boats than this.' We stayed for a long time talking about the wonders we had seen, and which we hoped to see – we did this a great deal while we were on the sea, because we had plenty of time to spare, whereas on land we had little spare time.

After leaving Lamu we went right out into the deep sea, which reaches as far as Aden, and is called the 'Ocean'. The meaning of the word 'ocean' is a large sea with no islands at which to stop. On this day I first noticed the officers of the ship; they do not remain in one place, but go from side to side, keeping a look out, and looking also ahead. They observe the stars at night, and the sun and moon; all these they look at that they may see the course on which the ship is travelling. They look at these through a telescope of a different kind from the ordinary ones, and which has many glasses on it; I myself looked through it at the sun, which looked round like an orange, and very red. We noticed that the colour of the sea was like blue (washing blue), and the foam was very white, just like the foam of the soap used in the final washing of clothes.

My friends, I cannot tell you about all the beautiful and wonderful things the English have in their boats, because it is impossible to explain them in a book. A foolish man who did not know of the existence of God, when he saw the miraculous things made by the Europeans, would call them God, and would not think they were made by men: though one would have pity on him on account of his ignorance, since even clever men are amazed at these things, unless they themselves have had a share in the making of them. One pities a foolish man, because he does not understand the difference between earthly and heavenly things.

Later on in the day Mr. Millar took me to look at the engines, and I saw a long way below us one of the engineers, who looked like a little boy on account of the distance; if one looks at these engines being driven by the fire, one soon gets giddy. I went and told the Katikiro about all I had seen,

* English = little basket. Baganda peasantry and others, not being able to remember English names, usually call the Government official by some nick-name. Mr. Prendergast got this name because he usually wears a straw hat.

as he was ill with a headache, and was constantly sea-sick, and never left his chair except to eat and to be ill, and very often he had his meals in his chair. I was very glad that I was not ill or even giddy, so that Mr. Millar had only one invalid to look after. He used constantly to come and ask us how we were getting on, though the Katikiro was always ill. Mr. Prendergast asked Mr. Millar how it was I was not ill, and he told him that it was because I was accustomed to the lake in Uganda; though this was not the real reason, which was that I was differently constituted to the Katikiro.

There are many different kinds of people in the world; some are constantly being sick when they see things they do not like, or smell things they do not like, or eat things they do not like – many are like this, while others can eat everything without any trouble, and so it is in all nations of the world; but because a man is accustomed to our Victoria Nyanza it is no reason he should not be ill on the sea. A great many Europeans are always travelling about on the sea, and yet they are ill; these ships are very different from our canoes, and the ocean is a very different thing from our lake, for the waves of the sea are like mountains, and I do not think one can get used to these by travelling only on lakes like ours.

On the morning of May 21st I found the Katikiro had slept very badly, and was very unwell, as he had not been able to eat anything, and what he did eat he could not retain. He asked me if I had prayed that he might be able to retain his food, and I told him I had not done so, but had merely prayed as usual for protection against all dangers on the way; and in this prayer really the other matter was included, since this illness was one of the dangers, as if a man could not eat he would not fail to die. After I had left him I went back to my cabin and prayed earnestly about this matter, and did so morning and evening all through the journey.

I asked Mr. Millar how far it was from Mombasa to Aden, and he told me it was about sixteen hundred miles; and I perceived that there was more water than land on the earth, just as I had seen in maps. I asked him if there were crocodiles and hippopotami in the sea, and he told me there were none, but that there were whales and fishes. I asked him what a whale was like, and if it had legs like an elephant; and he told me it had not, but that it was like a very large fish, and had a tail; he told me also how they were killed.

After this I played deck-quoits with Mr. Prendergast, and then Mr. Millar took me on to the top of the vessel, and I saw how it was steered, and how the officer on the top kept watch all round to look out for any danger, and how the ship was steered by compass, so that it did not lose its way when the sun and stars could not be seen. When they pass another vessel they can talk to it by means of flags, each of which has a meaning. I cannot tell you all about these things, as there is nothing in our country to which I can compare them.

The things of the Europeans are always amazing; and I thought to myself that if we were always wondering at these things which we saw while we were still on the way, when we reached England itself we should be like the Apostle of our Lord who was called St. John the Evangelist, when he saw the wonders of God which he had never seen before; and when he wrote them down in his book he had just to compare them to the earthly things they knew, though they were not really like them; because if he had not compared them to these earthly things, how could they have understood all these wonders? I, in the same way, in telling you these things, must just compare them to the things you know, though really they are not like them at all, as there is nothing in Uganda to which one can compare the English things; however, we are fortunate in one thing, and that is that some of these things will not fail to be brought to Uganda, and so will be seen by those who never saw them in England. Already we have seen the wonderful telegraph, which is the greatest thing that has yet come to us; the second is, perhaps, the steamers: these are the two wonderful things the Baganda have seen.

The next morning, May 22nd, the Katikiro saw the coast of Somaliland, and so felt better and walked about a little, and later on in the day Mr. Millar got from one of the passengers some medicine to cure sea-sickness, and the Katikiro took four doses and was cured; and so we could talk a long time together. He was very pleased at being cured, and we talked a long time about our country, and how Christianity spread over the world, and about the things we were going to see in England.

On May 23rd we passed several ships. One can understand that the sea is like a hill, as one first sees the smoke of a distant ship as it rises up into the air, and then as it comes up to the top of the hill you see the masts, and then when you get near to it you see all the ship. The Katikiro went all over our vessel with Mr. Millar, and came back and told me all he had seen; Mr. Millar also told us that in this part of the sea there are large fish that eat men who are swimming in the water or who are shipwrecked; they draw men down under the water and eat them. They live and breed in the water. You see the wonderful things that there are near Europe! He told us also a good many things about the different European races; and also told us to get ready the things we most required, as we should reach Aden in the morning.

The next morning, May 24th, at ten o'clock, we first caught sight of Aden, and saw a great hill like an island. We reached the harbour at twelve o'clock, and found in it many steamers and small boats. The houses on shore are round the foot of the hills, and are all of stone. The hills have no grass on them, and are all joined together just like the walls of a fortress. The houses look from a distance like mushrooms, and are white. The Katikiro attracted my attention by saying, 'Look at those dogs drawing carriages'; really the animals were horses, but owing to the distance they looked like dogs, and the camels looked like calves. A great many Somalis brought out their boats to take men and goods ashore; and when they reached the landing-place they were paid their fare. This custom will not fail to come into Uganda, as many large boats are sure to be built, and so little boats will be needed to take the cargo on and off.

The Somalis are very like our Bayima in every way, both in customs and in dress, for they have little sense of decency.[15] These Somalis have long been in contact with Europeans, and their country is near Europe, and yet they have never left off their evil habits; what makes them the harder is that they are Muhammadans, and therefore they harden their hearts and hate the Europeans. They come to serve the Europeans because they are poor and want to make money, not for any love of them.

The Europeans are wonderful people. The whole of Aden is one mass of rock; there is no grass and no green thing. If you see anything green, it has been planted there – you know how the Europeans plant things in places where they will not grow naturally – and every green thing if left to itself withers away.

They brought some boats alongside and we went ashore, and passing the custom-house went to the Hotel de L'Europe, which was kept by a Turk, and where we were to stop three days for the steamer that was to take us on to England.

In the evening we went out for a drive, and passed along the sea-shore, near which the people have built a great many houses. There are all nation-alities – English, French, Germans, Arabs, and Jews; these last chiefly sell ostrich feathers to the Europeans who pass Aden; they cheat them very much, as the Europeans are very fond of buying things that come from other lands.

[15] The association of the Bayima (commonly known as the Bahima) with indecency is a radical departure from colonial mythologies and taxonomies, since the cattle-owning caste in Western Uganda, Rwanda and Burundi had been instituted in colonial literature as a superior ruling class. In *The Journal of the Discovery of the Source of the Nile* (1864), John H. Speke advanced the notion that the Bahima were a 'Hamitic race' who had migrated to East Africa from further north. Evidence of their superiority was supposed to be their 'European' features and 'advanced culture'. Mukasa's condescension here is a mark of his confidence in the superiority of his new Anglo-African culture.

My friends, you had better let the Europeans teach in all lands, so that the people may escape from their ignorance.[16]

The English have cut through the hills at Aden and made a tunnel through which carriages pass; and lamps on each side take the place of the sun. They make their carriages go up on to a high hill in the way which I mentioned when I was describing the hill of Lumbwa, so that when you go up the hill you cannot tell when you arrive at the top; and at one end of the tunnel there is a fort with guns that will carry a distance as great as from Mengo to Sowe (ten miles). This statement would seem to be untrue to any one who did not know the miracles which the English do; there are some guns that will carry twenty miles, and though I may seem to you to be not telling the truth, yet there are things more wonderful than those about which I have told you, so that I am not ashamed of what I have written. The hill on which these guns are placed is as high as if one was to root up the hill of Rubaga and put it on the top of Namirembe. We saw also the tanks which had been made in the time of King Solomon, and had been repaired by the English. It only rains about every five years, and then the water comes down from all the hills and fills these pits, which are twelve in number. I did not see many cows at Aden, but the goats and horses and camels and fowls were everywhere in great numbers.

As May 24th was the Queen's birthday, all the lamps were lit and all the ships were lit up at night, and the whole town glittered with them.

When we got back to the hotel we had dinner, and then went for a walk and admired the houses, which were beautifully built, one house (row of houses) was as long as from Mengo to Kampala (half a mile).

I asked Mr. Millar why they still remembered the Queen as she had been dead so long, and he said it was because they all loved her so much, and had not yet forgotten her, and also our King Edward had not yet been crowned.

The next morning, May 25th, was Sunday, and we went to church. We found that most of the congregation were soldiers, who had their rifles with them in church – each man had his rifle beside him; they guard this place very carefully, and therefore all the soldiers take their rifles to church. We two were the only two black heads in the church; all the others were white. When the service was over Mr. Millar told us to come outside quickly, and we saw the way the soldiers all held their rifles in the same way, and all

---

[16] If one of the problems raised by Mukasa's text is how the colonised can identify so easily with their coloniser, this paragraph contains a useful explanation. Throughout the text, Europe is associated with teaching (enlightenment), and peoples who exist outside the orbit of this form of knowledge are defined as ignorant. But both terms – enlightenment and ignorance – are moral rather than epistemological categories in this context: enlightenment is conversion to Christianity; ignorance is the inability or failure to be converted.

turned round together without any one making a mistake, and all their feet reached the ground together. Mr. Millar read us the laws of the place, how no one was allowed to take photographs of the forts. The laws were written in English, French, German, and Arabic, as this place is in Arabia.

We then went back to church for the Holy Communion, after which the chaplain came out and greeted us, and asked us if our church was like that one; and we told him that ours was larger, and made of brick, not stone. At half-past four the Katikiro went with Mr. Prendergast and Mr. Millar to see the Consul; I did not go with them, but when they came back the Katikiro told me all he had seen and how they had had tea, and how they had not stopped long, and how the Consul was a very old man with a white beard.

If any one came to Aden who was not used to great heat, he would perhaps die in about ten days. Many of the inhabitants leave their houses, and all sleep outside on account of the heat; we ourselves spent the day in our loin-cloths only, in the house, and when we were called to have a meal we dressed properly. In all the houses they have large fans to make the place cool, and these fans are fastened together with ropes, and then a man stands a long way off and pulls the rope, and all the fans sway to and fro and you get a little cooler; there is no day or night to this heat – it is always hot.

The next day, May 26th, we sat on the verandah of the hotel, and in the evening went for a drive past the forts and down to the sea-shore. There are a great many children in Aden, though the English send their own children to England to be educated while they are still very young, as the heat is too great for them.

Chapter III

S.S. Manora – *The Red Sea not red* – *The Katikiro ill* – *Suez* – *The Suez Canal* – *Port Said* – *Athletic sports* – *Nearing Europe*

The next day, May 27th, we packed up our things as we heard that our steamer was going to arrive, and at half-past seven it reached the harbour. It was about twice as large as the one which had brought us from Mombasa, and was about 125 yds. long and 45 ft. wide. We went on board after breakfast, and the ship stayed a long while taking in cargo – skins, flax, ivory, etc.; they took on board about 5,400 bales of goods of different kinds.

We had lunch in the saloon, which was as wide as the space between the centre pillars of Namirembe Cathedral, and held about a hundred passengers.[17] When dinner-time came we put on our best clothes, and as we entered the saloon all the passengers turned round to look at us, and kept their eyes on us all the time we were there, and we wondered if they were looking at us to see what we were eating, or whether they wondered what country we had come from. After dinner we walked up and down the deck, as is the custom of the English to stretch their legs.

There were a great many Jews on board, going from Aden to Egypt with their wives and children, and they were very much bullied by the sailors, so that I felt quite sorry for them; they abused them and struck them and tormented them in every way; they never walked about on the boat like other deck passengers, and even the small children bullied them. They were all very timid, and ran away from any one who threatened them; they were like defeated soldiers, afraid of everything. These Jews, however, are great cheats when they trade; a thing worth two rupees they sell for ten, though if you know their customs you can get it for five or six; they chiefly sell silks

---

[17] Namirembe (see note 10) serves both as a point of reference in Mukasa's attempt to translate the European 'other' and as a sign of how this 'other' has been contained within Bugandan culture. In other words, for the intended audience of this book, Namirembe is the space in which they have tried to rebuild new institutions in European terms; serving as a figure of the native and foreign, it functions as a bridge between Britain and Buganda.

and ostrich feathers, and are not ashamed to overcharge for them, and take them to every ship that comes into the harbour.[18]

There was on board the boat a very fat man, as fat as Nakatanza and Kaima* rolled into one. It is difficult to tell you the size of some of the English; when they see a man as fat as Nakatanza, they say, 'In a few years that man will be fat.'

The next day, May 28th, we reached the Red Sea, though it is not really red; the water is quite black, and we were surprised that a black sea should be called 'The Red Sea'.[19] We asked the captain why it was called the Red Sea, and he said that perhaps it was because the inhabitants of the coast were red in colour, and so it was called the sea of the red people, and thus the name got changed to the Red Sea. It is a very large sea – 1,308 miles long, and from 80 to 150 miles broad.

We passed the island of Perim, on which were some houses belonging to the English; there are no natives on the island; the people are only there in order to guard the passage, just as they are at Aden and Gibraltar, to stop bad people passing; this is what I think myself. We also saw an island of rock, only with no earth on it, and on this a tower had been erected, with a lamp at the top, to warn ships to keep away from the rocks: this sea has many rocks in it that break up ships, but now-a-days there are not many accidents, as the whole sea has been examined, and so they know what it is like, and can go through safely by means of the compass and the stars, which show them the right road.

The next day, May 29th, after breakfast the captain came to us and asked us how we had slept. He only knew English, and asked the Katikiro if he was learning it, and the Katikiro said 'Yes', and he said he hoped he would know it by the time he went back to Uganda. Mr. Millar then came up, and the captain took us up on the bridge and showed us a map of the Red Sea, and also a very old map of our lake, the Victoria Nyanza, made in the time of King Mutesa. He showed us a great many other things, and later on we saw some water under a microscope, and in it was a thing like a caterpillar, which was invisible to the naked eye. We were amazed at the cleverness of the Europeans in thus being able to see things invisible to the ordinary eye.

---

* These are the two fattest men in Uganda.

[18] The figure of the Jew occupies an ambivalent position here and serves as an example of the conflicting sources of Mukasa's knowledge. The author's familiarity with the Jews comes from the Old Testament. Their story here – of genesis, ecumenical authority, conquest and exile – is a familiar one for the African reader; it is the basis of empathy. But as the rest of the paragraph indicates, Mukasa's education in Christianity and Englishness has made the grammar of anti-Semitism accessible.

[19] The image of the Red Sea is a dramatic one in both the Old and New Testaments.

Things such as this one cannot tell to an ignorant man, because they would appear as idle tales to him. Mr. Millar said, 'Do you see that caterpillar? That is the reason we boil our water'; and we from that time saw why water ought to be boiled.

Later on it became very rough, and the Katikiro and I returned to our cabins, and had our food brought to us; he was very ill, but I was not actually sick myself, though I felt uncomfortable.

At one time the ship got a little out of its course without the steersman noticing it, and the captain at once rushed up on to the deck and abused him for his carelessness. I saw this myself, and understood how the captain was looking well after the boat.

The next day, May 30th, Mr. Millar came and asked us if we were not going on deck, and we went up; but it was very cold and so I did not stay there long. Another reason that prevented me from stopping there was that the English ladies and their children were sitting all over the deck, and there was hardly room to pass, and I did not like to keep forcing my way past them. The Katikiro soon also came down below, and was very ill during the day with six different illnesses, cold, fever, sore throat, indigestion, gum-boils, and headache, and I was very distressed about him, but he consented to eat a little food. Mr. Millar asked the doctor to come in and see him, and he gave him some medicine. The former also came in seven times during the night to see him, and this showed me how unwell the Katikiro was, and I kept awake all night to see after him, as he was continually tossing in his berth.

Mr. Millar helped us a great deal in everything we required, and would not sit with the other Europeans, but always sat with us, and covered the Katikiro with his own rug when they sat together, so as to keep his knees warm, though other Europeans would not do such a thing as that; and he was not afraid of their despising him. I think there were two reasons why he did this: first, because he was a real Christian; and secondly, he followed the customs of his nation in their kind government, and did not want to bring shame on this nation, because the English rule righteously in all lands, whether of wise nations or of ignorant nations, and they honour men who do not themselves expect to be honoured. This nation is a truly peaceable nation in all its laws, which are in many ways like the laws in the Bible.[20]

---

[20] It is interesting to note that biblical law is given a certain antecedence over British law. It is also important to note that whenever the author is confronted by events that seem to contradict his own ideal notions of Englishness, he turns to moral laws or customs as the golden standard against which the Europeans are to be judged. Against the disjunctive particularity of the culture he encounters, Mukasa seeks universal codes that might connect people above their manifest differences.

The following day, May 31st, Mr. Millar came to ask us to go on deck; but the Katikiro would not go as he had not slept well. However, I said I would come up after him; but when I reached the deck, I could not see him – there were only ladies and children, so I went down again, and kept quiet, and the Katikiro got a little sleep, and I too slept a little, and then we both went on deck and found Mr. Prendergast and Mr. Millar, and talked to them for some time, and asked them where all the passengers came from; and they told us that some of them were soldiers, some missionaries, some tea-planters, and so on, and that they were all going to England to rest. At night we asked a great deal about the various customs of the English, and wrote them all down, so that we should make no mistakes, as every nation has its own customs. In the evening the wind dropped, and the sea got a little calmer.

The following day, June 1st, we passed an island with a lighthouse on it, the light of which was turned up and down by clockwork, and in the evening reached the town of Suez, the lights of which were like stars. The governor of the town and the doctor sent us a message that they would come and examine us in the morning; and that we were not to go away until we had been examined. Our captain was very angry, as he wanted to get on his way; but doctors are held in great honour, and one cannot disobey them, so that, although the captain was angry, yet he had to obey.

The next day, June 2nd, at six o'clock, Mr. Millar called us, saying, 'Come and be examined; the doctor has arrived', and so we went on deck quickly. They first examined the Indians, because there was plague in their country, and then they read out the names of the Europeans, and then we were told it was all over, and we were very pleased. We thought that perhaps, owing to the Katikiro's illness, we might have to leave the boat, since he had been ill for seven days; and even a person who was not a doctor could tell how ill he was, as he had got very thin from eating so little. They took off two sick people to keep them until they got well, and then they would let them go on by another steamer, since steamers are constantly passing.

They gave us an electric light, which was very strong, and hung it over the bows of the ship to prevent us from running into another one; the light from this lamp was much greater than that of the sun, and one could not bear to look at it. It was brighter than the sun at its brightest. We met another ship in the canal at night, and I tried to look at its light, but could not do so for more than a part of a minute; it was so bright it made our ship look as if it were whitewashed. Mr. Millar took me down to show me the engine that made the light, but when he began to explain it I was just like a little child in being quite unable to understand it; the machine made 9,000 revolutions a minute.

This canal is a marvellous thing, and shows how the Europeans can always do whatever they set about doing. It is as long as from Mengo to Wakoli's, eighty-seven miles, and is all cut through the sand, and is so deep that it will take vessels seven stories high. It is not wide – one could throw a stone or an orange across from side to side; and when two ships meet, they tie one up to posts on the bank to let the other pass. They always tie up a ship coming from Europe to make room for one going to Europe, as the latter has on board tired people going home to rest. There are all manner of different coloured lamps along the canal, each with a meaning for the sailors. We found workmen widening it in some places, and saw how camels worked in carrying away the sand; each camel knelt down till its panniers were filled, and then got up and went away when it was ordered to do so.

The town of Suez is built on the breakwater, and there are rows of trees planted and watered as in Aden, so that the inhabitants may have shade. As you pass along the canal you come to a wider part, on which is the town of Ismailia, and near this is the road along which they brought our Lord when He was young and His parents were fleeing from Herod, who killed the little children in Bethlehem.[21]

The houses of the Egyptians are high and fine, like those of the Europeans, but not so much decorated. I cannot compare the beauty of the English houses to anything else – you will hear about them later on.

At midnight on June 2nd we reached Port Said, which is on the Mediterranean Sea, which St. Paul crossed when he went to preach the Gospel, and in which are the islands of Cyprus and Crete, and also Sicily, which is near Rome. Port Said is a large town not far from Alexandria, where the Nile flows into the sea; we did not expect to see towns like this in Africa – we thought we should only find them in Europe.

The next morning, June 3rd, the Katikiro called me to look at the town and see what it was like, as at night we had only seen the lights. Some of the houses were as much as six stories high, and the whole place was very well laid out, and there were a great many people about. After we had finished taking in coals we left, passing many ships in the harbour and numbers of small boats.

We left Cyprus and also Jerusalem to the right, and did not see these places, though we should very much have liked to have done so, because they are very famous in the Bible.

I was a little unwell during the day, and the Katikiro was rather worse in the evening, but did not wish to see the doctor.

---

[21] The journey through the Middle East and the Mediterranean has, in effect, become a confirmation of the narratives Mukasa has read in the Bible.

Chapter III

The next day, June 4th, we were on the sea near Crete, the island on which St. Paul left Titus to be the bishop of the church; Captain Sanders showed us the island at about two o'clock, when it appeared like a cloud in the distance, but at five o'clock we got near to it and passed by the side of it. The Katikiro was very much worse and ate nothing during the day; he went up on deck to look at the sea, as he was tired of stopping in his cabin, and thus he got a chill and was worse; however, Mr. Millar persuaded him to come to the dining-table, and he ate a little lunch and then had a hot bath. I was much amazed at the cleverness of the English, because the steward first turned a tap and let in cold water from the sea, and then turned another tap and let in steam from the boiler, which made the water hot.

One wonders more each day and each hour that one sees the cleverness of the English, which is never ending. They are not white men for nothing; in all countries white things are considered very beautiful, and so also the English deserve to be held in honour, not only on account of their white colour, but because to their whiteness they add very wonderful wisdom, and just as a blacksmith or a carpenter is given praise on account of the good work he does, so they should be praised on account of what they do.

The Katikiro was worse in the evening, so I went for Mr. Millar, and he came down with the doctor and Mr. Prendergast, and found that his temperature had gone up to 102°. The doctor gave him some medicine, and he perspired gently during the night. He was a very obedient patient, and did whatever I told him without arguing, and was not troublesome as some other people are.

The following day, June 5th, the doctor gave him some more medicine, and he got a good deal better, and was able to go on deck to see the sports. They had a race in which the people collected potatoes and put them into buckets; and another in which they raced, each one having a potato in a tea-spoon, and many other kinds of races. I noticed the honour they gave to the ladies, as a lady was chosen to give away the prizes.

There were about eighty Europeans looking on at the sports, and one would not have believed that such things could be done on a ship, as all the time the sports were going on the ship was not standing still, but going on its way.

The next morning, June 6th, we caught sight of the coast of the mainland of Rome, and first saw a large hill near the town of Reggio; we soon passed through the sea which divides Italy from Sicily, which was as wide as from Munyonyo to Kisinsi. On the island of Sicily is a high hill covered with snow, which is behind the town of Messina. After we passed the straits we went near an island called Stromboli, on which was a sharp-pointed hill, from which a great deal of fire comes out and also smoke.

On this day I saw how the Europeans dance to the piano, a thing which they like doing very much. When they dance they jump up and down and twist round, men and women holding on to each other in pairs; for my own part I preferred the music to the dancing, which I thought was a shameful thing, for men and women to dance thus together.[22] They danced in many different kinds of ways, a different way for each tune.

After this the Katikiro called me to come and see the machine that makes the cold to prevent the meat going bad. I took hold of some of the lumps of cold stuff (snow), which was like hail, and I wanted to take it away, but Mr. Millar told me it would melt, so I left it; it made my hands very cold indeed, so that they nearly cracked with the cold.

[22] Why does Mukasa find men and women dancing together shameful? It would be tempting to read this as a sign of his incomplete acculturation, but it is more accurate to interpret his moral qualms – his puritanism – as a product of his strict interpretation of gender and sexuality in the New Testament. His authority here is, of course, St Paul.

Chapter IV

Naples – Pompeii – Marseilles – European trains – France – Arrival in London – The Westminster Palace Hotel

The next day, June 7th, we arrived at Naples at five o'clock, and saw all the large houses. Mr. Millar told us to get ready to go on shore, and we went off before breakfast and got into a little steamer, which took us ashore, and then a guide came to take us round Naples, and also to show us the town of Pompeii, which was destroyed in the times of the Apostles. We got into a carriage and drove along, looking at the large houses and the beautiful streets and the numbers of people, and the many horses and donkeys and cattle that were drawing the peasants' carts. If one was to lose sight of one's friends for four minutes, one would be lost, as all the streets and all the houses are alike.

We drove to the railway station, and then went about seven miles by train, and our guide bought us some breakfast, and we paid him for it, and he then bought some 'tickets' to enable us to pass along all the roads. These tickets are small bits of paper, which are signs of the permission you are given to travel everywhere, and without them you cannot go anywhere. After we had bought our tickets the guide took us to Pompeii. The Romans enclosed all the place after they had dug it out, and arranged to take tribute from every one who wished to see it, since a wonderful thing like this would not fail to bring sightseers, and it cost a great deal to dig out. Even now it is not yet all dug out. They showed us many little hills, which they told us were all houses. The mountain from which the fire came to destroy this town is about three miles off.

We first went into a house in which were bodies that had been dug up; men, horses, bears, cows, cats, dogs, etc., and everything was just as it was in the old times. We saw all the evil practices of the people in those days. We went into the town and saw what the roads were like, and entered a great many houses.[23]

[23] This paragraph reinforces the point that Mukasa's moral authority – and his ethnocentrism – comes from, and is secured by, his Christian conversion. For Victorian Britain, the ruins of pagan Rome may be insignia of Western civilisation, but for the colonial subject they are reminders of 'evil practices'.

I want you to understand, my friends, how that the evil of this city brought its terrible judgment on it, and its sin was like that of Sodom and Gomorrah. We saw many unspeakably bad things. God is very long-suffering, though men are foolish; and though they have seen this town, yet many do not repent of their evil habits, or leave off spoiling their cities, though God will execute His judgment on them in His own time, and therefore we all should remember that there is nothing more valuable than our lives.

Our guide then took us to the station, and we had to wait there about half an hour, and while there we saw a telegraph that wrote down everything; afterwards the train came in, and we went to Naples and drove round the town. When Mr. Millar saw how we were surprised at the number of people, he told us we should see many times more than these in London; and we could not understand this, although it was true. He would not allow us to speak to the people we saw, because some of them were beggars, and others would have abused people like us; so he took care of us and showed us everything, and we did not get very tired. After this we went back to our ship, which left in the evening.

The next morning, June 8th, we passed the islands of Corsica and Sardinia, and they called us to see a whale; but when we reached the deck the ship had left it behind, it was going so fast.

The inhabitants of Corsica are very lawless, and are always fighting with one another, and will not obey any of their rulers, and do not like strangers.

After passing Corsica the wind became very strong, and the sailors had to take down the awnings as the waves came on to the ship. I stayed some time looking at the waves, and then went to call the Katikiro to look at them; but he could not stay long – it was too cold. At night I could not finish my dinner, and the Katikiro could not eat anything, on account of the rough-ness of the sea.

The next morning, June 9th, found us nearing Marseilles, the port of France where travellers land from Africa. There were a great many ships in the harbour, large ships, and men-of-war, and small steamers. When we got into the harbour a man came alongside, who did a great many acrobatic tricks with his daughter and a dog, and we were surprised at all the different things the Europeans learn to do – one is always finding something new.

All the goods for Marseilles were then taken off the steamer, and our things were taken on shore with them, as we wished to get to England quickly, and so were going to cross France by train, a journey of one day only, whereas to go round by sea would take eight days.

Mr. Millar told us to get ready to leave the boat, and after lunch we went with the guide, who had asked us to allow him to show us round the town. He brought us a carriage drawn by a horse, and we got in and went to see what Marseilles was like. He first showed us the very old wall of the town, which had been built by the Romans, and a very ancient church, a fine building of stone.

We then went to see the greatest church in the land, which was three thousand years old; it was built in 1098 B.C., and was first a temple, where they used to offer up their children, but afterwards it was made into a Christian church, as it is now. We then saw the large harbour, in which were a great many ships, perhaps seven hundred; the masts of them were like a forest of dead trees, and we wondered with an unending wonder, because wherever we went we found something new to wonder at. After this we went up a very high hill to get a general view of the town; we went up a precipice. They took us into a room which they called 'lifet' (lift). They make a thing like the room in a house, and a man comes and turns a handle, and a great deal of water comes out, and when all the water is finished, the room goes up by itself.

When we got to the top I looked down at the carriages and horses which had brought us, and they looked like goats. We then looked over the town, which is very large indeed, and contains a great many people, who are very busy in their different occupations. They are like locusts in number. At the top of the hill they have built a very beautiful church; it is impossible for me to tell you about the ornaments outside and the paintings on the roof. The floor is of black and white pavement, and looks like a piece of cloth, but if you walk carelessly you fall; I myself nearly fell down, as it was so slippery. Inside they put also many of the objects of their religion, all of gold, and also a great many very beautiful pictures. After we had seen the church we went back the way we came. This lift is put there to make money, because there are a great many people who come to see the church, as it is so fine, and many come from the town to service; and when a man sees that if he goes all the way round he will take a long time, and he has the money to pay, he will not fail to go up this way, and pay to do so, as we did, because we did not wish to go all the way round, and this was the shortest way, and everything costs money.

We reached the bottom and paid for our journey – Mr. Millar always did the paying, as we did not understand how to do it – and then got into our carriage, and our guide took us to see a house of remembrance (picture gallery), in which were pictures of all the ancient saints of God, and of the old kings of Europe and other lands, such as Africa and Egypt; there were pictures also of the chief men of these lands who had done great deeds, and of all the bishops, and of the different battles of old time. We also saw a great many pictures which were not worthy of being exhibited, as they were of people in a state of nature, and were most shameful!!!

This building was a very large one, and tired us a good deal. After this we went to see the water they carried underground, and which came out through the mouths of statues of many animals – lions and cows and horses and men – they made the fountain thus to gladden the eyes. The water fell at last into a pool, from which it returned whither it had come; it was very cold and splashed like a waterfall, but a waterfall has more water in it. After this we went to look for a house where they sell food (hotel), and then after dinner went to see if our train had come.

We had been a short time at the station when we heard it whistle, and when it arrived we got into our compartment. We four had a compartment to ourselves – Apolo Katikiro, Mr. Prendergast, E. Millar, and H. Mukasa. Our friends were very kind to us, and gave us the best places, and we had beds to sleep on. When I saw how fast the European trains went I understood that there was nothing to which I could compare them. For want of anything else I might compare them to the way a bullet travels, as I know how fast that goes; failing this, there is nothing else to which I could compare them. Well, let me ask you what sort of a thing is it that only takes one day from Mengo to Mombasa? If you can think of anything that does this, you can compare the rate of a train to it, because this is the distance across France as far as Calais, the port on the other side.

The next morning, June 10th, we woke up as we were travelling through France, and saw how the country people had built themselves very nice houses, and how well they had cultivated their land. The country is a very fine one, and is divided up into pieces; one field we saw as long as from Mengo to Munyonyo (eight miles) not divided up into pieces, and sown in different parts with different kinds of seed, red and yellow and green and white all mixed up, and when we looked at it from a distance it was very pleasing to the eye.

At 8 a.m. we reached Paris, the capital of France, and wondered at the large houses and wide roads and many horses, and the men like ants in numbers; the houses resembled hills in their height and size. We saw also a tall pillar they had put up, with the figure of a man on the top standing on one leg, with wings and with a sword in his hand; when you look at the top of it you hold on to your hat so that it shall not fall off, it is so high. If you go to the top of it you can see all over the city, but we did not do so, but only saw it from below. This pillar was put there as a memorial to remind people of the prison into which their king used to put them (Bastille); when they removed the prison they put this pillar up, and wrote on it all about what happened at that time, as a memorial. We stayed two hours in this town and had breakfast, and then got into another train, and went to Calais, the port for England; and as we went we admired the country, which was one to be desired, as it was pleasing to the eyes.

When we got to Calais they brought a steamer with two paddles, one on each side; it went on the water like a horse gallops on land; the distance across was as far as that from Entebbe to Lulamba, and took us an hour and a half, and then we reached Dover, which is the English landing-place from France, and saw the long pier which they are making out from the land, and alongside of which the ships land their passengers. It goes out into the sea a distance equal to that from Munyonyo to the island of Bulinguge, and is all of stone, and we were amazed to see it. We got quickly into the train, and it took us to London. As it went we looked at the country and the houses, and reached London at 7 p.m. But if it were possible for the eyes to be sore from seeing so much, when we came back to Uganda you would have seen how sore our eyes were, and would have understood and said, 'Yes, we see you; you have indeed seen many marvellous sights.'

When we arrived we found Sir Clement Hill and Captain Hobart waiting for us at the station, which was called Victoria; as Mr. Prendergast had telegraphed to tell them of our arrival. We thought Sir Clement Hill, who is such a great man, most kind thus to come and meet us on our way, and we perceived we were among friends, since we had thus been met. After Sir Clement Hill had welcomed us he told Captain Hobart to take us to where we were to live, as he had been appointed to help us in everything connected with our visit to England; and Mr. Millar was our interpreter. Captain Hobart took us away in a fine carriage to the place where we were to stop, which was in a house for strangers, called a 'hotel'; the name of our hotel was the Westminster Palace Hotel, and it was in the road called Victoria Street, near the Houses of Parliament. When we entered that house it was as if we were going into the house of the King himself; it was magnificent and beautiful beyond praise, and we looked about from side to side admiring it. Though one is praised for restraining oneself and not looking about, it is impossible not to do so in England.[24]

We went into the room which takes people to the upper floors, and after we had got in the servant shut the door, and told us to sit down, and we sat on the seat; the servant then pulled a small rope and the room took us up, like the thing did at Marseilles, about which I told you. We soon reached our rooms on the third floor; the number of the inner room in which I and

---

[24] 'Though one is praised for restraining oneself'. Although Mukasa deploys many of the tropes associated with wonder in travel narratives, he also operates within a Victorian moral economy in which restraint is considered to be a virtue.

the Katikiro slept was 208; that of Mr. Millar was 209. They showed us everything; the dining-room, and the bedroom, and the bath-room, and everything else, and then we sat down, and all the servants, both men and women, came to hear what their work was to be. They know that every visitor has his own habits as to eating and as to drinking tea; one wants to drink every hour, another does not do so; one likes many different kinds of food, another likes a few kinds; they showed us also the things that call the servants to bring the food, or water, and we learned all about them. The work of the servants is this: the men do the cooking, the women make the beds and bring the early tea, and water for washing the face, and clean the boots, and they turn on the bath-water – but we would not let them do this, but did it for ourselves; they also washed our clothes, and lit the fires for us when it was cold – not every day.

Captain Hobart stayed a long time talking to us, he was very fond of us, and we knew him; he had learned Luganda, because he had been two years in the country, and had been questioned by Mr. Fletcher, one of the C.M.S. missionaries, and had been passed by him while he was in Uganda.[25] After a while he went away and we had dinner; and as it was very cold the chamber-maid lit the fire, and the room got warm. After dinner we sat at the table and wrote our letters.

[25] The Church Missionary Society (CMS), the largest Anglican missionary society, was synonymous with Protestantism in Uganda during the early colonial period and its evangelical preferences explain many of the moral codes in Mukasa's discourse. Apart from its missionary work, the CMS was responsible for building a constellation of cultural institutions, including hospitals and schools. Its missionaries were prolific ethnographers producing the first written accounts of history, society and culture in Uganda. Their works provided models for Sir Apolo Kagwa's ethnographic texts, but, as noted in my introduction, the Katikiro was also the missionary's chief 'native informant'.

Chapter V

The next morning, after breakfast, our friend, Sir H. Stanley, came to see us; he had come to Uganda long ago, while we were still children.[26] After the Katikiro had greeted him he thanked him for the letters he had written to Zakariya Kisingire (Kizito), urging him to teach the people of our land all the things one can learn in this life that are helpful to body and soul. We talked to him a long time about the present state of affairs in Uganda, and how things were in the old times of Mutesa, who was king at the time he visited the country. We talked a very long time to him and to his wife, who had come with him, and who is as kind as her husband. She would have liked, had it been possible, to have come to Uganda to see the country.

Sir Clement Hill next came to see us, and talked to us a long time about Uganda affairs, and we told him all the things that seemed most important to us, and about which we had wished to tell him; he also asked us about the country of Kavirondo, and about a great many other matters. He asked us what we thought of what we had seen in England, and what most astonished us, and we told him. He asked us if we wrote down what we saw, and Mr. Millar said to him, 'Ham Mukasa writes it all down every day'; and he said that we ought to get our book translated into English and printed, because a great many people would like to read it and would buy it; and I said that it would be difficult to get the money to print it. He said that it would cost us nothing, and Mr. Millar undertook to translate it into English.

---

[26] The rest of the world may remember Henry Morton Stanley from his discovery of Livingstone ('Dr Livingstone, I presume'), but for the Baganda, a more momentous and memorable occasion was the meeting between Stanley and Kabaka Mutesa on 5 April 1875. Stanley's letter to the *Daily Telegraph* inviting Christian missionaries to open shop in Uganda ushered in the events that would lead to the conversion of both Sir Apolo and Mukasa.

After this a reporter came to see the Katikiro and get some details of his early life; and then Captain Hobart took him away to write his name in the King's visitors' book, while Mr. Millar and I went to the shops to buy things.

When we got into the shop (Army and Navy Stores) my eyes itched with wonder at the beautiful things. The way they decorate their shops is most wonderful; it would be difficult to find anything they do not sell there – all kinds of clothing, for men, women, and children, everything of every kind that you may want you find there; I saw also a room filled with people drinking tea. The people who had come there to buy things were like those who were going off to a war, some going upstairs, some downstairs, and some being carried up in little rooms like the one I have told you about in which they took us up in the hotel. I saw a great many people, both men, women, and children, staring at me, for in that house there were perhaps ten thousand or more people, and I was the only black man. There was one old man who came quite close behind me to see what I was like, and when he saw that I had turned round to look at him he turned his eyes away quickly; but when I saw he was ashamed to go on looking at me, I turned away my eyes so that he could have a good look at what I was like, and he stayed a long time looking at me; and this led me to understand that since he had become an old man he had never seen a black man, or perhaps he might have seen one at a distance, but never so close as I was.

When we got back we found the Katikiro had returned, and he told us about what he had seen in the King's palace, and about the King's soldiers and what the palace was like, and I told him what I had seen. After lunch we opened the windows of our room and looked at the people in the streets outside our house, and saw people and carriages going to and fro like locusts; one would think they had no place of their own, and were busy walking up and down, although really every one is going where he wishes to go.

We were very much surprised at the number of English people in London, and remembered what Mr. Millar had said to us in Naples and Marseilles, 'These people whom you think so many are really very few; you will see many times more than these'; and we saw that what he had said had come to pass. In this city the people walk about till one or two o'clock in the morning; the English sleep very little, and therefore they get very rich, because 'A sluggard will not fail to beg of him who is not a sluggard', the meaning of which saying is that a lazy man begs from a man who works hard, and therefore all our nations require many things from the English.

In the evening we went to dinner with Captain Hobart, and he and his wife and sister and aunt and mother welcomed us and were very kind to us;

his aunt played for us very beautifully on the piano. After dinner we went over the house and saw the things he had brought from our country of Uganda – spears, and skins of animals he had shot. When we got back to the hotel, we said we would not use the lift, but go up by the stairs, to see what they were like in these high houses. We went round and round; the stairs went up by a gentle rise; they were not at all steep, and we took a long time getting up, and said, 'If we had gone up by the lift we would have been there sooner', though we climbed the stairs by our own wish.

The next day Captain Hobart took us to buy some things with Mr. Millar. We went to that fine shop (Army and Navy Stores), and they bought us macintoshes to keep the rain off, and we bought some clothes for ourselves, and walked through the house and saw what a great number of people there were in it; the one house was as large as one of our towns, as besides its length and breadth it was also very high, and there were a great many people in it. The number of things that were in it was wonderful – coats, hats, bedsteads, chairs, sticks, umbrellas, boots, socks, ladies' clothing, looking-glasses, clocks, footballs, exercise-books, picture-books, and all kinds of things for young and old to play with. I cannot tell you about all the things the English have – I must just leave off; the things I have not told you of are innumerable.

We also visited other places, and the Katikiro went to the house where they talk over matters (Parliament), and saw a great many chiefs debating in the place where they debate about their government, which brings peace in their country and in the countries of others. When he came back he told me how he had seen those houses, and where the members of Parliament sat, and I very much wanted to write down all he had seen, but he could not tell me properly, and said he had forgotten some of the things, and we agreed to ask leave to go together in future, so that if one forgot the other might remember.

At night we went to dinner with Sir H. Stanley, and found him with a great many people; Lady Dorothy Stanley and he greeted us warmly, and he called his child, Denzil Stanley, to shake hands with us; and introduced all the people to us, giving our names and the name of the person who was introduced to us, and we then sat down and Lady Stanley talked to us, and told us how interested she was in our country, and asked us a great deal about it. She also showed us a cup which had been made for them, and on it were figures of a black man and of tusks of ivory and of spears from our country, and also a picture of the whole land of Africa.

After this we went in to dinner and ate the food that had been chosen for us, of a great many different kinds, after the fashion of the English; there were also ripe bananas, which we did not eat. After dinner the ladies went away and the men only remained, as is their custom everywhere, and we talked to the master of the house, and he told us of a great many things that bring peace and prosperity – such as teaching the people how to work, and teaching all the children, so that they can afterwards do work that would make them rich. We were pleased at what he said, because he is like our father from having been in our country, and from having told everybody about what he saw; he therefore talked to us as to his children.[27]

After this he took us to see a picture of our old King Mutesa, which he had drawn; it was exactly like him, and the Katikiro said, 'If you have many copies of the picture I would like one'; and he said that he had only this one picture, but that he would get a copy made and give it to the Katikiro. After this we went upstairs, and Lady Stanley got out her machine which talks like a man, and which is called a 'fornegraph', and we all spoke into it. They told me to sing some of our songs into it, and I did so, and they were all very pleased. After this they took us into another room, and Lady Stanley got ready a large piano and played to us on it; this piano played by itself; you trod on the bottom part of it like you do in similar instruments, and it played by itself. After she had finished, first the Katikiro and then I played on it, and soon after we went back home.

The next morning, June 13th, it rained all day; Mr. Samwili (Herbert Samuel, M.P.) came to see us – he was the man who paid a short visit to Uganda, and then returned to England; two of the leaders of the Church Missionary Society also came to see us, and then Mr. Ernest Gedge, who had been in Uganda long ago, and from whom we got the name 'geji', by which we call our small Sneider rifles. In the afternoon we went to tea with Captain Hobart, and then the Katikiro went with him to see the Duke of Norfolk, and Mr. Millar and I returned home. When the Katikiro returned he told us of all he had seen, and what they had said to him (the Duke of Norfolk was not at home), and how kind Captain Hobart's father was, and how he had given him two books about the coronation. The Katikiro and I then told Captain Hobart how we wanted in future to go together, because one man cannot see everything, and forgets a great many things he has seen; but Captain Hobart said that when only one was invited it was hard to take others and so we let the matter drop.

The following day, June 14th, we went to the house of images of all kinds (the British Museum), which contained many wonderful things of long ago, statues of the old kings of all countries and of Egypt. We saw also the body of a man said to be eight thousand years old. We could not understand

---

[27] Sir Stanley's paternalism here seems welcomed because he is considered to be one of the founding 'fathers' of Ugandan Christian culture (see note 26).

whether this was true or not, because we see in the Bible that those who calculate the time from the Creation make it out to be nearly six thousand years; and after this one is told that this body is eight thousand years old! Is not this a thing to be wondered at? We saw also other remains, 5,000, 4,500, 3,700, 2,000, 2,500 years old. On every statue they write its name, its age, and the country from which it comes, so that people can understand.

This house of images, the British Museum, is very large indeed, about twenty times as large as the Namirembe Cathedral; you can understand the size of it if I tell you that when you walk about in it it is just as if you were not in a house at all, and you think you are outside. The posts that support it are very large, as large as one of the largest of our trees, but of dressed stone; the outside posts are twice as high as the eaves of our cathedral.

The bodies in there are looked at in a very ingenious way. They make glass boxes and put the bodies inside, so that they shall not be damaged or touched; they also write up notices, 'Do not touch.' You can see through the glass whatever is inside, and this is the custom throughout. When we were at Pompeii we saw how the hands of those who had come to draw water at the wells had worn down the stone – it was quite worn down where they took hold as they drew water; and this is the reason they do not let people touch what is exhibited, because they do not want the things spoiled, since numbers of people go to the Museum every day, and if each one caught hold of the things they would be worn out in a month.

We saw there different articles from our country; some had been brought by Sir H. H. Johnston, who had given a great many things, and others by other Englishmen: the Rev. J. Roscoe had given a great many, the Rev. R. P. Ashe had given a great many, and others too had given things from our country of Uganda.

After seeing all this we went home, and Dr. B. W. Walker, the brother of Archdeacon Walker, came to see us. He is very much like his brother; you could well go up to him and say, 'Good morning, Archdeacon Walker', mistaking him for his brother, they are so much alike. Mr. Millar's brother also came to see us; his name was Charles Millar, a very kind man. He laughs and jokes with people, and is very cheerful, and every day is the same as he was the day before.

We afterwards intended to go and see the boys drill (inspection of Boys' Brigades by H.R.H. the Prince of Wales), but Captain Hobart never came to take us; and when he did come he wanted to take the Katikiro to see the King, and had merely come to tell him when he would take him, and went away saying, 'I will tell you when the time comes.' He said that the King's secretary had told him that they would send him a messenger when he was to bring the Katikiro. However, when the King saw he had not time to see the Katikiro, because he had so much work, he said, 'I cannot see him now; I will see him to-morrow, when I have finished my work.'

We then went out to see the wonders of England. We went with Mr. Millar and his brother, Charles Millar, and first went in our carriages to see the wonderful railways that go through the town underground. The English truly are marvellous people! The railway was called 'Central London', and is a hundred feet below the ground; we saw many roads, and trains passing, and the people who were there were like locusts in numbers. If your friend were to leave you for some time, you would get lost owing to the numbers of people. The roads there are very fine and wonderful; they have electric lamps, which shine and act as suns. If any one were to take you there, and did not tell you that you were going underground, when you arrived you would not know that you were under the earth because the roads are so fine and the electric light is so bright, and the people are like locusts in numbers; and all these things make you silly, so that you would not understand that you were underground.

We also went under the river which is in London and is called the Thames; we left it above and passed underneath it, and came up the other side without knowing this, as we went in the train. When I asked Mr. Charles Millar, 'Where is the River Thames?' he said it was over our heads and we would see it when we got out of the train, as we should pass above it going back. When we got out from underground we climbed up the steps to see where we had come, and to understand the depth of the earth to the underground roads, and then we saw how the River Thames was above the tube; the river was like an ocean in size. We then got into a carriage and crossed a bridge over the Thames, as we had passed under it just before, and we wondered very much at the work of the English, which is above praise. After this we went home, and our friend Mr. Charles Millar said good-bye to us, after he had taught us an English saying, 'Buck up', the meaning of which is 'Come back soon'; we learned it on that day, and liked him very much.

After we got back Captain Hobart took the Katikiro off to have dinner with him at half-past seven. Mr. Millar and I had dinner together before this, but the Katikiro did not eat with us, as he wished to leave a place in his inside for the dinner where he was going; and when he came back he told us of the many kinds of nice things he had eaten.

The next morning, Sunday, June 15th, Mr. Millar told us to get ready to go to the great church of St. Paul's, and we did as he told us, and Captain Hobart came to go with us. We went along the road called the Thames Embankment, which is near the River Thames, and he pointed out all the different houses on the way. We reached the church at the same time as a great many little boy soldiers (Church Lads' Brigade); there were about three hundred of them. An attendant, who had a staff of office, came outside to fetch us, and took us in and showed us our places, and then went back to his work. We were in seats near those of the great people, and not far from the Communion table. When the soldiers were about to enter they blew their bugles; they blew so well that one would have liked to march with them. We were a long time waiting for the service to begin, and wondered at all we saw; the church is covered with pictures of men, and of our Lord and the Virgin Mary, and of brave men who are buried there. The pulpit is very high; there are a great many seats in the church, perhaps from 3,500 to 4,000, and they are all filled on Sundays.

While we were waiting they began playing the great organ; we did not at first think it was an organ, as the sound was like the sound one hears in the sky when it is about to rain; this organ thundered like that, and the seats we were on shook, and the ground shook. When the clergy entered they came in a large procession of singers, little boys and young men and old men, and sat in their appointed places where no one else may sit. Each man had a lamp in front of him, for the church is rather dark owing to its size, and therefore they had many electric lights and gas lamps all over it, and also very long wax candles on the Communion table, but these were put there in accordance with the custom of the place – if it were not for this custom the electric light would have been enough. When they played the organ all the singers and every one else joined in, and the whole place was filled with the sound of the voices and the sound of the organ.

My friends, that organ is a wonderful thing; it has iron things (pipes) which they put on the wall to increase the sound; these iron things are like the stem of a green banana, and inside they put things that sound like a harmonium, and when they play the organ these things sound, each sounds from its own place, and the sound thus fills the building and reaches even those who are farthest away. The singers and every one else in everything they sing follow the organ, and in all the Psalms they follow the organ, and when they say 'Amen' they follow the organ. I counted the singers near the organ: those with nice voices were twenty; the old men with deep voices that give tone to the voices of the young were four in number.

The building is several times larger than Namirembe Cathedral, and is all the one church of St. Paul.[28] The preacher preached from Heb. iii. 17, and preached very well, in a loud voice, and spoke plainly, and not indistinctly like some others do. After service we returned home, and found the streets

[28] African Christians sought to build institutions which would equal their European counter-parts, hence the linkage between Namirembe Cathedral and St Paul's.

full of people who had come from other churches. The others went the way we had come, but Mr. Millar and I went along Fleet Street, and he showed me all the different places we passed.

A short time after lunch we went out – the Katikiro went with Captain Hobart, and I went with Mr. Millar to see the little soldier boys (Boys' Brigade), who had been collected from all over the country in their turn, as is the custom. We walked all the way there, a distance as far as from Mengo to Bulange (a mile and a half), and as we went I got a good look at the River Thames and saw what it was like; it is like an arm of the lake is some parts, although it is only a river.

After crossing a bridge we went along by the side of the river, and by the side of the hospital called St. Thomas's Hospital, and reached the house of the Archbishop of Canterbury; and I saw a great many little English boys following me to see what a black man was like, and wanted to talk to them, but Mr. Millar told me not to, and so I left off and we went on; perhaps there were as many as eighty looking at us. At last we reached the place where the boys were: they had put up an iron fence and inside had pitched their tents, and the people who had come to look at them had to remain outside the fence. One of the officers came and welcomed us and showed us the kitchen, and what the tents were like. The boys had a very nice band, which played well. After we had seen these things they took us to Mr. MacConnell, the head of the camp, and we had tea with him. There were about two hundred boys; the names of their officers were J. R. MacConnell, W. M. Alexander, and Mr. Parker, the Adjutant. After tea the head of the camp said to me, 'If you would say a few words to us now we should be very pleased; just say what you like'; and I thought it would be well to do so and consented, and they blew the bugle, and some of the boys came quickly and stood up in a line, and I spoke thus:

'My friends, I am very pleased to come here and to see what you are doing, but most of all I thank God for uniting us with you in spirit; though there is a difference in our bodies, yet our hearts are one in the sight of God, who made us one in His Son, and I therefore thank Him for this. I want you to understand that had it not been for this, people would never have come to such a distant country as ours, to tell the words of God; and so we are very pleased to come amongst you, just as if we had known you before, though this is only our first visit. If, however, you were to tell one of the heathen in our country that you would take him to England, it would be the same to him as saying you wished to kill him; and therefore, my friends, I thank God for all that He has done for us, and may He increase His peace in this land and in our land, that there may be perfect peace. If God does this we shall all be pleased, and shall be able to visit one another just as we have now come over to visit you, both I and Apolo Katikiro, whom you would call the Prime Minister; he is the greatest chief in our land and I am his secretary, and came over with him to write down all we saw. Well, may God be with you always.'

After I had said this the head of the camp spoke in the same way, because he was a true Christian.[29] After this he sent for a cab to take us back quickly, because the people would have hindered us. He went with us a little way, and then we went back to the hotel and found Apolo had returned, and he told us how he had had tea with Captain Hobart's mother, and I told him all I had seen as I have described.

The next day we went to buy some of the things we needed at the shop called 'Army and Navy Stores', where there are a great many things, and whatever any man may want can be found there. We bought some note-books and writing-cases, and then went back and had our hair cut.

At half-past one we went to see Sir H. H. Johnston, and he welcomed us very warmly; we found there his wife and his younger brother, Captain and Mrs. Hobart, and Lady Johnston's mother. After lunch Sir H. H. Johnston took us to see the glass room in which he did his writing, in which were birds and other things, and many things that had come from Uganda. He showed us many kinds of animals he had got from other countries, and pictures of the different tribes through whom he had passed, and made his phonograph sing for us; it sang a Kinyamwezi song thus: 'Fundula malole Bwana Wiswe', which means, 'Take off the spectacles from your eyes, O our master.' The song is much longer than this, as the Wanyamwezi are greater singers than any of the peoples to the west of the lake. This phonograph made us laugh a great deal. Sir H. H. Johnston also gave the Katikiro the book about our country which he wrote when he came to bring 'mairo' into our land.* He wrote a great deal about Uganda, but we have not yet fully understood all he wrote, but have only seen the pictures. I have heard,

---

* Sir H. H. Johnston changed the whole system of land tenure in Uganda, and arranged that each chief should have a certain number of square miles as his freehold. A freehold plot of land is hence now called in Uganda a 'mairo'. Under the old system all the land was held feudally from the King.

[29] Speaking like 'a true Christian' has a certain implicit value: it presupposes a unity of spirit among people of different nations and cultures, it underscores the authority of God, and it prays for the peace that makes the universal Christian church possible. It is within the universality of a common religion that the author seeks to establish affiliations with the British other.

however, that he said that all the Baganda were short, and there were no tall men, but that the Katikiro is the only tall man in Uganda. This is not so. Perhaps he forgot; I do not think he made this mistake on purpose, because there are a great many tall men. All our ancestors were tall men, and at the present time there are many tall men. He has written a great deal in this book about how the people speak in different parts of the country, and has also printed some of the best songs of the Basese, who paddle our canoes, and has a picture of our King, Daudi Chwa, and pictures of some of the chiefs.

After we had looked at this book he told us to come with him and see the wild animals, and we went with him and the others. We walked as far as the Zoological Gardens, and saw a great many kinds of animals that we never see in our country. We first saw wild horses and wild cattle, and lions, and tigers – which are the leopards of India – and elephants, and hyenas, and giraffes, and chimpanzees. I cannot tell you the names of all the animals; I can only tell you we saw sixty-three different kinds or more, beasts and birds and snakes and small creatures. It is difficult to find an animal that is not there. After this the superintendent of the gardens took us to his house to show it to us, and also to show us a picture of his father, who was the first superintendent; he himself was a man sixty-five years of age, and had taken the place of his father in looking after the animals.

They gave us some biscuits to give to the elephant, which took them out of our hands. We also threw pieces of biscuit into its mouth, and it ate them. It was wonderfully tame and did what it was told, just like a man; they told it to stand on a stone, and it did so; and to put up its trunk, and it did so. We also played with the chimpanzee; its keeper was nursing it like a baby, and he told it to shake hands, and it shook hands like a man. We also saw wonderful snakes; two boas from India were as large as the middle of a crocodile, and each eats a goat every day. I also saw a turtle as large as a pig, and a giraffe that was much taller than an elephant; perhaps it was as much as 20 or 22 ft. high, and it was still young. We saw also a pelican thirty-eight years old, and another thirty-four years of age.

A great many people come in to see these animals, perhaps as many as a hundred thousand every day; I do not quite know, as one meets numbers of men, women, and children wherever one goes. Do not think they can just walk in – not so at all; they first have to pay something, and they can then go in and see the animals. There are always people coming to see them; every day different people come.

After this we came away with Sir H. H. Johnston and his younger brother, who knows a little Swahili. Sir H. H. Johnston himself knows it very well, and speaks it much better than many people. We next went to a place where they sell tea, and there Sir H. H. Johnston and his brother said good-bye to us and left us, as did also the superintendent.

After tea we went home, and after our arrival Captain Hobart came to say he had an invitation for the Katikiro to go to the New Zealand dinner, and the Katikiro accepted it.

Bulwagi na musumbira Kyai
mukulu. ngaaua emunyonyo
ela namusumbira emeu ma
muu no mulabiji u ape
ela abayungu bali buwebati 37
abaga nda twali muwenda 9
netwa nyuka nyo kumbaga
eyo. ate I nkuwebiga
etwitama omuwendo gua
baba nabayalihua.
naye eseoz muwambi ysba
ela yatapayo abamu muwasuu
ela nabahuade bangi nyo
ela betaga okudukayo abakya
bi abala muu katano
tuamala okububya kubalgi
nti abesese bagla Ikudukayo

nagamba nti namala okubiro
woya ndihadamu
Kalemo welaba batonda
abuhume nje apalo Katihiu

Bano lebafu abafa

Mumugi May 31. 1904.

Musujja	85
Mongota	862
Kaumpuli	37
Kawali	157
Kifuba	50
Nyoka	89
Kidukano	7
Munyu	232
Kabotongo	25
Enduwade endala	356
	1900

Bano lebana abagalibwamu 508
Kaleno welaba Nze
Apolo Katikiro

Translation of Letter from Apolo Katikiro to Rev. E. Millar.

MENGO, UGANDA, *June 24th*, 1904.

TO MR. MILLAR.

MY DEAR FRIEND,

Many thanks for your two letters about the death of Sir Henry Stanley. Many thanks for attending his funeral, and for telling me how honourable a burial he was given.

I had your letter copied on my typewriter and sent it to all the chiefs, that they might read it and hear all about the funeral.

Things here are going on well. There were about ten thousand people present at the dedication of the cathedral; we were a very large number.

When our friend Mr. (T. F. Victor) Buxton reached Uganda we welcomed him warmly, and I had tea ready for him on the way up from Munyonyo. I also gave a banquet to him and to our bishop – there were thirty-seven Europeans and nine Baganda present, and we enjoyed ourselves very much.

I send you the numbers of births and deaths. On the Sese Islands Muwambi (chief of Kome Island) is dead, and seven other chiefs have died, and a very large number of people are ill, and those who are still alive wish to leave the islands altogether.

We told the Commissioner that the Sese Islanders wished to run away from their islands, and asked his advice; and he told us that he would consider the matter and let us have his answer.

Well, good-bye; may God protect you.

I am,
(Signed) APOLO KATIKIRO.

The following is a list of those who died in the month ending May 31st, 1904:

Written by the Katikiro's clerk.	Fever	85
	Sleeping sickness	862
	Plague	37
	Small pox	157
	Pneumonia	50
	Internal disorders	89
	Dysentery	7
	Infantile diseases	232
	Specific diseases	25
	Other illnesses	356
		1,900
	Children born	508

This only is the Katikiro's own writing.

Well, good-bye.

I am,
(Signed) APOLO KATIKIRO.

Chapter VI

Interview with the Church Missionary Society – The Bible House – The Bishop of London's garden party – Dinner with Mr. Herbert Samuel, M.P. – A Board School – 'Ben Hur' – The Hippodrome – Lunch with Sir T. Fowell Buxton, G.C.M.G. – The London Hospital – Visit to Hampstead – The Crystal Palace

The next day, June 17th, we went to see the rulers of the Church Missionary Society; the Katikiro and the Rev. G. K. Baskerville went in one carriage, and I and Mr. Millar in another, and we reached the Church Missionary House, where we were greeted by Prebendary Fox, the chief secretary, and our bishop, Bishop A. R. Tucker, who had come to the door to meet us. They escorted us in, and we found a great many ladies and gentlemen, about one hundred and fifty, who all stood up as we entered, in order to give us honour and welcome us warmly. All the Uganda people sat together, Bishop Tucker, the Revs. G. K. Baskerville and E. Millar, Dr. A. R. Cook, and ourselves, their Uganda pupils.[30]

After we had sat down we prayed to God, and the President, Sir John H. Kennaway, said a few words, and then asked the Katikiro to make a speech, and he and Mr. Millar (as interpreter) stood up. He spoke for a long time, and said how he had at first come to learn to read because Mr. Mackay and Mr. O'Flaherty gave him food; but afterwards he went on learning because he saw that Christianity was a good thing, and so he no longer thought of the food. He said a great deal, and after he had finished Bishop Tucker, our bishop, spoke for some time, and told how the Katikiro had helped the Uganda Church; he also spoke of my having written a commentary on St. Matthew's Gospel. After this Sir T. Fowell Buxton said a little, and then the bishop prayed, and all was over.

We then shook hands with many who were there, both men and women,

---

[30] While the colonial relationship may now appear to us as a vertical arrangement between the governors and the governed, Mukasa represents it primarily as a network of people connected by religious and cultural associations; by the same token, his Englishness is derived from his membership in the Anglican church. The whole of this paragraph is a commentary on the ecumenical nature of colonial relationships.

and went to have some tea. After this they showed us the store from which books in all languages go out. We saw the room in which Namukade and Kataluba (the envoys sent over by Mutesa in 1878) had lived, and also saw the man who had looked after them. This room is now a store for Luganda books.

(They then went to the Bible House, and saw the secretaries of the British and Foreign Bible Society.)

They told us that every day eight thousand books are sent out, and go to all parts of the world; and we saw old Greek books on parchment, from which they get the books we read now. We also saw Hebrew books made of skins. All these old books they put in glass boxes, so that people should not handle them; but they can be seen quite well through the glass.[31] We saw also a press for printing books for the blind, who cannot see at all; and we all worked it to see how it printed, and the impressions which we ourselves took were given to us to take back to Uganda to show to our friends. We also saw the portraits of men long dead, who had done good work, and who are thus commemorated. After this we went home, Bishop Tucker and his wife escorting us as far as the door.

After a short rest we went to see the Bishop of London, and there found a great many people, perhaps three or four thousand; there were a great many carriages belonging to the visitors whom he had invited. We went through on to the lawn with the other visitors; we two and an Indian were the only black people there. The Bishop of London is a very cheerful and kind man, and greeted us very warmly. We went all round his garden, and saw beds of flowers and of different kinds of vegetables. After we had walked round and seen everything, we said good-bye and came home; and after a short rest the Katikiro went with Captain Hobart to the New Zealand dinner, and Mr. Millar and I went to see a wonderful conjurer, who did some very clever tricks which quite puzzled me.

He produced a boy out of a cloth, and a bear out of a piece of paper; he got fire out of a cloth, and caught little fish in the air; he also produced a large water-pot full of water out of the cloth, and lifted a man up without holding him, so that he remained lying down in space with nothing above or below him; he shot at a lamp on one table and it appeared on another, and did also a great many other things. When we got home we told the Katikiro what we had seen, and he told us about the New Zealand dinner.

---

[31] The symbolic economy of books has special resonance for the travellers: literacy and writing are a source of the authority and privilege bestowed on them as the representatives of their culture at the coronation of Edward VII; the existence of Luganda texts in British libraries is evidence of their community's admission into modern culture.

The next morning Captain Hobart took the Katikiro to Ascot, the place where the horses race, and Mr. Millar and I went to a great many shops. I saw a wonderful house where people store their money (National Safe Deposit Company), which has been very cleverly built of extremely hard steel; it is built with two circular walls which are extremely strong, one of stone, the other of burnt brick. The doors are very strong, and as thick as a hand's breadth, and close by themselves, and no man is able to open them, or to cut through the circular wall of stone or of burnt bricks, which are very hard. Policemen walk about all the time round the walls; there is water above and below to protect the place from fire, and this water is like a lake in volume, and is all round the building. Inside there are many holes, in each of which is a box, where every man who wishes to do so can keep his money, and every one who keeps his money in this house has many private signs given him, so that no one else may take his place, and by his cleverness steal his money.

After this we returned home, and after a rest we went to see Mr. Herbert Samuel, who spent a short time in Uganda, and gave the King a toy steamer, that went on the water just like a real steamer. He also took many photographs of our country, and of different kinds of people, peasants and chiefs, and of the King and of the old kind of houses which are being done away with at the present time, and of our different styles of clothing; all these things Mr. Herbert Samuel did when he was in our country. When we reached his house we found he had asked a great many people to meet us; in all there were twelve of us. The Uganda party consisted of the Katikiro, the Revs. E. C. Gordon and E. Millar, and I, Ham Mukasa. After dinner he showed us a great many photographs from Uganda and the neighbouring countries.

The next morning, June 19th, they took the Katikiro (on Lord Onslow's motor-car) to see the statue of King Albert and of those who were great men in his time (Albert Memorial); this is not the Albert who is king at present, but one of a long time ago. The Katikiro told me this when he got back, and I wrote it down.

After this we went to have lunch with Dr. B. W. Walker, the brother of Archdeacon Walker the friend of Ham Mukasa, and he cooked a fine luncheon to welcome us, and took us all over his house to show us what it was like: we noticed that the kitchen was on the lowest floor. We sat down ten to lunch, Dr. B. W. Walker, the Revs. E. C. Gordon and E. Millar, Apolo Katikiro, two other men and three ladies, and Ham Mukasa.

Later on we went to see over a children's school, and when we arrived they took us all over it, and showed us how they were taught many different kinds of wisdom. They are first taught to read and to do arithmetic, to do carpenters' work and to swim, to jump and to run, and to cook like ladies and married people, to keep the house in order, to wash clothes, to make the beds properly, and to wash up everything that requires washing when it is dirty; to sweep out the house, and to do every kind of work that people must learn to do for themselves. Every kind of work necessary for men and women is taught there, so that when they grow up they know all about it, and can choose whatever occupation they wish, and the work which one leaves another can do, as he knows about every kind of work.

They teach them from three or four years old for seven years; others are taught till they are fifteen; the children of rich parents are taught everything. We went there at twelve (2 p.m. really), and came away at a quarter to six, and they gave us samples of the carpenters' work that they do, and we took them home with us. There were a great many children in that school; we saw from three to four hundred. When they saw that we were going away a great many of the little ones came to see us off, and wanted very much to have a good look at us. I wished to speak to them, as about eighty of them were following behind, and rolled up my coat-sleeve to show them what my arm was like, because many of them wanted to see it, and they came closer and each child wanted to shake hands with me, because they were so pleased. Some were at first afraid, but when they saw their companions talking English to me they too came close up, and I played with them and picked them up with one hand, and so on. When they saw we were going they all came to say good-bye, but Mr. Millar said, 'Leave them alone, there are too many of them', and so we got into our carriages and went home, wondering as we went at the houses and carriages like locusts in number.

After dinner we went to see a game ('Ben Hur') in a place called Drevy Len Banker (Drury Lane Theatre), and we saw how they dressed up in a great many different ways.[32] They first dressed themselves up like the wise men from the East, following the star to seek for our Lord; after this they brought on the city of Jerusalem, and the priests dressed in their proper costumes; after this they imitated the way the Romans used to row their boats when they ruled the world and attacked the city of Jerusalem, and crossed the sea to get there and fight against it. After this they imitated Judah the Jew and the men who rebelled with him. After this they brought on the spirit the Romans worshipped, Apollo by name, and their marriage customs, and the way they went to their weddings; and they brought on a wicked woman, who enticed away the man she had set her heart on, and

---

[32] Mukasa's puritanism does not allow for the value of play for its own sake, hence the elaborate imposition of moral meaning on this representation of a performance which was perhaps intended to be pure entertainment.

took him off in a boat to her place. They next brought on horses that raced in chariots, and then they showed the healing of some lepers by our Lord.

The people who were there were perhaps as many as six hundred; it was a very large house, and they had put in it shelves for all the sight-seers to sit on, and these were from the bottom to the top of the house, and there was a great space left for the people to play in.

They made the place like the ancient Romans used to make their amphitheatres, in which they saw beasts fight with prisoners, and this is the way they make all their places of amusement; they sang also the songs of Apollo, the god of the Romans, just as they used to sing them when they were still heathen; they collected a great many children and women and men, and these sang as the people used to sing.

The next day, June 20th, at half-past nine in the morning, the Rev. J. Roscoe and Mr. Millar's sister came to see us. Mr. Millar's sister came with her little girl, who very quickly drew us a pencil-sketch of a horse, and we were pleased to see the way the English teach their little children. We also went with the Rev. E. C. Gordon to Dr. Oppenshaw to look for a boot for my bad leg, and we met Dr. Walker there, and they told me to speak into a thing called in English a telephone, and I spoke to another man four and a half miles away. Then Dr. Walker left us, and we went with Mr. Gordon to the manufacturer of (surgical) boots to see if he could find a boot for my bad leg, but he could not find one of the kind I required in his stock, and promised to give me an iron thing that would make my legs of equal length, and then to make a boot for me.

After lunch we went to see a most marvellous performance in a place called 'The London Hippodrome', but it is difficult to tell you about the things we saw there, because if you tell a clever man about these things, in his stupidity he thinks you are not speaking the truth at all; however, I will try to tell you, as well as I can, what we saw. First, there was a woman in a carriage drawn by a horse all spotted like a leopard, which was called in their language Leopard Horse (Leopard was the name of the horse). This horse marched along with its carriage just like soldiers march to a band, and the band played and the bugles blew and the flutes played a tune for it to march to. Then there was a dog that walked round between the horse's legs, as it was walking, and neither of them made a mistake as it passed in and out just like a man who had sense, and we were very surprised at the way they had been taught.

After this came a man who played at catching bullets nearly as large as a football, a wonderful man; he also picked up a man and put him on his hand, and the other man stiffened himself and he lifted him right up with only one hand. After this came a man who played with his feet with very large barrels, lying on his back on a couch; after this he brought three things as large as drums and put them one on the top of the other, although they were not flat, and kept them together by his skill, and played with them with his feet, and they did not fall, although they were round. After this he lifted up seven dogs on a piece of wood that was like a stick with seven branches, and had a dog sitting on each branch; he lifted these up on his head and they did not fall.

After this they brought on some boys and girls, each on a single bicycle wheel, without anything to hold on to in front, like other bicycles. One of them picked up a boy of about twelve years of age and held him up with one hand as he was riding, and we were amazed at his skill; and then the boy put one hand on the other's head and pointed his feet to the roof, while the other rode the bicycle round. After this the rider took his bicycle to pieces as he rode it, and remained with one wheel only, as when he first came on; in the same way he put it together again as he was going. After this they brought on an elephant and gave it a big drum, and it played it just like a man; and they gave it a gun and gave the words of command, and it drilled just like a man, and put its gun wherever it was told to; and they ordered it to fire, and it fired just like a man.

Some elephants also put a man on a couch just as if he were ill, and carried him where they were told; one of them was told to fetch the medicine off the table, and it did so, and gave it him to drink; and the sick man told it to bring a candle, and it did so; and he told it to light the candle, and it fetched the matches, and struck them, and lit the candle. It also lay right down on the ground with the man underneath, and stretched itself out on him; it also stood on a wooden chair, with all its four legs together, and got down when it was told. It always did as it was told; it wiped the perspiration off the man's face, and fanned him because he was hot, and blew out the candle, and made a fool of itself, as if it was mocking at people who talk into the telephone – it put the receiver to its ear just as people do who speak to one another through the telephone; it also played the cymbals very nicely, just like a man. After this they told it to trumpet, and it did so.

Then they brought on a great deal of water, just like a large pond; the water came out of the ground, and we could not see where it came from, and it became a great lake; and they made a bridge and brought on to it horses and a carriage with people in it, and fired off a great many guns, imitating a war, and the horses and carriage fell into the water with all the people and they swam ashore; and we wondered very much at all this, which was hard to understand. After this Mr. Herbert Samuel (who had taken them to the Hippodrome) took us to a traveller's house, and bought us some tea, and introduced us to his wife, and showed us a photograph of his child. We went home at 4.10 p.m., and afterwards Bishop Hanlon came to see us and stayed till five o'clock.

The next day we went to have our photographs taken, and when we came back we rested for a short time, and then went to see our friend, Sir T. Fowell Buxton, G.C.M.G. When we got there we found Bishop Tucker and another bishop who had been in Australia, and who was called Bishop Montgomery. He was a very kind man indeed, and made great friends with me, and said, 'I want you to stay in England; you can go back later on'; and I refused, saying, 'That is difficult, sir'; because, though he said this, he only said it jestingly in his kindness, as he knew I could not stop behind. We had a very nice dinner; they had made a fine feast to welcome us, and we were fourteen at table.

After dinner Sir Fowell Buxton took us to see a hospital, called James's Hospital (London Hospital), and we got into his carriage and said good-bye to our bishop and all our friends, and went away, looking as we went at that part of the town through which we travelled. We crossed the River Thames on a bridge supported by chains, and went a long way round and saw many places and roads (following the route of the coronation procession and over London Bridge), and at last reached the hospital called James's Hospital. They took us round a great many places in the hospital. The ladies who do the work, and who are called sisters, first took us round, and afterwards the chief doctor came and showed us a great many things; some rooms were upstairs and some downstairs.

After this they showed us a thing that reveals an invisible disease. They brought a boy with his clothes on, and we could see all his bones; and we put up our hands, and could see the bones of our hands. They showed us a picture of a man who had been shot long ago, and the bullet remained in the leg, and they made the leg transparent and took the bullet out. We saw also photographs of the palms of the hands of people who had got needles stuck in them, and they made them transparent and took the needles out; there were many of these. This machine works by electricity. They have a glass through which the power of the electricity – that is, its light – passes, and shows you everything that is in your body; but it is hard to understand it – one can only marvel at it.

After this they took us to write our names in the visitors' book; we all wrote them, and any one who goes there may see them, because they are put away there. They then gave us tea, and then Apolo Katikiro said, 'I beg that you nurses will come to our country and help in our hospitals; because the nurses are few, and the sick many'; and they replied, 'That is true, we might come, but here we are not without work; you have spoken very nicely, but even here the sick are many in this hospital, and those with broken legs are many, who have had their legs broken by carriages or by powerful machinery.' I noticed the chairs like carriages that take about the sick; they are like beds, and have on them things that hold books for those sick people to read who have no strength in their hands.

We then went downstairs, and they said good-bye to us, and we got into Sir Fowell Buxton's carriage and went through other streets to the carriage which the Government had lent us. When we got to it, we said good-bye to Sir Fowell Buxton and he went home, and we went to visit Mr. Millar's brother at Hampstead, and arrived at 6.30 p.m., and found him waiting for us. He welcomed us into his house, and we found there our friend the Rev. G. K. Baskerville and other friends of Mr. Millar's, who had come to greet us for his sake, and we sat down and talked for a long time very happily.

He is a very kind man, and has brought up all his little children very nicely, and their mother is as kind as their father; I used to call her my mother, in their language 'mother', because she was so kind. Mr. H. E. Millar took us up and showed us where we were to sleep, and we then came downstairs and had dinner, to which Mr. Baskerville stopped; and we went on talking with our friends about everything we wanted; and Mr. Millar showed us a great many photographs of people in our country.

The next day, June 22nd, was Sunday, and we went to church. We all prayed in English, and there was no difference between us all in language, but only in our bodies, although we could not understand all the service.[33] There was a very fine organ there, which had a beautiful tone – they have tubes that look like banana stems, and put them on the organ, and when they play it the air that comes out makes these things sound, and increases the music, so that all the people can follow it; and therefore in every church in England they have organs like this.

When we came out of the church a great number of persons both small and great, who were not accustomed to black people, came to look at us as we were going home. After reaching home we rested a short time, and then went to see Mr. Baskerville and his father and mother and brothers and sisters, and had tea there and then returned. In the evening we went to a service for young people, and there they showed us what the organ was like; it was a very large one; any one, whether big or little, could get inside it, it was so large. The Katikiro and I went inside and saw a great many things there which the makers in their wisdom had contrived.

We saw also how orphans are looked after. They are collected into one house and have guardians appointed to look after them; boys are looked

---

[33] We can note, once again, how Mukasa tries to overcome differences 'in our bodies' by appealing to the 'universal' language of prayer.

after by men, and girls by women, and they are all dressed alike; the girls have blue dresses and white hats; any one dressed differently is one of their guardians. We also saw a number of ladies who were being trained to go out as missionaries; and when they showed them to us, the Katikiro said, 'We want you all to come to our country of Uganda'; and they replied, 'We cannot go where we ourselves would like, but where our leaders send us'; and we replied, 'That is so – you cannot do as you like; but we want you very much indeed.' After this we went back to the house in which we were stopping.

The next day, June 23rd, we went back into London at half-past ten, and after a short rest went to see the glass house (Crystal Palace), where they keep only the most beautiful things.[34] There are figures of all the kings, and many great men and brave generals, like Sir Lord Roberts, who conquered the Transvaal at the Cape. There are also copies of all the things made in their land; they pick out one thing, and put it there to show people how things are made in different places to which they cannot go themselves. We saw there live fish, and birds of all kinds. They chisel out stones and make them just like people, and put them there to remind people in after years what they were like. There were a number of statues of the kings from early times right down to the Queen (Victoria) and Edward VII, and of generals who had won great wars right down to Sir Lord General Roberts, who conquered the Boers while the Queen was still reigning. There is a statue in stone representing him on a horse; one wants to salute it and say, 'Good morning, Roberts', though really it can neither see nor hear.

We saw how they bore gun-barrels, and saw also a slide for canoes in the game they play with them (waterchute). They make a large pond on a hill, and they make a slide of boards, which the canoes run down to get into the water below. They rush down very fast; a giddy person could not endure it. We saw also a great many people who had come to enjoy themselves, and there were many amusements, players on flutes, organs, and banjos, and many other instruments. We saw a very tall tower from which one can get a distant view over the city; perhaps you could see twenty or twenty-five miles – that is, as far or farther than Entebbe. The tower is four or five times as high as Namirembe Cathedral, because when you are at the top men below look like little children. We saw also large and small fish, and fish of

---

[34] The African travellers seem particularly fascinated by institutions which serve as depositories of custom and tradition such as Crystal Palace and the Natural History Museum. This interest is an indication of the way the colonised were appropriating colonial categories for their own use; for if what made a nation distinctive was its establishment of a usable past, the travellers were in Britain to learn how this was achieved.

all kinds in glass boxes, into which they pour water, and in which the fish live; when you look at them you would not think there was any glass there, as you can see them playing. When we saw all this we were amazed at the care of the English, who can feed unfeedable things like fish and keep them alive many years in their little lakes. The English are a wonderful people.

We also saw how they dig for gold. They had a model showing how gold was dug out. Some of the figures were on the top of the hill, and some were down underground digging, and they had iron baskets and chains, and there were pulleys, and the chains drew the baskets up and let them down; some men were cutting out the earth, whilst others were collecting what was dug out and putting it in baskets, and the pulleys were taking it up to the surface, and the men on the top were doing their work with it. When you see things like this you wonder very much. It is difficult to tell you about them, and even those who make them cannot explain the matter properly, for you cannot fully understand their explanations.

There was also in that building a woman who showed us a machine for sweeping up the rubbish in a house, and wanted us to buy one, and we thanked her for showing it us; but our friend Mr. Millar made us laugh very much, because he thanked her in Luganda, and said, 'Webale kulika nyabo' ('Thank you, I congratulate you on it'), and we laughed very much, because he did not understand he had made a mistake; and when he saw I was laughing at him, he said, 'What are you laughing at, Ham?' and I said, 'Because you thanked that lady in Luganda, and she did not understand what you said; what will she think?' and he said, 'I forgot.' And this was true, because usually among other English people he spoke English; but on this occasion he forgot that English people were not Baganda, because he had learned Luganda so well that it had become a part of himself.

We left at five o'clock in the evening, after having been there about an hour and a half. The building in which we saw these things was called the Crystal Palace.

Chapter VII

The next day, June 24th, they came to take the Katikiro to go and see the
King; but as we were waiting they told us that the King was ill, and then
again that he had had an operation, and our hearts were very sad on account
of the King's illness, because the life of the King is of great value, since he
rules over so many people, and therefore his illness filled all hearts with
sorrow.[35]

When the visitors received the news they all went to write their names in
the King's book to show their sympathy. There were a great many people
who had come from all lands who went to do this, kings and princes and
great men from the lands ruled over by the English, and from lands that are
merely on friendly terms with them. Our chief went also – he went with
Captain Hobart, because only the leading men were called thither – and
when he came back he told me all he had seen.

On this day also we went to visit Said Ali, the prince of Zanzibar, who is
now king, having succeeded his father, who died during his son's stay in
England. Four relatives of Archdeacon Walker also came to see us, and in
the evening we went to see the wonderful conjurer about whom I told you
before; Apolo did not go the first time, so we went again, that he too might
see with his own eyes. If one sees the wonders of England by oneself, and
then tells others, one is disbelieved for lack of a second witness, like Mika

---

[35] This paragraph calls attention to the gap between the figure of the king as the symbol of regal
authority and his bodily nature; the precarious health of Edward VII is notable because
it parallels a crisis in imperial culture which Mukasa's text is unable to inscribe. One of the
ironies that inform the colonial relationship is that the British had occupied Buganda in the
twilight of the imperium.

Sematimba,* who was not believed since he was all by himself when in England.[36]

The next day, June 25th, we went to see a doctor, because the Katikiro was not feeling well. He went with Mr. Millar and me, so that we were just the party that had left Uganda together.

After lunch Captain Hobart came and took us off to the fort of the kings of England from old days, which is called the 'Tower', and when we arrived there we saw many relics of all kinds from the time of their ancestors, old spears and swords, and knives and cannon, and guns with slow matches and flints and caps, and ancient clothing of iron, and helmets of old time, and fire-baskets, and the old rooms in which the ancient kings slept, and their old dining halls, and the guard-rooms of the old soldiers, and the old prison cells without doorways, and with windows so small one could not get one's hand through them – some had no windows at all – and the old staircases that twist round, and the passages in the houses. We saw also the ancient kings, and the way in which they were dressed; and they showed us all the good kings and all the bad kings, each king and the way he ruled. We saw also the place where the king called Charles I was beheaded, because he would not listen to his nobles; we saw also slaughter-places, where the common people were killed; we saw also the ancient church, where all the nobles who were beheaded for treason were buried. They had put up a brass board on the wall of the church, and on it had written their names and their crimes and the year in which they rebelled; their graves are under the floor; if you look on the ground you see the inscriptions on each grave and can read them.

We also saw the axe and sword that cut off the head of their king, and the different kinds of fetters in which criminals were fastened; these fetters fastened the hands and feet and head together. We were also shown how they fastened their women to strong trees and stretched them like a cow-skin is stretched, and the trees tore them in half. We saw also the bell that used to be tolled in old days when they were going to kill a man. But in all lands the ancient people were very evil indeed in their customs, to torture people thus cruelly. We climbed to the top of the Tower, and looked out over the whole city and the River Thames, and saw many houses, and many ships on the Thames. We saw also a most wonderful thing. They have made a bridge across this River Thames which flows through the middle of the

---

* He came to England in 1892.

[36] Aware that Sematimba's eyewitness account of Britain had been met with incredulity, Mukasa continuously warns his readers about the problems inherent in representing a landscape of 'marvels' and thus pre-empts their doubts.

city of London, and this bridge is made of iron, and they put on it great hinges, so great that I can compare them to nothing in our country; the width of the bridge is as wide as the Entebbe Road near Muwanga the blacksmith's (40 ft.), or perhaps wider. Captain Hobart told the men who look after it to show us how it went up when ships wanted to pass, and they pulled over the levers that lifted it, and it came in half, and one half went up on one side and one half on the other, and the ships went through with their masts; and after they had passed, the bridge came back and joined itself up, and the carriages and foot-passengers passed over it just like you pass over a bridge that cannot be raised, or that does not move. It is a very large bridge, as long as from the King's gate to that of the Katikiro (100 yds).

We passed over it in our carriage and went to the place where they make things for African travellers – tents, and chairs, and tables, and flags, and ropes for boats, and small tents for servants on the march and for soldiers. We saw there many women, both old and young, all sewing tents by hand, and we thought they were very industrious and very strong to sew such hard cloth, although they were women. They were making tents, and bags for tents and bedsteads; we had always thought that men made the tents, though it was really women. But, my friends, you ought to be struck with that wonderful bridge that goes up by itself as you have heard; such a breadth and length is a marvellous thing. It is called the 'Tower Bridge'.

After we had been to the top of this factory of which you have heard; and had seen the city and the trains which were close at hand, we went home with Captain Hobart, because Mr. Millar had not come with us, as he had gone to a meeting to pray for the King. When he came back he asked us what we had seen, and we told him everything as I have described it here, and he told us about his journey; we were also told that the King would take about three months to recover fully, and that on account of his illness the coronation was put off. The Rev. H. Clayton also came to see us on this day, and arranged with Mr. Millar to take us back to Uganda, because he wanted to stay in England to rest. We were very pleased, because Mr. Clayton is a nice man, and we like him very much, and we hoped he would explain all our difficulties, because he is a very clever man.*

The next morning, June 26th, Captain Hobart took us to see some soldiers who fight on horseback; we drove to the railway station, and went by train, and when we arrived, we found the chief of the soldiers had brought us a two-horse carriage. He made two soldiers ride in front of us, while he himself rode at the side of the carriage, and gave us very great honour; his name was Colonel Wallis. When we arrived at his encampment

---

* This arrangement was not carried out: Mr. Millar went back with them.

he showed us many things of different kinds belonging to the soldiers. He first showed us how the horses were fastened up, and the doctor's house and all his things, and the soldiers' kitchen, and what their tents were like inside, and their uniforms. He also made them mount their horses to show how they fought, and they all mounted, officers and all, and went through their drill, and fired a great many guns, just as they would do in a real war; there were about two hundred and fifty horses in all. He showed us how the horses are taught not to be afraid of the firing, and to retire when commanded to. After this we were photographed with four of the officers; and after lunch we went home, being escorted on our way by Colonel Wallis and some other officers, who treated us with great honour.

The next day, June 27th, we went to see a fire brigade display, and saw there a Chinese prince, the heir to the throne, who also had come to see how they put out fires. We saw all the different kinds of apparatus – ladders that joined themselves together, horses that galloped very fast when going to extinguish a fire, and squirts that sent water right up to the tops of the houses. They put a pipe into a pit in which water is stored up, and turned a tap, and the water rushed out to a great height. They showed us how they climb up the houses to get people out who are kept in by the fire, and how they get them out when they are senseless and bring them to the ground. We saw also a steam fire-engine that went along the ground like a train, and also how people jump from the second or third stories into a sheet, which is stretched out below. We also saw where they make these fire-engines; and the telegraph that calls them to put out fires; we were also shown a map of the district over which they put out fires – the size of it is forty square miles. We saw the helmets of those who had died in putting out fires, and we were told there were eighty fire-stations in London.

In the afternoon we went to see the soldiers who had come from all lands; all kinds of Africans to the number of four hundred – Soudanese, Swahilis, Baganda, Kavirondo people, Abyssinians, Masai – and other nations from Asia; Chinese, Indians, and a great many other tribes we saw there. We saw also English people like locusts in numbers who had come to see what black people were like, for all kinds of people were there in this place called 'Alexandra Palace'. There was a very large building there which was full of people; if one were to fall down he would be trodden to death. This was about seven miles away, but it is in a part of London.

The next day, June 28th, we left London, and Captain Hobart took us to his place in the country to see the King's Fleet, which had come together for the coronation. We went by train, and as we went we admired the country; we passed forests of trees that had been planted, and houses of rich and poor in the country just as we have. We passed also Sir Henry Stanley's estate, in which were lakes that he had dug out, which had many tame white birds on them; and at last reached a town called Southampton, which is on the sea and has a very large harbour. There were a great many very large ships there – some would take five thousand men on board; altogether there were about three thousand ships or more – I could not tell the exact number. We went over two large ones and were very tired, as the captain took us into every part of them. After going all over the harbour we got into a little steamer which took us to the other side, where Captain Hobart lived.

We landed at the end of a very long pier made of boards, about as long as from Munyonyo to Bulinguge (one mile), and walked down it to the shore, where we found Captain Hobart's carriage, which took us to his house. Every one in those parts gives him great honour, because his father is a very great man, and is honoured by many people. Captain Hobart's house is a very beautiful one indeed; we had tea there, and then he took us all round his garden with his wife and his steward, and showed us all his vegetables and flowers, and showed us also where his horses live, a very nice house which we at first thought was his church; but when we got into it we saw our mistake, though from the outside it looks like a country church. He had six horses and three carriages. We then saw his landing-place, which is at the side of his grounds, and returned to the house, and he showed us our rooms, which were on the second floor.

At eight o'clock he called us to see the lights of Southampton, which were like stars or comets. These lights can be seen five miles away. After looking at these lights we got very chilly, and went to bed. When one hears the ships trumpeting any one who knows how cows bellow that have been raided in war would understand when I say they bellowed like that, though I only compare them to cows on account of the numbers – the noise they make is far greater, greater even than the trumpeting of an elephant; they go on all night, coming in and going out, and never leave off their noise; the ships trumpet as they come in and trumpet as they go out, and you hear a great noise all the time with the large ships and the small ships, and the moaning of the sea and the noise made by the screws of the ships as they go by.

The next day, June 29th, we went with Captain Hobart to see the fleet and the men-of-war that had come for the coronation, and were going away again on account of the King's illness. We went in a very small steamer – perhaps it was twice as big as our Uganda steamer the *William Mackinnon* – and saw a great number of vessels, which had been arranged in lines of a hundred in each line. We passed between them, and were amazed at them; there were in all about six hundred. We saw many of the guns they carried; some had twenty, some fifteen, others ten, others eight; they were very long indeed, and could carry a distance of fifteen miles, some ten miles, others eight or seven. Is it not an amazing thing that one could fire a gun from Entebbe and the shot would fall in Mengo? When the sailors play on the bugles and flutes and violins and cymbals and drums one would want to have four ears to hear better, and four eyes to see better.

We also saw the King's palace called Osborne in which the Queen died, which is on the island called Wight; her son has now given it to the country, and any one who likes can go there and sleep in it. We were amazed at the sea in this place, because it twists about like the Victoria Nyanza does round Busi. We also went to see the river in which they used to build ships; there is a forest near at hand which is called the New Forest, in which they used to cut the timber for their boats in old days; but when we got to the river our steamer got mixed up in the rubbish, and we were delayed about fifty minutes. After this we landed some of our passengers and went back to the starting-point; and as we went we looked again at the ships, though these were only the ships at one place, Portsmouth, which is near Southampton, and is not such a big place as other larger harbours. We then went home, and found it very cold though there was no rain. After we had rested a while, we went to visit our friend Mr. C. Z. W. Fitzgerald, who cooked a very nice meal for us, and also gave us some presents; the Katikiro he gave a thing for counting the days, and me he gave a china cup with a picture on it of the King and his Queen, which had been made to celebrate the coronation. Mrs. Fitzgerald is a German, but very kind; one would not think she was born in Germany, because the Germans are not at all kind – there are a few kind ones, but they are hard to find, for the many we saw were all ruffianly; but this lady was not like them except in her accent; she played for us on the piano, and showed us how they put pretty things on the walls from all lands and of all kinds to rejoice the eyes.[37] After seeing her we went home.

The next day, June 30th, we went to see our friend Lord Montague, and drove there in Captain Hobart's carriage, a distance of seven miles. On our arrival he welcomed us and showed us all over his house and garden, and showed us also his artificial lake. He showed us the house that used to belong to the monks – his own house had been the chapel of the monks in old days, but the king had given it to him, and he had made it into his house, and now it is six hundred years old; the present church used to be the dining-hall of the monks, and had been made into a church. He also showed us the site of the ancient abbey of the monks; the ground plan can be seen, and is like that of Namirembe Cathedral.

---

[37] This narrative was produced at the height of a bitter rivalry between Britain and Germany over the control of East Africa; the image of Britain as the model of civility demands the invention of the uncivil German body.

After seeing all round his grounds we went back to Captain Hobart's by another road through the forest, and saw a great many trees that had been planted there; some of them were very fine and tall. When any one cuts down a tree he has to plant two or three others in its place.

The Katikiro was very ill with fever on this day, and ate nothing for lunch or dinner, and though he took medicine four times during the day he did not get any better; and so Captain Hobart took me instead of him to see his father, and I went all over the house and saw many curiosities that his son had brought from our country – guns, and shields, and spears, and arrows, and harps, and horns, and skins. He also showed me an old chest for storing money, made in 200 A.D., and told me that his house was a hundred and fifty years old, and showed me where his cows slept in winter; – in the summer all English cows sleep outside, as do the horses of some of the country people. He was very sorry that the Katikiro could not come, and his wife sent him a photograph of the house so that he could see what it was like, even though he had not been there himself. When we got home we found the Katikiro was worse, and so we gave him more medicine, and he got a little better, though he did not recover properly.

The next day, July 1st, after breakfast we left Captain Hobart's house in Hampshire, and crossed by the steamer to the other side, where we found the chief of the place waiting for us, and he took us all over the harbour and showed us the ships that bring the soldiers from India, and we saw how large they were. We saw all over one of them, which had in it stables for the horses, kitchens, and hospitals for men and women. After this we left Southampton and soon arrived in London, where we found Mr. Millar awaiting us at the railway station. He congratulated us on our safe arrival, and we told him how ill the Katikiro was, and then we went home, and did not go out again on account of the Katikiro's illness.

The next day, July 2nd, was a great day, because the King had sent in his place his eldest son, George, the Prince of Wales, with the Queen, to review the Indian troops, since he himself could not review them on account of his illness. There were about a thousand soldiers, all Indians, with perhaps sixty English officers in charge of them. They had large bands with cymbals and bugles, and it was a wonderful sight; many men from many nations had come together to see these Indians and the Queen and the Prince of Wales.[38] There were Germans, French, Spaniards, Italians, Japanese, Moors, Abyssinians, Egyptians, Chinese, Danes, and many other peoples,

---

[38] The author admires the Indian troops both because of the spectacle they present and the idea of commonwealth that empire has made possible: within the symbolic economy of empire, Africans and Indians find kinship they would otherwise not have found.

and they all sat on a frame-work of boards that had been put up. Perhaps there were a hundred thousand people there, without counting those who were standing in the roads, waiting to see the Queen and the Prince of Wales; perhaps in all there were one hundred million (!) including those in the roads and on the staging and on the roofs of the houses – I am not sure of the actual number; they were like ants on a journey. The Queen and the Prince of Wales came in all royal state, and we saw them well, because they came close in front of us, and so we had a good look at them, as our seats were in the second row from the front; the authorities showed their love for us by giving us such places of honour. I can compare the kindness of the English to nothing on this earth.

The soldiers came and took up their appointed positions in line, and then we heard the Queen and the Prince of Wales coming, and the crowd cheering them very loudly – for there were people all along the road by which they came to the courtyard of the Foreign Office (Horse Guards Parade), in which we were all waiting. The Queen came first in a carriage with two princesses; the Prince of Wales was on horseback, with many famous people accompanying him, General Roberts being just in front of him, and they marched slowly round to greet every one.

The Prince of Wales then got off his horse and stood up, and they brought the officers of the Indians up one by one to be introduced to him; he shook hands with each one, who then retired backwards. After this he again mounted his horse. He first returned the salute of the soldiers, and then went round again a second time in the way in which he had entered, bowing as he went, and we all bowed and took off our hats; the ladies did not do this, for it is not the custom in Europe for ladies to take off their hats. After he had said good-bye to us he went home, and we thought the kingdom of the English was a marvellous kingdom.

As we were going back we saw the children of the Prince of Wales, the grandchildren of the King, getting into their carriage to go home, for they too had come to see their father reviewing the Indian troops.

Chapter VIII

Birmingham – Steel pen making – Making rifles – Liverpool – S.S. Oceanic – Liverpool Town Hall – The Cotton Exchange – The landing-stage – Cambridge – 'The tutor of the world' – The University Press – The University Library – 'One cannot have everything' – St. Joseph's College, Mill Hill – Hampstead – An English wedding – Carlisle – Canon Rawnsley's sonnet – The Agricultural Show – Cows like hippopotami – Sheep-shearing

After a short rest we left for Birmingham, the city in which Miss Dallison, the nurse in Mengo hospital, was born;[39] and after we had settled into our hotel, which was called the Queen's Hotel, we went to see her father. We found he was out, and her mother had a slight attack of fever, so we saw her brother and sister, and then came home, passing on the way a large house that had been built for poor people to live in, and of which Miss Dallison's father was the chaplain. He came himself to see us at night, with four of his children.

The next morning, July 3rd, we went to see the factories of Birmingham. We first went to a place where they put gold and silver coatings on all kinds of things – rings, spoons, kettles, basins, pots, cups, medals, forks – and many other things that are gold and silver-plated. We saw how all these things were made, and then went to a pen factory.

This pen factory was a marvellous place; there were in it 2,200 workpeople; and we there saw a great number of women working only at making pens. There are a great many different operations, and each is carried on in its own department. Let me try and tell you them as well as I can remember.

1. Cutting the steel into long strips for making the pens.
2. Softening the steel to make it suitable for working.

---

[39] Mengo Hospital had been established by Sir Albert Cook, a member of the Church Missionary Society, in 1897 and had quickly risen to prominence as a medical centre in East Africa. The connection between Mengo and Birmingham may appear incidental here, but it is a subtle reminder of how Mukasa makes Britain comprehensible to his readers through analogy.

3. Examining, to see if the steel is suitable for pen-making.
4. Cutting the steel into strips the size of a pen.
5. Cutting off pieces at the sides to make the point.
6. Pointing the pen.
7. Splitting the point.
8. Printing the lettering on the pen.
9. Examining the pens to remove imperfect ones.
10. Weighing the pens into packets.
11. Making boxes for the pens.
12. Baking the pens over the fire to harden them.
13. Putting them into a mixture to temper them when red hot.
14. Putting them in sawdust to polish them.
15. Seeing that they are flexible and not brittle.
16. Putting the boxes of pens into paper wrappers.

All this work has to be done to a pen, and each kind of work has its own set of workmen, as I have told you; but I have not mentioned a good many other operations that are gone through. The head of this factory (Perry's) was a very kind man, and took us round a great many places, and gave us many different kinds of pens made there, and a picture of the factory, to remember it by.

After this we went to see a factory where rifles and bicycles are made (B.S.A.), and found there three thousand workpeople, men and women, in this one factory.[40] On our arrival the manager very kindly gave us a man to take us round, and we first wrote our names in the visitors' book, and then our guide showed us all the different parts of a rifle; each part has a special anvil and bellows and hammer to make it, and as each part is made it is handed on to other workmen, who continue the operation. The hammer was as large as the base of a large drum; when they hammer with it, a man moves a lever, and the hammer works itself, and in the anvil underneath are sockets of different shapes, each one shaped like the forging that has to be made in it, and the one hammer makes all the differently shaped things. The whole building was full of belts and machinery, all working by the power of the engine that turns all the machinery and keeps on working till 5 p.m., when the workmen rest. We saw how the barrels are bored, and how the stocks are made, and how the screw-holes are made. They also fired off some of the rifles to test them, and we all three fired them at the target.

We also saw where they made bicycles, and saw a great many different parts being manufactured; there were a great many women in the workshop,

[40] Bicycles and rifles had become indicators of modernity and power in the colonial scene.

and we were amazed at the strength of English women that enables them to work like men, as in every kind of work one finds men and women. After this we had tea with the manager, and while we were at tea the time arrived when work was over for the day, and we saw all these three thousand workpeople, men and women, going away, and the whole road was blocked with them, they were so many. Every week they make fifteen hundred rifles, but during the Boer War they were making five thousand a week. My friends, one never ceases wondering at the English; when we heard this, we shook our heads like a man suffering from hunger.

The next day, July 4th, we left the city of Birmingham and went to Liverpool, where we arrived at 2 p.m. We went to the North-Western Hotel, and after lunch went to see the ships in the harbour, as Liverpool is the largest port in England; the town also is very large, but not as large as London, which stands alone, no other town on earth approaching it in size. We got into an electric train, and reached a very large ship, the largest in England; it was called the *Oceanic*, and was 704 ft. long, and 70 ft. wide, and 60 ft. high, and will take 2,300 passengers; the anchor was 4,000 tons in weight (!), and each ton is 2,240 lb., so you can understand what 4,000 tons is. There were 350 men in the crew, and it had two screws, and every hour travelled twenty miles, while other ships go only fifteen, fourteen, thirteen, or twelve miles per hour; this is the quickest ship of all. We were taken all over it, and saw it all above and below. There were eight stories in this ship.

We saw the engines that drive the screw, but I cannot explain to you what they were like – I can only say that they were marvellous; one would think that such large engines would be only found on dry land. The people on board were very kind, and gave us tea. We got as tired in that boat as one would do in a town on land; going up the stairs is like climbing hills on land, and that is the reason we got tired, though we did not go all over the boat, but only into about forty rooms. The rooms on the boat were just like the rooms in the houses in a town, but the eating-rooms and recreation rooms were very large, and higher than those on land. Apolo tried to reach to the top of one of these rooms with his stick, but could not do so, even though he is a tall man; and though he added another stick, still he could not reach the roof, and we wondered without ceasing. The floors of these rooms were made of black and white indiarubber, and were so beautiful we did not like to tread on them. We saw another ship that will carry seven hundred head of cattle; it was built only to carry cattle, and would appear very large to any one who had not seen the *Oceanic*; it had three masts and two funnels; but we did not go on board, but merely looked at it. We saw also the gangway along which they take things on board; any one who saw it would not know he was over the sea, as it is so large and wide, and rests one end on land and the other on the sea, where all the ships come; it is all of wood. We went back again by the electric railway, the carriages of which were as large as on an ordinary railway.

The next day, July 5th, our friend Councillor Dart came to take us over the town of Liverpool, and we saw the great buildings and assembly rooms. We saw there a very large organ; the pipes that took the wind to it were like the funnel of a steamer; there were about six hundred seats in the hall. We next went over the Town Hall, a very fine building indeed. We first saw the chief man of the town, who was called the Lord Mayor, and he gave us a guide to show us round, and we saw the place where the town council meet, and the law courts, the criminal court and the civil court, and the place where criminals go who are condemned to death, and where those go who are not yet condemned, and where the visitors sit. We saw also another room with three large lamps in it, about ten thousand pounds in weight, and two large mirrors, one on one side and one on the other; if you look into them you see yourself everywhere.

We then went to the Cotton Exchange[41] to tell the merchants about Uganda, and found there a great many people. Mr. Dart spoke first, and told them who we were and what our country was like, and then Apolo spoke a little, and when he had finished they all clapped their hands and took off their hats. We next went to the landing-place and saw how they had very cleverly made there a floating bridge which was like an island; one would not know it was a bridge, though really there was water below. When a ship comes alongside it they put out planks, and such heavy things as horses and carriages can embark and disembark.

We saw some carts that had come from Ireland (Birkenhead) and were full of casks of beer, about twenty in each, and they disembarked while we were there. After this we went to hear the large organ, but almost as soon as it began we had to leave to catch our train; and so we left while the organ was playing, and got into the train for Cambridge. On our way we met at Leicester the father of Mr. A. B. Lloyd and his mother and brother and sisters, who were very like him; they had got some tea ready for us, and after tea we got into another train and arrived at Cambridge at 9.30 p.m., and found the Rev. J. Roscoe waiting for us at the station, and went with him to the Bull Hotel, and were given our rooms where each was to sleep.[42]

---

[41] It was through the cultivation of cotton that Uganda was to enter the colonial economy, hence the value of the Cotton Exchange.

[42] The Reverend John Roscoe was the author of some of the earliest works on the culture of Buganda and had worked closely with Sir Apolo. The two came to control the way Bugandan society was read and deployed in the legal and cultural framework provided by British colonialism.

The next day, July 6th, was a Sunday, and we went with Mr. Roscoe to a church that was about eight hundred years old. In the afternoon we went to visit the Master of Trinity and the Rev. T. W. Drury, Principal of Ridley Hall, both of whom are great men in the city of Cambridge. We had dinner at Trinity College with a large number of those who were under instruction, and with Dr. Aldis Wright, who helped in turning the New Testament from Greek into English; we saw him at the same table as ourselves and the Master of Trinity. We saw these great colleges where the sons of the rich are taught, and where they learn all manner of things, both theology and earthly wisdom. Now-a-days they are taught engineering, carpentering, and about all kinds of machinery, and also nautical knowledge and other things which are profitable to men in this life, after they have learnt religion. Our friends whom you know, Archdeacon Walker, Revs. R. P. Ashe, W. A. Crabtree, R. H. Leakey, E. Millar, H. Clayton, Mr. G. L. Pilkington, Dr. A. R. Cook, and others were all taught here, in the places we saw.[43]

This city is a very famous one on account of its learning, because it teaches things that are much to be desired by all men on the earth, and though it is not as large as other cities, yet I call it 'the tutor of the world'; and though there are many tutors in Europe, yet there are none to equal Cambridge; perhaps Oxford comes next to it. After dinner the Master of Trinity escorted us as far as the gateway of the courtyard, and said good-bye to us very kindly, and we went home. To this city many nationalities come, wishing to learn wisdom, and I therefore call it the tutor of the world, and even though students pay heavily to be taught there, there is a reason for this, for 'Who feedeth a flock and eateth not of the milk of the flock?'

The next day, July 7th, we went to see the house where books of all kinds are printed (University Press), and saw some wonderfully clever printing presses; you will understand how clever they are when I tell you that the only work that has to be done by hand is to put in the paper; the press prints by itself, takes off the paper itself, inks its own type, and cuts up the paper, and oils itself – all this we saw.[44] And though we had seen many wonderful things, still this was more wonderful, as it did its own work just like a man

---

[43] Trinity College had produced some of the most prominent clergy in the Church Missionary Society and this list contains the most influential. Mukasa's description of them as 'Our friends whom you know' points to the latent politics of his text and its intended audience: he assumes that he and Sir Apolo are part of an Anglican network which is perhaps privileged in the colonial culture; that his ideal reader is Bugandan Anglican; and that the reading of his text will solidify this connection.

[44] Both Mukasa and Sir Apolo were prolific writers and Cambridge University Press (which had printed many of the books read in the colony) fascinated them as a powerful agent of colonial modernity.

who has the spirit of life in him, though it was only made by man's wisdom. We were again amazed at the cleverness of the English, which is unending. We went over a great many rooms in which printing work of different kinds was being done, and then went to see the store of books that had been printed.

After this we went to see the building in which they keep every book of every kind, one copy of each (University Library). Of every book that is printed they take one copy, and put it in this building as a remembrance. We saw there a great many books some fourteen to seventeen hundred years of age, and they told us there were about half a million books in the library. Is this not amazing? If you count the number of books in the Bible from Genesis to Malachi, how many would you find? then, again, how many are there from Matthew to Revelation? Well, this is the way they count their books; one book of every kind is stored up, just as Apolo Katikiro wrote *Basekabaka Bebuganda* ('Kings of Uganda'), and they took one copy and kept it; in this way the number of five hundred thousand books is made up.

After this we rested a short while, and then went to visit Mr. Roscoe, and stayed a long time talking to him and his wife and children, because his wife is just as fond of the Baganda as if she had been born in Uganda, though she has never been there, and it is only her kindness. If it were not for her children she would have come out there long ago with her husband. She is as kind as he is, and their children are equally kind.

In the evening we went to see the Master of St. John's, and had dinner with him and his students and great men; but the number of students was small, because a great many were away at this time, as it was the vacation. After this we went to see Dr. Frazer, who also was in Cambridge, and he gave us coffee.[45] There were a great many people there – among them two very clever ladies, sisters, who are well known, and who have travelled in many parts of Asia, and on Mount Sinai found a portion of the Gospel of St. John, which they were at work upon at that time, and they gave us a photograph of it. They have learned Arabic, and can speak it, and write it in its own characters. They wanted very much to come to Uganda, but they made us laugh by saying, 'We very much want to come to your country, but we are afraid of the man-eating lions'; and we said, 'There is now a railway, so that the lions do not eat people'; and they said, 'We heard that the lions had taken a man out of a railway carriage and eaten him', and we laughed

---

[45] Mukasa's visit with Sir James Frazer appears cursory, but this is only because he takes the famous anthropologist's connection to colonialism for granted. Many of the missionaries trained at Trinity had been Frazer's students and several produced ethnographic monographs on the people to whom they ministered; the line between fieldwork and Christian conversion was often thinner than we might think.

very much at their wanting to come to our country and being afraid of lions, because there are a great many ladies now in Uganda, and they have not yet been eaten by lions; and this made me understand that one cannot have everything. These women are very clever indeed, and yet they are afraid of animals they have never seen. They are very much alike, and very kind, and are both widows; but their wisdom and their joy of heart are now to them in the place of husbands. After a time we went home, being very tired, as we had been visiting all day.

The next day, July 8th, we left Cambridge, and went with Mr. Millar to visit the Roman Catholic Bishop of Nsambya (Uganda), whose name is Hanlon, and found him waiting for us at Mill Hill Station with a carriage.[46] I forgot my fez in the train and Mr. Millar telegraphed for it, and they brought it back; but I was very much ashamed of being bare-headed in such a great country, and to be like a little child, though a full-grown man, and so I covered my head with my pocket-handkerchief. We first visited the nuns, of whom there were six who hoped to go to Uganda; and they showed us all round their nunnery, and collected about a hundred and fifty little children from three years old and upwards, and one of the nuns played on a harmonium, and all the children stood up in front of us and sang very nicely. We sat on a very nice lawn at the back of the house, which was on the top of the hill, so that we got a fine view.

After the children had finished singing we thanked them, and went to see the church, which was very fine and large, and then we saw a number of men who were under training as priests to go out as missionaries. They collected them together to hear about Uganda, and Apolo told them what was going on in our country, and Bishop Hanlon translated for him. After this we had lunch and rested, and then we were photographed behind the church, and were taken all round the grounds, and saw there some pigs as large as calves; we then had afternoon tea and went away. They brought us round a carriage, and after we had got in all the priests said good-bye to us very kindly, and cheered us loudly; and when we waved our handkerchiefs they all cheered again until we got out of sight among the trees. Bishop Hanlon went with us as far as the railway station, and we then went to our

---

[46] This passing gesture to Catholicism can be read as an attempt to gloss over the sensitive religious politics of Uganda. For during the period of colonial conquest and rule, the newly colonised found themselves divided between Catholics, referred to as the BaFranza (the French) because the main Catholic mission had been founded by the French White Fathers, and the Protestants who, because they were mainly drawn from the Church Missionary Society, were called the Bangereza (the English). This association between nations and denominations was broken when Bishop Henry Hanlon founded a Mill Hill Fathers mission in Buganda in 1895.

place in Hampstead, Mr. H. E. Millar's house, which we regarded as Uganda, as we could always rest there; and both he and his wife and children were very kind indeed, just like Mr. and Mrs. Roscoe were.

The next day, July 9th, was the wedding day of the Rev. G. K. Baskerville of Uganda, and we got ready, and at one o'clock went to have lunch with him, and found there his father and mother and three brothers. After lunch we went with him to the church, and after we had waited a short time the bride arrived with great honour, and was beautifully dressed, just as all brides are; her train, which trailed after her, was about eight or nine feet in length, and was of very fine material. She walked very slowly; where an ordinary person would take one step, she took four, because she walked slowly, as is the custom of brides. When she entered the church we all got up and sang, and after we had sung and prayed, Mr. Baskerville's father united his two children, and after they were married they asked the Katikiro to write his name in the register as a witness. After this was over we went to have tea, and then went home and wrote our letters for Uganda.

At eight o'clock we went to the Hampstead Town Hall, because Mr. H. E. Millar had made a great feast and collected a great many people, perhaps three hundred of his friends and others whom he wanted to see us. We stayed there a long time; the building was a very fine one, built after the custom of the English. Hampstead is like a town, though it is not a town really, but a part of London; just as Namirembe, Seguku, Rubaga, Natete, and Kampala are a part of Mengo, so also there are many districts in London. Hampstead is about as far from London as Munyonyo is from Mengo (eight miles). The following of our friends were at Mr. Baskerville's wedding: Revs. E. C. Gordon, H. Clayton, E. Millar, Mr. H. Maddox, and Mrs. Maddox.

The next day, July 10th, we left Hampstead at eleven o'clock and went to Carlisle to see the great beasts (Agricultural Show), and arrived at 5 p.m., since it was 299 miles off, and so were six hours on the road. Well is not a journey half as long again as to Toro a long journey?

When we reached the station we met our kind friend Mr. Miles MacInnes, who had brought a two-horse carriage to meet us, and took us to sleep in his own house. When we arrived his wife and daughters and friends greeted us very warmly, and his daughters made a fire for us, as it was very cold. They also played on the piano, and showed us a dog which had been taught wisdom. We went up to our rooms and admired the house very much indeed, for it was a very fine one; but one gets tired of praising the English houses, they are such grand ones. We sat down twelve to dinner, six ladies and six men, amongst whom was a very kind friend called Canon Rawnsley, who wrote a sonnet to Apolo:

Though I should never see your dark face more
Nor hear your murmuring soft Luganda speech,
My prayers, my hopes, my memories still shall reach
Across the forests of your native shore;
And I shall see you adding store to store
For your young King, proclaiming each to each
Justice and right, and urging men to teach
In life and death the Saviour's precious lore.

Farewell, brave Katikiro, farewell, friend;
Go to your people, tell them we revere
A man whose honour for the spoken word
Is stronger far than power of spear or sword;
Tell them we love a man of heart sincere,
And Britain gives you hand-grasp to the end.

After dinner it had become dark, and we sat on talking to our friends, and went to bed tired at about 11 p.m.

The next day, July 11th, Mr. MacInnes took us to see things of many kinds, animals, and things made by hand, both of wood and iron, and all kinds of seeds, etc. We drove in Mr. MacInnes' carriage, while his children walked. We soon reached the place where all these things were collected. We first saw a statue of the Queen, which had been unveiled on July 9th; it was a very good one, and an excellent likeness. We next saw pumps and mowing-machines, and thrashing-machines, and machines for cutting grass for horses, and that tied up the bundles just like a man would. We saw also sheep-shearing machines, butter churns, machines for making cloth, carriages, and movable wooden huts for police to sleep in. We saw too all kinds of food and of vegetables and flowers. We saw some very large cows that looked like hippopotami, and horses like buffaloes; our Uganda horses are about as large as an English horse only a year old. We saw too a horse as small as a goat, which they call a pony; and this is its natural size. There were about seven thousand animals in all, cows and horses.

We saw there how they shear sheep; when they are shearing it, the sheep does not move till all the hair is cut off; and so we understood what we had heard in the prophecy about our Lord: 'He was brought as a lamb to the slaughter, and as a sheep before her shearers is dumb, so he opened not His mouth'; for we saw it being done. They shear the sheep every year, because the sheep are the bark-cloth trees of the English, which they beat out, and their wool makes the clothing that they all wear, as cotton clothing is not much worn; but cotton cloth is used for other purposes. After this we went back to Mr. MacInnes' house, after we had been photographed at the shearing place, and we have copies of this photograph at the present time.

After a short rest we went on to Scotland, to the city of Glasgow. Mr. MacInnes and his family all came to the station to see us off, and bade us a very kind farewell, and we went on our journey and arrived at Glasgow.

Chapter IX

Glasgow – Visit to the Lord Provost – The municipal buildings – A prison
– The University – The Cathedral – A coal mine – Steel works – Greenock
– Sugar refining – The city councillors – Dumbarton – Shipbuilding –
Edinburgh – The Forth Bridge – Luncheon with Sir William Muir –
Paper-making – Holyrood Palace – Reception by the town council

The next morning, July 12th, we went to see round the city, and to see the great men and the important buildings that were in the centre of it. The Lord Mayor of Glasgow had given us his representative to take us round, and we first went to see him himself. He welcomed us warmly and showed us a little of the Town Hall, but could not be with us long, as his office brought him much work; and so he left us to the City Chamberlain, whom he had asked to see after us and to show us round. We saw the hall where the chief men met, in which were eighteen seats; and the hall where the others met, in which were seventy-seven seats, and saw also other rooms.

In the banqueting-hall there were a great many lights; the weight of them was over a ton, the lights being about two hundred and fifty in number, and each was in a glass bulb and could be turned on separately, as they were all electric lights, and the wires shine by themselves without any oil as we have in our lamps. They turned on these lights to show us how brilliant they were. We did not go over the whole house, which was about ten times as large as that of Kisingiri (third regent). They had valuable stone on the walls, which resembled scented soap or blotting-paper, and was much to be marvelled at.

We then went to see the prisons, and were taken round by the Governor himself. We first visited the male prisoners. The prison was like this: they make a large stone building with iron doors immensely strong; which have very small holes in them, through which the jailor can see what the prisoner is like as he sits inside; they put in each cell a small prison table and a prison bed, which is not a nice one; all the furniture of the cells is common, and suitable for prisoners – very common prison chairs, very common prison clothing, very common prison blankets, very common prison spoons, not like ordinary spoons; they take a cow's horn and make a very thin spoon out of it, and all the prisoners eat with these; for they are afraid of them killing themselves if they had the ordinary metal spoons, hence they make them thus – they make them thin as they are afraid that if they were thick the prisoners might be able to kill themselves. The building itself is very fine and the cells are nice, but very narrow; the bedsteads are narrow and so not nice; the prisoners' clothing too is common, and their windows are very bad as they are very small, but they let out the bad air and let in the good. The jailors look after them very well, and give them books to read – every one can have the book he wants; but they do not let them receive private letters, or tobacco, or intoxicants, or anything else unsuitable; they have rules forbidding all these things.

They have arranged very cleverly too what to do when the prisoners' friends or relations come to see them. They have made two iron gratings – on the side where the prisoner comes there is a grating, and where his visitor is there is also a grating, and there is a space of about ten feet between the two, so that they cannot stretch their hands across; and a guardian of the prisoners stands between the gratings listening to all that is said, so that nothing shall make the prisoner more unhappy during his imprisonment, and that he shall not obtain a letter or anything that is not allowed, and this is the reason they have to converse through iron gratings.

Both the prisons, that of the men and that of the women, are alike; perhaps the only difference is that the women are given looking-glasses, as they like looking at themselves in the glass every moment; and they are guarded by other women and not by men. I thought to myself that when a poor man or woman is brought into that prison he would be glad at all he gets there, because at home he would not have a looking-glass and clothes and good food; the only thing that he would not like would be to be called a prisoner; perhaps there may be some other reason to make people unhappy in prison, but of those things that I saw I do not think there is anything to make a man unhappy, unless he happened to be a man who had occupied an honourable position – such a man might be unhappy; but the kindness of the officials and the way they look after the prisoners are very good – not for those evil ones who do not want to give up evil habits, but for those who have done wrong and do not like having done so, and repent.

At the door of every prisoner's cell they put up the reason of his captivity, whether he be a man or a woman. The Governor told us there were 460 prisoners in the prison – 270 women and 190 men.

After leaving the prison we went to see a church which was eight hundred years old, having been built in the year 1102; it was very fine indeed, and very large. We then went to see the University and the hospital. We saw over the University and the place where the chief men sit, and from their seat we got a view over the whole town, and saw the River Clyde, which runs through the city. We had not time to go into the hospital, but went back to the Lord Mayor and had dinner with him, and then went home in the heavy rain.[47]

The next day, July 13th, was a Sunday, and we went to the Scotch Cathedral of Glasgow, and found there a great many people; they did not have many prayers, but read the Psalms and had a few extempore prayers, and a sermon and a hymn, and then all was over. They put a box in the doorway, and every one who came in threw in his rupee, and was given a paper. Inside they also had a collection, so that the outside collection was merely to count the number of those who came in – we understood it thus. When we left the Cathedral we walked home, looking at the streets and the houses as we went, and so reached our house, which was called Caledonian Railway Company's Central Station Hotel, Glasgow, and was the hotel at the railway station itself. The Katikiro had fever, so we did not go out again that day.

The following morning, July 14th, we went to see how they dug coal; we went some way by train, and then drove to the house of our friend Mr. Sholto Douglas; his secretary, Mr. T. Stockdale, went with us to show us all we did not know. When we reached Mr. Douglas' house, Mr. Stockdale gave us some English clothes to wear so that we should not dirty our own clothes; and we left our own clothes behind and got into the carriage, which took us to the train, which was only the fireplace that pulls the carriages along. We got on this, and it took us to the place where the coal was washed. It is difficult to explain how they do this. After leaving this place we went back to where they dig the coal.

They first explained to us all the machinery above ground, which was not understandable, and we then got into the room in which they go down to where the coal is dug. We all got in – Apolo Katikiro, Ham Mukasa, Mr. Millar, and Mr. Stockdale – and arrived safely at the bottom, and there found a great many people in the bowels of the earth, both young and old, each one with a lamp on his cap to give him light as he worked. They gave us lamps also, and told us to fasten them in our caps; but we were afraid of burning ourselves, and so we kept them in our hands, all of us who did not

---

[47] Universities and hospitals feature prominently in Mukasa's narrative because they were considered to be the ideal and most desirable signs of modernity. Both Sir Apolo and Mukasa were active in the establishment of Makerere College, the first centre of higher education in East Africa. In 1945, when there was talk of transferring the college to Kenya, Mukasa wrote an article in which he described the college as a sign of the progress Uganda had made 'in wisdom and knowledge' since the first teachers arrived in Britain in 1897.

belong to the pit; but all those belonging to the pit, including the small boys, fastened their lamps in their caps. We walked a good distance, perhaps about three hundred yards, and got to the end of the part where they were digging; but other diggings were longer. There were rails along which the trucks of coal ran to take the coal away from the place where it was dug, and to carry it to the surface. They told us to dig a little; the Katikiro would not do so, as he was tired, but I dug out a little, which I have brought to Uganda to show the Baganda what it is like, because they hear of it, but have never seen it.

After this we went back, and I asked the depth we were underground, and they told us we were seven hundred yards down, and had gone three hundred yards along the passage, making a thousand yards in all. We then went home and washed the black off ourselves, and put on our own clothes, and went to lunch with a lady who lived near; she was about seventy years of age, and was very kind to us. Her husband was away; we should have liked very much to have seen him, but we could not. They had a very nice house, and there were numbers of wild rabbits about, which even came quite close up to the house.

We next went to see a great smithy, and saw how they make the wheels of railway carriages, and the iron plates for ships; they make there plates for ships of all kinds, and we understood that Glasgow was a city of men who were clever at building ships. We saw, too, wonderful machines that lifted the blocks of iron, etc.; some could lift 672,000 lb. Is not this marvellous? Who would ever think that such a weight could be lifted? We saw a piece of iron of this weight being lifted, and were much surprised at the cleverness of the British. We saw also a machine that squeezes out iron into long plates; they take a large piece of iron about a yard long, and squeeze it backwards and forwards till it becomes a plate ten yards long. If you try to look into the furnace where steel is melted, you cannot do so unless you have a piece of blue glass; and if you were to try you would lose your eyesight.

After seeing these things we went home, and very shortly afterwards five of the judges of Glasgow came to see us – Messrs. D. M. Stevenson, John Ferguson, Simon Dallas, and two others; and asked us a great deal about our country, such as, 'Are there many drunkards in your land?' and the Katikiro told them how there were some, and how they were stopped. And they asked, 'How do you punish them?' and he told them that they were imprisoned for two months, or, if they would not give it up, for six months, if they went on drinking. They then asked him, 'What do you do to drunken women?' and he said that in our country we do not usually imprison women, but only men; but there was one woman who used to get drunk, and received ten strokes as a beating, and her husband was told to stop her from getting drunk. They asked him, 'Do you have drunkards in your Parliament?' and he said, 'A drunken man cannot come into our Parliament', and they asked him, 'What do you do to chiefs and to peasants who get drunk?' and he replied that a chief is fined 75 rupees (£5), and a peasant 6 rupees (8s.), and is imprisoned two months.

They were very pleased at hearing that drunkards were not allowed in our Parliament, and that the Parliament itself did not like there being drunken men in our country; and told us how they themselves imprisoned drunkards for two or three days, and said, 'We wish to punish them more severely, because they do not leave off getting drunk, and others we send out to work in the country.' They also asked us what kind of traders came to our country; and we told them that there were Germans there, and Italians, and Indians. They then left us, and the Rev. H. W. Pembridge, the vicar of St. Silas' Church, came to see us, and we talked to him for about forty minutes; he was very anxious we should come and see his church, but we had not enough time.

The next day, July 15th, we went to see how they boil sugar in a town called Greenock, which is near Glasgow, and which is the place where they boil the sugar that comes from sugar-cane. When we left our hotel we went by train to Greenock, which is by the sea-shore, and went first to the manager of the factory, who greeted us warmly, and then took us all over the works, and showed us how each part of the work was done. They first showed us specimens of the different kinds of sugar, and the different processes – about twenty-five in number – through which it passed.

They boil the sugar, and pass it over the burnt bones of cattle and other animals; these bones are all burned and become charcoal; one can only wonder at the use they make of these bones – one cannot explain it. We then went to another department and saw the boilers and engine that drives all the machinery; in all factories the engines are alike, and though there is a difference between the different engines, it is difficult to tell what it is when one merely looks at them. The owners know the difference, but the whole building is full of noise above and below, and there are great wide belts always turning round. We saw the bags through which the sugar is strained, and the place where the pure sugar runs out, and the huge pots in which it is boiled, which are made of iron, and are very tall; this boiling takes away all impurities. In this place we saw the workmen had only got on very small cloths round their waists and nothing else, on account of the heat which there was where they worked.

There were many other processes which it is difficult to describe in making this sugar, which was very sweet and in great quantities; but those who make it have to work very hard. The machines of the English are many, and are all over the land, but they cause a great deal of work; and because the English work so hard, therefore machinery spreads into all lands. We all understand that perseverance increases one's wealth; but laziness does not do so in any kind of work, whether it be done by the hands or not. All you then who read this should not be lazy when they teach you different kinds of work.

When we left this place we went to a room where women were putting the sugar into tins, in which it stays altogether, and is then sent out everywhere. English women work wonderfully fast, just like their husbands; we were amazed at them. After this we went below and saw a great many men with simply bits of cloth on them, like the Kavirondo people or the Bahima; they dress like this on account of the heat, because if they did not take care of themselves they would soon die.

These English factories are as large as the space in front of the King's enclosure in Uganda, or larger, and small factories are as large as the fort at Kampala, but all one building.[48] After seeing round the factory we went into the office and washed our hands, for all the buildings were very dirty inside, and all the workmen had faces like black men, because the charcoal made them very black. After we had entered our names in the visitors' book we drove to see the chief man of the town; and a great many people, both men and women, young and old, came to see what we were like.

When we got to the Town Hall, we found the council were holding a meeting, and they received us very kindly. The man who came with us told them in a few words who we were, and then all the councillors who were assembled there clapped their hands – they were twenty-five in number; and after this Apolo Katikiro spoke a few words, and we all clapped; and then the chief man of the town said a little, and again we clapped; and then we went away, since on our arrival we had found them occupied in discussing their business.

After this we returned to our hotel and had lunch, and then went to see where they make ships. When we arrived we saw a great many things – screws for ships, and the way iron plates were pierced and bent, and how boards were shaped; we saw, too, planes of many kinds, that cut in a most wonderful way by themselves. We saw one plane which cut off a shaving while we were there, and this shaving was just like a sheet of paper; we asked the manager of the works to give it us, and he did so, so that we could show

---

[48] British factories were other significant institutions of colonial modernity and by describing their size or spaciousness, Mukasa was also calling attention to their absence in Uganda. In this instance, factories are compared to the king's enclosure (and a colonial fort) because there were no factories in Uganda.

it to our friends, and not only explain in words what it was like; and at the present time we have it, and show it every day. We then went to see where they build ships, and how they do all the work, from the keel upwards. We saw one just finished, and about to leave the yard; it was very beautiful.

They also showed us a thing in which they first try what the ship will be like. They make a model of the ship in beeswax and other things, such as fat, and have a large house in which is a very long ditch full of water, and in this they put the wax model, which is about five feet long, and exactly like what the boat is going to be, and has the same proportions. They showed us the way they made these models, and also a model which was complete, and which was in the water; and we got on board this one, and they showed us how they tested it, to see if the shape was a good one, or in what way it was not right. The length of the ditch was about twenty or twenty-five yards from end to end, and both the Katikiro and I travelled all along it in the boat, and then came back along the side on foot; the boat is drawn along by a cord, but whether it was a steam engine or an electric one that pulled the cord I do not know. Again we were amazed at the cleverness of the English.

After tea we were taken to see the models of the old ships made by the ancestors of the present firm; and we saw how as they went on making ships they invented new things up to the present time. They have a large building in which all these models are shown, with large glass windows. We saw also the portraits of the founders of the firm (Denny, Dumbarton). After this we went away (to Edinburgh), and the manager of the works went back to his work.

The next morning, July 16th, we went to see the Forth Bridge, which is one of the wonders of the world – a marvellous thing; there is nothing like it in any other land, but it is the only one of its kind and is near Edinburgh; it was made in 1890.[49] We first went to see the chief who looks after it, and he asked us to write our names in his visitors' book, and then accompanied us, and we walked over it to see what it was like. We saw the huge iron pillars, larger than any tree in Uganda, and 351 ft. high; they went up to an amazing height. Some railway trains full of numbers of people passed over the bridge while we were there. We saw one trainload of eight hundred children, who were going out to play in the country, and they waved their handkerchiefs when they saw us as the train rushed past, and were very anxious to see us black people – if they had not been in the train they would all have come to look at us; and we reached the other side, a distance of one or two miles. Seven trains passed us while we were on the bridge, and they

---

[49] If civilisation is conceived in terms of biblical codes or civility, modernity was clearly manifested in technological marvels such as the Forth Bridge!

were going very fast, so we got to one side; but the rush of wind they made would have been enough to throw us over if we had not resisted it. I cannot tell you how fast the English trains go, and as we were only about two feet away from them the force of the wind was very great, and the bridge shook with the weight of the trains. The part of the sea which is bridged is about as far as from Munyonyo to Kisinsi. We then went down to the shore to look up at the bridge, and saw a very old well, perhaps a thousand years old, and I drank some of the water from it; we also saw a woman knitting socks, and I asked her to let me try, and I knitted a little, and then we went away. The chief of the bridge, Mr. A. Hunter, was very kind indeed, and wanted to take us across the water so that we could see the bridge from below; but his steamer was out of order and could not take us, so we went back by train by the way we had come on our feet, and when we got to his house he said good-bye to us, and put us into another train, and we went home and rested a little while.

After a short rest we went to have lunch with our friend Sir William Muir, a very old man, eighty-three years of age, but still very strong, and with a good appetite; he rides a horse and a bicycle, and talks with an exceedingly strong voice. All the questions which he asked us were very clever ones, showing that his mind has not got old. He said to us, 'Next time you come you must bring your wives, and I will look after them for you in every way'; and we thanked him very much for his kindness, for we saw that though we thought his time of departure from this world was near at hand, he did not think of this owing to his affection for us, and thought of future events as they concerned us, and not as they concerned him. He had three daughters, who had lunch with us, and after lunch we went to see how paper is made.

The Lord Mayor (really Bailie Brown, as the Lord Provost was away) of the town of Edinburgh took us in a two-horse carriage to the place where paper is made, and there we found the manager, who greeted us very warmly, and showed us over his paper-works. We first went to see the grass from which paper is made, and which is like the grass which grows beside our lake; we saw how it is first cut up and boiled, and pounded up in a machine to make it soft and to squeeze out the water. We saw how it was steeped in water a second time, and how the impurities were taken out, and how another machine made the paper white, and how the material became consistent and like a well-dressed goat-skin, and then became like real paper. We then saw how it was made smooth and nice like real paper, and how it was rolled up on a roller, and how the great rolls of paper were cut just as if they were merely one sheet.

We saw women doing paper up into bundles just as you see it; and a great many other things also we saw that we could not understand in this one work of paper-making. After seeing all this I asked for some specimens of the grass and paper to show to the Baganda, and we then went back to visit the Lord Mayor.

He first took us to see the palace of Charles II (Holyrood), which is four hundred years old, and was very fine; the Queen (Victoria) used to use it and was very fond of it; it was built in 1503.[50] We saw the kings' beds, and the chairs of the ancient kings, and all their blankets, etc., and a great many other things. We saw the bedstead of Mary (Queen of Scots), which had a very old blanket on it which was like a pocket-handkerchief in size. There were visitors' rooms and a council-room, and a room where great men sat after they had dined with the king, or were summoned by him. After this we went to have tea with the Lord Mayor, and saw his robes and chain of office, which was worth £900, or 13,500 rupees for the one chain. He made the Katikiro put on all these things to show him how they wore them; he was a very cheerful and amusing man.

After this he made a long speech, praising our country and saying how much they wished to be our friends, and how anxious he was that our land should increase in wisdom. After he had finished the Katikiro spoke, and said how we were the friends of the English, and how we had always wished to be on friendly terms with them from the time of Mr. F. J. Jackson (1889) to the present time; he told them also how the country was getting on at present. After this we went home to our hotel. On this day also Mr. Millar's sister came to see us, and also some traders, who told us how they wished to make something from our bark-cloth trees, and how they wished to come to Uganda and build where the Nile flows out. They asked a great many questions about our country. Apolo told them about the things that grow there and the things that do not grow there; and after learning all this they went away.

---

[50] The African travellers were perhaps unaware of the political turmoil written into the facade of Holyrood Palace and the complicated history of the restoration. The connection between Charles II and Queen Victoria seems a natural one for Mukasa to make, for empire represented itself as a dynastic realm in which different monarchs represented the meaning of Englishness across time and space. For this reason, Mukasa and Sir Apolo are travelling through Scotland oblivious to the country's difference from – and troubled relationship with – England.

Chapter X

The following morning, July 17th, we went to Newcastle,[51] where they make cannon, a distance of forty miles from Edinburgh, and there we found our friend Mr. William Cruddas, who took us to sleep in his own house, and did not make us sleep in a strangers' house, which they call in English a 'hotel'.

He brought us a very nice carriage with two horses and took us to his house, where we found his two daughters waiting for us at the door. They greeted us very kindly, as is the custom of English ladies, and we went in and sat down for a little while, and then they showed us where we were to sleep; and after we had washed off the dirt of the journey we went down to lunch, which we enjoyed very much, as the English always feed their visitors very well.

After lunch we rested a little while, and then went to see the works where cannon are made. We went in the carriage which our friend had lent us – we were Apolo Katikiro, Ham Mukasa, Rev. E. Millar, and Mr. W. Cruddas; and when we reached the works they introduced us to the overseer, who was the second in command and not the manager of the whole works. He took us over the whole of the works, and our heads ached and our faces got black, as we went in and out through all the workshops, which were very smoky, as these workshops always are. We first saw how they bored out the barrels of cannon, and how they twist round them on the outside iron bands, which are like wire, only much wider. We saw the gun-carriages and the bullets, which were as tall as I was and were larger in size. We saw, too, where they forged gun-barrels, and also a hammer as large and as high as a hill made by white ants. Do not think that men hold these

---

[51] Newcastle had already developed a reputation as a major industrial city closely associated with imperial expansion in the form of armaments, shipping and railway stock.

hammers and work with them; this is not so at all. In England a great deal of work is done by hand, but this is usually the case in the country. In great factories machinery is their servant; and their wisdom and strength are put into these machines, so that they become like human beings to work by themselves, and hammer and oil themselves, and lift up other machines and cut other pieces of iron, and do all kinds of work just like men.[52]

We saw a man-of-war, which was made for their wars which they wage with one another, when they fight with some other European nation.[53] It had in it another house, which is put there to carry the big guns, and which the bullets of another ship cannot pass through. Inside it there were ladders. We went inside and were wonderstruck and amazed at it. It contained some guns that would carry fifteen miles, and other guns that would carry thirteen miles. It was just like a house on dry land; its length was ninety-five feet. After this we went to see a finished gun; and they brought three practice cartridges and put one in the breach of the gun, and told Apolo Katikiro how to fire it, and he did so; they then put in another one, and told him to fire it by electricity, and he squeezed the electric thing and did so; they then put in another, and gave it to one of the daughters of Mr. Cruddas, who was with us, to fire, and she did so by electricity.

After this we went to see the store where all these things were stored up, and saw all kinds of cannon, and patterns of all kinds of work – bullets, electric machinery, etc., all were there. We then went to look into a fire-place where iron was melted, but could not look in with the naked eye, but only through blue spectacles, which they gave us to look through. All the iron looked like water, and was in motion; and after we had looked in they closed the doors, because there were doors over the holes through which we looked in. After having tea with the manager we went home, I taking with me a shaving from a cannon which I had asked for in order to show to the Baganda; the Katikiro was given a thing like the inside of the barrel of a gun. The whole works were as large or larger than the space in front of the King's enclosure in Mengo, and there are twelve thousand men employed in them, and they come from every part of the country and keep changing.

The next morning, July 18th, we went to see how they make plates of earthenware for the rich. We saw the manager, who greeted us very kindly, and then took us round the works. He first showed us the stones which they use, and the earth, some of which resembled clay, though it was not clay;

[52] At a time when the culture of modernism was castigating the machine for usurping human agency and objectifying labour, Mukasa seems in awe of machines which act like human beings.
[53] The man-of-war and the cannon are here venerated as insignia of British power.

another kind was like our white earth, though it was different. He showed us the furnace in which the stones were burned, and the machine which broke them up and mixed them with water and earth, and filtered the mixture to take out the bad earth.

We saw many places where the pottery was being made, and many machines for making it; and they made some things in front of us to show us how it was done; and we saw every kind of ware, cups, tea-kettles, slop-pails, and flower-vases that were like our hand-drums in Uganda. I took away with me some stones and some of the earth which is used in the pottery, in order to show it to my friends in Uganda; they gave us also some of the powdered stone to take away. When we reached the store we saw what really beautiful things were made there, such things as we see in the shops in our own country, and we thanked the manager for showing us such beautiful work.

After this we drove home, and then to the railway station, where we found the mother and two sisters of our Miss Glass, who married Mr. Fraser, and I gave her the letter of introduction which her daughter had given me, to say that I was one of her friends. We then got into the train and went to Hampstead, and left Newcastle, the birthplace of Miss Glass, the wife of the kind Mr. Fraser.

On the following day, July 19th, we went into London, to the shop where they were making an iron boot for me, and there met Dr. B. W. Walker. I tried the boot on, but it did not quite fit; and then we went to a doctor to have Apolo Katikiro examined, as he had a bad chest. The doctor examined him very carefully, as he was a very clever man, and told him that he had an adhesion in his inside, and that was what pained him, and that there was nothing the matter with his chest or anything else. The Katikiro then gave the doctor his fee and we left. I went home with Dr. Walker, because he was a great friend of mine through his brother Archdeacon Walker the friend of the Baganda; and the Katikiro went away with Mr. Millar to buy some things.

After lunch Dr. Walker took me (Ham Mukasa) to see the building called the Natural History Museum,[54] where they keep dead animals which they have bought and sewn together, so that they look as if they were alive.

---

[54] Mukasa had been properly educated in the value of history and antiquity by British missionaries, and he and Sir Apolo were firm believers in the preservation of historical artifacts, hence their admiration of the Natural History Museum. What is apparent here, however, is that colonial historiography promoted a temporality that stretched the genealogy of Englishness way back into the Old Testament. It was by establishing kinship with the biblical texts and cultures they taught that the colonisers could claim legitimacy as the agents of Christian conversion.

We walked a short way, and then got on to a carriage of two stories which is called an omnibus, and reached the building I have told you of, and wondered at all the animals. Any living thing that is not there has never been seen by an Englishman, or it would have been brought there, whether it were bird or creeping thing or precious stone; all things from all nations, whether white or black, were there. It was there that I saw the whale that swallowed the prophet Jonah, so that he should go to Nineveh.

Let me try and tell you the names of what I saw: lions, bears, tigers, elephants, giraffes, hyenas, apes larger than men, which are called gorillas, hippopotami, rhinoceros, different kinds of antelope, zebras, wolves, buffaloes, jackals, kangaroos, and another animal like a horse that came from Ruwenzori and which Sir H. H. Johnston brought; it has legs striped like a zebra, though it is not a zebra. We saw also birds of every kind from all over the world; I saw a crocodile which they found inside a rock which they had split open, mice of all kinds, and the largest tree in the world; they had cut off a section of the trunk and brought it there. I saw too the largest elephant's tusk in the world, and stones of great price called 'diamonds' that are put into rings, and many other kinds of stones also. I saw also a bird the bones of which had been found, though it does not exist now, but was destroyed long ago. It was like an ostrich. However, I cannot tell you about all we saw; I can only tell you a few of the things which Dr. B. W. Walker showed me. We went round the place together; it is open every day, and about ten thousand visitors go there daily.

After we had been round the museum we went back to tea at Dr. Walker's house, and he sent for a friend of Archdeacon Walker's to come and see me; however, after waiting some time, as he did not come, they called a cab and gave me a letter to show where I was going, and some medicine for the Katikiro, and I went home to the house of Mr. Henry E. Millar at Hampstead, which was called Heathdown; and called Mr. E. Millar, and he paid the cabman, who had driven a distance as great as from Munyonyo to Mengo (eight miles). I then told the Katikiro about what I had seen, just as I have described it here, and he told me his adventures, which were as follows:

After he and Mr. Millar had left us they went to buy some things and then went home, and after a short time went to visit the Prime Minister of England. They found there a great many kinds of people, Chinese, Indians, Moors, South Africans, and a king who was black like we are, and who had come from near Lake Nyasa; his name was Lewanika, but he was not a Christian, and did as he liked. There were about three thousand English people there drinking tea as they stood up, as is their custom. The Prime Minister asked the Katikiro about Uganda, and he told him all about what they asked him, and then Lord Salisbury told his son to take the Katikiro over the house to show him what it was like, and he took him all round it. His son too is a person of distinction, and is called Lord (Cranborne). The house was built by Queen Elizabeth and given to his ancestors, and is a very beautiful one; the Katikiro saw in it chairs of gold, such as are in the houses of great people, and there is also a large church in it. After seeing all this they came back to Hampstead.

On this day we heard of the death of Saidi, the Sultan of Zanzibar. His son, who was called Said Ali, had been in England for the coronation to represent his father, and knew English very well, since he had been taught at Harrow School. He heard of his father's death on his way home, and was then chosen to succeed him as he was the only son, and he is the sultan at the present time.

The next day, July 20th, was a Sunday, and we went to church and rested the remainder of the day, and stayed at home; and all the time we were in England we never obtained another day like this one, on which we could rest right up to the evening, as we did in the house of H. E. Millar, the brother of E. Millar. He is a very kind man, and his children are very kind too, and his wife is a true English woman at heart, being really kind, as the true English are.

On the following day, July 21st, we went to Reading to see how they make biscuits. When we reached the railway station we found the Lord Mayor of Reading waiting for us, though he was not the real Lord Mayor, but only his deputy, who took the position when his friend was not there, as he himself had been Lord Mayor in a previous year. He was a very kind man, and had brought us a two-horse carriage in which we went to his place. He was wearing his robes of office in order to give us honour. When we reached the Town Hall we found the council settling the affairs of their town, and they received us with honour, and we stood up before them while the man who had brought us there told them who we were, and the Katikiro then said a few words to them about Uganda, and how we had come over to see what their country was like. After he had spoken we went away, because they were busy; and were shown all over the building, and saw what it was like.

We then went to see over some fields of valuable flowers (Sutton's seed works) of very many different kinds; the man who took us to see them was the head of the company that did business in flowers and in flower seeds. We went over some very large grounds, and saw also some flowers that did not like the cold, and so had glass houses built for them, in which were pipes through which hot water flowed, and the heat from the pipes went all over the houses, and was like the heat of the sun, and so the flowers grew in the heat. It is a beautiful sight to see a field of these flowers; they are very pleasing to the eye when one looks at them.

The rain came on and we left, and went to a building in which was a large assembly room. After a short rest we went to have lunch, and when we got into the dining-hall, we found there a great many English people who had been invited to lunch with us – perhaps there were as many as sixty of them or more, men and women; some of the men had beards as white as the beard of a colobus monkey, and very fine and beautiful.

When we had finished eating our host rapped on the table, and every one kept silence, and all turned their eyes and ears to him, and he told them all about our land; when he had finished another man spoke, and then another, until five people had spoken, and then the Katikiro said what he had to say, and told them what our country was like, and how it was doing, and how he wanted all the people to get wisdom of all kinds that is useful in this world, both spiritual wisdom and earthly wisdom that is profitable to people in this life. When they heard this they were very pleased at our anxiety to learn wisdom of the right kind and not foolishness.

After this the Katikiro stood by the door and shook hands with the guests as they went out, and then we went to see how biscuits were made. We saw a great deal of machinery in motion, which was very puzzling; but all the machinery of the English in all the factories is alike, and when it is all in motion you cannot distinguish the different kinds of work that are being done, though the workmen and owners know the difference. We saw how they begin making biscuits: they have a pot in which water is boiled, and the flour is mixed with it and gets quite soft; when it is soft they put it into a machine that squeezes it and makes it like paper, and then another machine cuts it up into lumps like biscuits of all the kinds which you see; every kind has a machine that cuts it up in the way in which you see it; all kinds are made in the same way, and get their shape from the machine that cuts them up. After the biscuits are cut out they are put into a machine which bakes them, and then they put them in water in which they are boiled; when they are cooked they rise to the surface; the uncooked ones sink to the bottom. I inquired how many different kinds of biscuits were made, and they told me that there were a thousand varieties, and that there were six thousand people employed in the works. I called this factory 'the stomach of England', because it feeds the whole land.

After this we went to see the father of Mrs. R. H. Leakey of Ndeje, Bulemezi, and we there saw the father and mother and one sister of Miss Pike, who used to be at Gayaza; we also saw Mrs. Gordon's mother, who had with her an orphan girl from Zanzibar (Mombasa), whom she had brought home to be educated.[55] She had already been two years in England, and the Church Missionary Society had taken pity on her and had brought her to England in their kindness, so that she would not be unhappy when she had grown up. She had two brothers in the Government service. Mrs. Gordon's mother told me that she had had thirteen children, or thirty-five including her grandchildren, and we praised God for His kindness to her and her husband in giving them such joy that was not for all, and could not be bought with money, even though one might be a man with uncountable wealth.

After this we went back to London, and journeyed as far as from Mengo to Busi, and went to the Great Central Hotel.

---

[55] The Christian missions moved early to establish schools to train a new Christian elite in Buganda. Among the most prominent of these schools was King's College, Budo, established by the Church Missionary Society at the beginning of the twentieth century and fashioned after British public schools; Gayaza School for girls was established by the CMS in 1905.

Chapter XI

Sheffield – Armour-plate works – Electro-plating – Brick-making by machinery – Cutlery works – Exhibition of ladies' work – Reception by the Lord Mayor of Sheffield – Manchester – Cotton spinning and weaving – Rubber works – A house on fire – Plate-glass making – Railway carriage works – Crewe locomotive works

The next day, July 22nd, we got into the train to go to Sheffield, the birthplace of Mr. C. W. Hattersley, who teaches the Baganda children writing and arithmetic, and who was the first to build a children's school in Uganda, and is therefore held in honour by all the Baganda, and has also taught a great many old men who at first could not learn to read.[56] When we reached Sheffield railway station we found the Lord Mayor waiting for us, and he greeted us very warmly, and took us away in his two-horse carriages; he and the Katikiro and Mr. Millar got into one, and I and Archdeacon Eyre went in the other, and they took us along with great honour, and made three policemen on horseback go in front of us. A great many people followed us – some went in front and some on both sides, and we went along in the centre in great state; and every one wanted to see what we were like, because the chief of the town had given us such very great honour, and therefore many people came, both old and young, to see what sort of people they were who were given such honour.

While we were still in London Mr. Millar had written a letter to tell the people of Sheffield, 'The Katikiro of Uganda will arrive on such and such a day', and this had been printed in the papers, and had been told to all the people in the town, so that they were waiting for us in all the streets which we were to pass through, and we went along through crowds of people standing in the streets; some got on the tops of the houses and looked down on us as we passed, to see who they were who were coming in such state: we saw the women lifting up their little children and running with them that they might see what we were like; there were a great many people, young

---

[56] Once again we can see how the significance of the British landscape is determined by its connection to Buganda and the social institutions (education, for example) which the people of the colony considered paramount to their future development.

and old, men and women. At last we reached the factory in which the Lord Mayor was interested, and, after writing our names in the visitors' book, were taken to see all the work they did; because in this city they make different kinds of things, such as wheels and axles for railway carriages, bullets for cannon, screws for ships, and plates for ships through which bullets cannot pass, and a great many other things which are not explainable in Luganda.[57] We saw also a machine for lifting other iron things, which would lift 2,560 frasila, or, as they call it, forty tons, and were very much astonished at it. After this we asked if we might go away, as we were very tired indeed, and they begged us to stop and have some tea; but we refused, as it was past our time for going home, and we wanted to rest. If you agreed to everything the English beg you to do, you would get ill and die a sudden death, because they are so kind they want you to see everything, and to talk to them all day long; and so their kindness tires you before you know it, and you are like a reed which is burning at both ends and so gets burned right up quickly.

They took us away in state with our policemen in front, and we arrived at the house of Archdeacon Eyre, where we were going to stop. He is a very kind man, very tall and big, and has eight children. At four o'clock the Lord Mayor wrote down for us the names of the places which we were going to see on the morrow, and said he would call for us at nine o'clock – that is to say, three o'clock in Uganda reckoning.

The next morning, July 23rd, we went to see the factories where they make knives and metal tea-pots, and spoons, and forks, and metal plates, and razors, and where various things are made of ivory, tortoiseshell, and horns of animals, and hoofs of horses, though we did not see any of these last, but were only told that horses' hoofs were used. However, we saw all these other things that I have mentioned, and saw also how they broke up a kind of stone which is like that which we have on the Sese Islands, and reduced it to powder, and then added water and made it into bricks. All this work is done by machinery; the only work done by hand is to take away the bricks. When they have dug out the stones they put them in boxes which are fastened on to a long chain, which is very cleverly made and is driven round and round, and so carries away the boxes and brings them back again without stopping; the machine which drives the chains round is also very clever. In the building is a great deal of machinery of different kinds: there is one machine which grinds the stone to powder, and another which breaks

---

[57] This statement has two possible meanings: that there are some British experiences for which Luganda words do not exist, or that the experiences encountered here are beyond the analogical schema which has helped the author so far in his representation of Britain.

up stones as large as those we use for putting our cooking-pots on over the fire – is not this a wonderful thing? – even if they put in three stones at once, it breaks them all up. When it has finished it passes them on to the machine which breaks up small stones, and when this one has finished with them it sends them on to the machine which grinds them to powder, and this one in its turn to the machine which mixes the powder with water; this last passes the material on to the machine which pounds it up till it looks like clay. Then it goes on to one which makes it up into a long roll, and then to a machine which cuts this roll up into pieces, and last to another that moulds these, and they come out very fine bricks indeed. The machinery never gets tired; the only things that get tired are the workmen who put in the stuff. As each brick comes out it is taken into a warm chamber, where it dries in the heat of the fire, not in the heat of the sun. When it is thoroughly dry it is taken to a chamber in which a fire is made, and there it is thoroughly burnt and becomes like a stone in hardness. This is the way in which we saw them making bricks.

We saw that the people in this town were very pleased to see us; a great many children, perhaps as many as three hundred, collected together at the brickworks and sang a fine song in praise of the King when he is crowned ('God save the King'). It was a very fine hymn, and made one shake one's head in time with the music, it was so fine; and we were very pleased indeed with these children.

We next went to see the knife factory, and when we arrived we saw that each man had his particular work: some forged the knives, others put them in the handles, others sharpened them, others polished them, others stamped the writing on them, others packed them away – each work had its particular workmen, all engaged in the one work of knife-making; and this is the same with all kinds of work – each operation has its own set of workmen, and we were amazed at all the different things the English make, as I have told you before. The building was full of rooms, in each of which different kinds of work were being done. We also saw the great store of ivory which is used for making the handles of knives, and a great many beautiful things which they make; we saw one knife with seventy blades, the value of which was two thousand pounds, and a blade of every new kind of knife which they invent each year they put into this one handle, each year and the corresponding blade. After seeing all this, they gave each of us a knife, and we went back to Archdeacon Eyre's house and rested.

After we had rested a little we were taken to see a building in which all kinds of work done by ladies were shown, work which they had done with their own hands. We found a great many ladies there who had come to see what other ladies had done, and to praise them, and to thank them for what they had done, and to say how it pleased them. You know the English praise very much any new inventions, and that is the reason they get wiser every year. Were it possible, it would be a good thing for us to do the same, and praise the work done by clever men in our country, so that they should be pleased and go on and invent something else another year; but it is difficult to learn to do this all at once. However, a city is not built in a day, and takes a long time, and so also one cannot learn all the wisdom of the English in a short time, but must do it slowly. 'He who goes slowly goes far.'

After we had sat down, our friend Lord Mayor G. Senior stood up and told those who did not know how we had come to see this exhibition, and when he had finished Archdeacon Eyre made a long speech, but before him the bishop (of Sheffield) told how we had come there, and also told the ladies how they ought to try and do useful work of all kinds.

There was one very rich widow lady there, whose husband had died and left her all his money, and she had no child. They told us she had forty million pounds, and there was a little child who gave this lady a basket full of flowers. We saw there a lady making some very beautiful cloth, and she made some for us as we were standing by, and we were very much astonished and thanked her very much for being so clever.

We left in great state with our policemen in front on horseback to keep the crowd away from us, and went to the Town Hall, where we found a great many people had collected together to see us. Lord Mayor G. Senior welcomed us very warmly, and asked us to stand near the door, the reason of this being that he wanted us to greet all the visitors, and so each one who passed shook us by the hand. We were doing this for about half an hour, and then were taken to the platform, and given seats in the front, and the Lord Mayor told the people a great deal about us and our country; and then Archdeacon Eyre spoke for some time, and made me laugh very much because he said I could sew very well indeed. He had found me putting a button on my white robe, and looked at me very carefully and asked me if I knew how to sew, so I said that I knew a little, and that is the reason he praised me. Truly the English make people glad in the work they are doing: the little I was doing he praised openly, that all might know how nicely I could sew; well, would not any one go on learning, so that he could get more praise?

After he had finished, the Katikiro spoke, and told the people how we wanted to learn to do work of all kinds, and wanted teachers; teachers both of the Gospel and also of handy work of all kinds – carpenters, smiths, builders, traders in cotton goods and other things, brick-makers, and coffee-planters. After he had finished, every one clapped their hands and cheered to give the Katikiro honour, and to thank him for the good things he had said, and for saying how pleased he was at all he had seen, and for liking their country so much as to ask them to send out people to teach the Baganda all kinds of trades.

After this we had tea, and then the Lord Mayor called us and gave each of us a knife for himself and one for his wife; we then went to the railway station to take the train for Manchester, and said good-bye to all our many friends who were there, Mr. C. W. Hattersley's mother and daughters, and Mr. T. B. Fletcher's brother. The Lord Mayor in his kindness went with us in state to the railway station, and said good-bye to us when we were in the train for Manchester, and then went home.

My friends, we were given wonderful honour in Sheffield; we were like warriors who had come back from conquering a great nation, because large numbers of people came to look at us and followed us wherever we went. We left Sheffield at half-past five, and got to Manchester at half-past six.

The next day, July 24th, we first went to the Town Hall of Manchester, a very fine building, but did not go inside it, as it was closed; we saw, however, a great many statues of their judges, who in English are called 'Lord Mayor'. After this we went into a cloth factory, where they make cloth of all kinds. We saw how they comb out cotton in a great many machines; there were about ten different kinds of these machines which make the cotton ready for making cloth, and about twelve more kinds to complete the manufacture of cotton sheeting in lengths. We saw about a thousand women at work in this cloth factory. In a cloth factory one cannot hear what one's companion says, even though he be quite close, on account of the noise of the machines, which make a noise like a large waterfall, or even a greater noise than that.

After we left the cloth factory we went to some rubber works, and there saw about fifteen different kinds of machines preparing the rubber. We saw how macintoshes are made: they take some cloth which looks like unbleached calico, but is strong; this they squeeze in a machine together with rubber, and the rubber enters into the cloth; after they have done this they cut up the cloth, and sew it into beautiful macintoshes just like you see in Uganda. We saw rubber that had come from all countries, America and Africa and other places. After this we said good-bye, and were each given a rubber thing with which ladies wash their faces in the morning.

We saw a great many other things on this day, and saw a shop being burned; it was a fine shop and goods to the value of about seven hundred thousand rupees (nearly £50,000) were destroyed. We saw how they fight with fire; they have a steam-engine which goes to help and pumps up water to a great height where the fire is; the water comes out with great force – perhaps if they were to turn it on the people it would kill them. The

English, however, are very much afraid to go close to a fire – their cleverness makes them appear to be afraid of it, because they stand a long way off to put it out; but when they are teaching the Baganda I see that they are not at all afraid of it – I am constantly seeing how little afraid of it they are. I see that there are many things the Baganda cannot do, but they are not afraid of fire.

Mr. F. Taylor, the father of Mrs. H. Maddox, took us to see all the things we saw in Manchester; he is a very kind man indeed – as kind as his daughter.

The following day, July 25th, we went to a town called St. Helens, to see how they make glass. We went by train a distance of twenty-one miles from Manchester, which is as far as from Entebbe to Kazo, and were accompanied by Mr. F. Taylor. The manager of the works showed us how glass is made; we saw the sand and charcoal and limestone, which are all heated up together in an earthen pot, and get very hot indeed, and the stuff appears like water. They make a brick oven as large as a small tent, into which they put the earthen pots; these pots are very large and very thick indeed – their thickness is equal to the length of one's thumb, about two inches; well, after they have filled these pots with the stuff I have told you about, they run them on wheels into these ovens, and then close the door and put in some coal which burns well, and pipes from bellows go in at the bottom and air is blown in so that the fire burns very strongly.

I cannot leave off praising the English. Listen! They make a coal fire very deep down in the earth, and from this they take pipes everywhere which give them heat for melting iron, and all these other things, sand and stones, which make glass – all these things are melted by the gas which comes from coals and which burns very strongly indeed, and we wondered with an unceasing wonder. The things of the English are amazing!

After all the things in the pot have become liquid they have an appointed time at which they take it out of the oven, and then it is put on wheels and taken to an iron table, perhaps 10 ft. wide and 15 ft. long, and some of the liquid in it is poured out. They seize the pot with very large iron pincers on each side to empty it out on to this table – the English are very strong, as these pots are very heavy. Well, when they have poured it out, they bring an iron roller like the trunk of a large tree, and run it up and down on this table, and it spreads the liquid all over the table; they then take this off and bring another thing, with which they cut off a part of the glass which has become hard; the plate is then put into an oven which has no fire in it, but is very cold, and there it stays for a whole day and hardens. The next morning they take it out and take it to the workmen who take off the roughnesses; and when these have finished with it they pass it on to the polishers, who make it shine; and they pass it on to the men who cut it up into the various shapes in which it is required. When this is finished they put a red substance on it, which prevents the light from passing through it, so that one can see into it from one side only – this work is done by women; it is next handed on to the people who fit the glass into frames, like you see everywhere, and the looking-glass is complete. I have not written down all the different kinds of work done to it, as it is difficult to describe them all.

After seeing all this we had lunch, and then went back home and rested for a while, and then went to see a place where they make railway carriages that are sent everywhere – some of the carriages for the Uganda railway were made in this place; we saw carriages of every kind, from passenger carriages to those in which cattle travel when they go from one country to another by train; we saw numbers of boards, millions of them; and then came home. The man who took us round was going to marry one of Mr. Taylor's daughters, and then go out as a missionary to India; he had been asked by Mr. Taylor to take us round, as he had himself been in these works for some six years, and having made his money in them was no longer working there. In the evening we had dinner at Mr. Taylor's house, and there met Mrs. Taylor and her daughters.

On July 26th we went to Crewe, where they make the 'heads' for railway trains, and there met the chief engineer, who gave us some one to show us round the shops.[58] We saw how they first forge large sheets of iron, and then pierce them with a great many holes, in which they put nails to join the fireplace to the water-tank; the holes for the tubes only were about eighty in number, and the tubes themselves were like gun-barrels. The strength of the piercing and boring machines was immense and incomparable, because they pierce and cut through iron as thick as a man's hand, or about four inches thick, and cut through it as quickly as one would cut through a banana stem. Those large nails that you see are all made in one machine, which cuts them and works them and puts the heads on them, and they come out complete. A man brings a hot bar of iron and puts it into the machine, and the machine itself does every little bit of the work. There were a great many machines of this kind in the workshop.

We saw some engines just completed, and others not yet finished, and some only just begun, and many kinds of engines that take about trains; for this is the fountain-head of the strength of all trains. After this we inquired

---

[58] The building of the Uganda Railway connecting the Bugandan heartland and the port of Mombasa was considered by the new African elite to be the most obvious symbol of their connection to the modern world; the railway engine was venerated as a powerful symbol of modernity.

the number of men at work in these shops, and were told there were 7,500. We then returned to the chief engineer's office, and they photographed us near the 'head' of the train that had taken us round; we were in all Apolo Katikiro, Rev. E. Millar, Ham Mukasa, and Mr. F. W. Webb, the chief of the workshops, and we were photographed in the clothes which we wore when on a journey. After this we went to see where they store up the lightning that gives light to the town, but when we got there we were not clever enough to understand it, and were simply amazed at the way they could store up in one place power enough to give light everywhere by means of electric lamps; each person had a wire going to his own house, even though it might be twenty miles off, and this wire brought him light even though he was so far off, and in every house, whether of a rich man or a poor man, there was electric light. Some have light from gas which comes out of coal, and that too comes from one place and is spread everywhere; the things of England are marvellous.

After this the people of Crewe saw us off, and we got into the train for London and went to Hampstead to the house of Mr. H. E. Millar, where we used to rest and escape the noise and rush that there was in the centre of London.

The following day, Sunday, July 27th, we went to Christ Church, Hampstead, and then came back home and rested. The father of Mr. C. J. Phillips, the store-keeper of the C.M.S., Namirembe (Uganda), came to see us, and we had a long talk with him; he was an elderly man, but not so big as his son, and gave us some match-boxes as a Christmas present. In the evening we went to a mission hall; our friend Mr. H. E. Millar preached and also played the organ, and when he had finished, Apolo Katikiro made a long speech, praising the kindness of the English, who invited us to stop with them; he also asked for teachers to come to our country and teach us all kinds of useful things, and said how much obliged he was to those people who always welcomed us. He spoke in Luganda, and the Rev. E. Millar, as usual, interpreted. After this we went to the Holy Communion in the church, and then went home to fasten up our letters for Uganda, and also to pack our things, because we were about to go back into London, as our friend Mr. H. E. Millar was packing up to go into the country, and his wife and children also were going there to rest.

Chapter XII

....

The Natural History Museum – Shopping – Lunch with Sir Benjamin
Stone – The House of Lords – The Guildhall – Visit to Mr. Burdett-
Coutts' stud farm – Visit to Warlies – Interview with Lord Rosebery –
Dinner with the King's guard – Changing guard at St. James's Palace –
Interview with Sir Clement Hill

The next morning, July 28th, we packed up our things, and after breakfast
got into our carriage to drive back into London; our friend Mr. H. E. Millar
and his wife and children said good-bye to us, and bade us farewell with true
kindness that had no hypocrisy in it, for they were all very sorry indeed to
say good-bye, both old and young, and the children had got to know us very
well and used to teach us their language, and we taught them our Luganda;
and they were just like our own relations, which they truly were in heart. A
great many people in their kindness never arrive at this stage, as some
despise those who look different from themselves; but these people and
many others we saw in other places were kind with true kindness of heart.[59]

When we got into London we first went to see my surgical boot, and then
went on with Dr. B. W. Walker, the brother of Archdeacon Walker, to see
a lady called Mrs. Lamb, who was very kind to us and took us all over her
house, which was six stories high. We then went to Dr. Walker's house, and
found there Mr. E. Millar and Archdeacon Walker's father, a very old man,
eighty-two years of age, but still very strong.

After lunch we went to see the house of the dead animals, which is called
the Natural History Museum; – you have heard of the number of animals
there are in it, when I went there before alone with Dr. B. W. Walker. I had
told the Katikiro about it, and so he was very pleased that we should go
there together, so that we could talk to one another about what we saw. We
saw a very great number of animals, and birds, and fishes, and creeping

---

[59] '[T]rue kindness of heart' refers to the absence of duplicity. Mukasa seems to consider
'kindness' to be a moral value of paramount importance in the mediation of relationships
between the coloniser and the colonised for a reason he leaves unstated in the text: the
incorporation of Buganda into the imperial orbit was characterised by promises made and
broken and treaties negotiated and negated.

things, and rocks and trees, and types of various nations. They collect there skulls of many races from all over the earth to show the difference between the various races. We went home with Archdeacon Walker's father by the railway that goes under the ground, and we saw how active he still was, since we got tired of walking about before he did. When we reached the Westminster Palace Hotel we had tea with Dr. B. W. Walker and his father, and they then went home.

The next day, July 29th, we went to buy the things which we wanted to take back to Uganda; Dr. B. W. Walker went with us, and helped us very much in choosing the best things to buy, as our friend Mr. Millar had gone to the dentist. After lunch Mr. Doggett came to see us; his son had gone to Uganda to catch wild animals, but he did not catch any – perhaps he found them too wild; I expect he will be more successful another time.

After Mr. Doggett had gone we went out again with Dr. Walker to buy the things we wanted, and later on in the day our friend the Rev. E. C. Gordon came to visit us, and slept in the hotel, and we talked a long time to him, and helped him in his translation of a book of Uganda folk-lore. We stayed up with him till very late, for he knows our language very well indeed, and so we stayed a long time talking to him.

The next day, July 30th, we went on buying our things for Uganda; there were four of us in all, Apolo Katikiro, Revs. E. Millar and E. C. Gordon, and Ham Mukasa, and we met Dr. Walker on the way, and went to a shop where they sell tools, and bought a great many things which we wanted.

After this we went to the 'Houses of Parliament', which is the house of the kingdom of England where all matters are discussed that keep the country in order, the house where the great council meets. We met there Sir Benjamin Stone, of Birmingham, who had invited us to lunch, and photographed us at the door of the Houses of Parliament which looks out on the River Thames, which is quite close, only about twelve feet off; he first photographed the Katikiro only, and then the Katikiro and Ham Mukasa, and then all three of us. While we were at lunch he said to us, 'I want to take you all round this place, and show you the chief house of our kingdom, and the pictures of the great men of old and the ancient kings who worked for this country.' When we heard this we were very glad indeed to think we were going all over this building, because it is held in high honour all over the land of England which is ruled from it.

He took us into a great many places. We first went into a very large room indeed, as large as the space in front of the enclosure of a Muganda chief,[60] and then went into the hall of the rulers who ruled in old times, and where

[60] The enclosure of a Muganda chief signifies his political power and moral authority.

all their pictures are kept; under each picture they write the name of the man and the office he held. After this we went into the courtyard outside, and saw the River Thames quite close by. We then went over many other parts of the building, and passed through the hall of pictures, and reached a long passage in which they put rebels who refuse to learn to be peaceable – they take photographs of them all, and put them there as a reminder; we then reached the room where the great chiefs leave their umbrellas and macintoshes and hats – each man puts his name on the peg on which he hangs his things. We then reached the Parliament Hall itself, where they sit to discuss matters of the State, and we looked all round it and saw the seats, three rows on each side, and five seats in each row; all the seats are together; they are not separated, but are like those in a school, except that of the judge who sums up the matters, which is between them and facing the King if he is present, but if he is absent it faces away from the King's throne, since the King is not there himself; if the King is present, it is not possible to turn one's back on him.

Behind the judge there is a table for the men who write down all that is settled, and behind the writers there are three rows of low seats, and above these they put the seats of the ladies, the wives of the great lords, who may want to come and listen to what is settled in the Parliament of their country. The throne of the head of the people, the King, is right in the centre, and that of the Prince of Wales on the right side, and that of another prince or the Queen Consort on the left; in front of the King's throne they put an iron railing, at which the children of the lords stand when they come to the Parliament. Well, I have told you all about this building.

There is also a robing chamber, and a hall in which the King meets the princes who greet him on his way into Parliament; the wives of the lords have also their hall where they greet the King on his way in. After this we went to the other side of the building and saw where they made King Charles stand – the king whose head was cut off because he would not listen to the Parliament.[61] We also saw where they beheaded him. We saw too a church underground in which they used to pray in old times, but which is not now used for the following reason. There was a rebellious murderer who wished to avenge himself on the rulers of the land, and brought some gunpowder done up in a cloth to destroy them; but a policeman saw him with it, and went to seize him; the man threw the gunpowder down and it

---

[61] Mukasa's reading of British history and politics is symptomatic of the way the colonisers represented themselves to the colonised. In this example, the beheading of Charles I is explained by his refusal to listen to parliament, an institution that colonial textbooks promoted as evidence of the democratic nature of British society.

caught fire, and as the policeman was carrying it out it burned him, and blew off his leg, and he died, and so up to the present they have given up using this church. After Sir Benjamin Stone had taken us so nicely all round, he said good-bye to us, and we went back home and rested awhile, and then went to Captain Hobart's, and stopped there till one o'clock in the morning, and then went back to the Westminster Palace Hotel, Victoria Street.

The following day, July 31st, we went on buying our things, because we could not buy them quickly, since we wanted to look at everything. In England it is hard to distinguish what is good and what is bad, as everything you see looks good. We went first to the house where they sell useful iron goods, and bought plates and kettles and cups, and many other things which we wanted. We then went to lunch in a house where they cook food for travellers; not out of kindness – you go with your cowrie-shells, and when you have finished eating, you go your way after giving them some of your cowrie-shells. They give you a small piece of paper, and on it is written the price you have to pay, and this is what you give them as you go out – one can buy all kinds of food in these houses.

After lunch we went to see the building where they try cases in the City of London (Guildhall). We went all over it, and saw it all; these English buildings are just like towns. We went into one room where they try cases, and found about forty people in it; they were trying a case about a building in which a man refused to pay the builders the price they had arranged; we could not understand the matter properly, as we only stayed a very short time. They behave very well in court, and do not all speak, but one man only speaks, and all the rest listen, and the judge himself writes down what he hears them plead. On our way home we passed a boot-shop and bought some boots, and then went to visit Captain Hobart, but did not find him at home; we stayed a short time with his wife, and then went back to our hotel.

On August 1st we went on buying our goods, and then went to Mr. Burdett-Coutts; he was selling about a hundred of his horses. When we arrived he first gave us lunch in a tent on the grass in one of his fields. There were about eighty people there, including three black men – Apolo Katikiro, Ham Mukasa, and an Indian.[62] After lunch we went to where they sold the horses. They build a rough house and put in it a great many seats for the buyers to sit on; they build also a pulpit, on which the man stands who prices the horses; this pulpit is high, so that the man's voice can carry well, and every one can hear. We sat on the seats which we found there, and

---

[62] This is one of the rare occasions when Mukasa calls attention to the travellers' racial difference, but it is interesting to note how this difference is represented as ordinary.

they brought the horses, one at a time, and the price of each was stated, and the buyers bought it. English horses are very expensive indeed, and are worthy of England; some horses were sold for £165, others for £120, or £100, or £80, or £70, but this last was a very old one, and so was sold for so small a price as £70 or 1,050 rupees – you see how expensive English horses are! We did not stop there very long, but went out by a back way, for one who is not a buyer should not stop where they are selling things; and then we went to a shop where we bought clothes for our children, and then went home.

In the evening the man who wanted to come to our country to plant bark-cloth trees came to see us, and asked us the best places for planting them, so that he might purchase the land or rent it; however, letting a rich man rent one's land is the same thing as selling it all, unless one is very clever. After he had talked for some time he went away. Our tickets for the coronation arrived during the day.

On August 2nd we went to choose a writing-desk for the Katikiro, as our friend Sir T. Fowell Buxton wished to give him one; the Katikiro bought me a writing-desk also, for which he paid £7. After this we went to give the packers instructions as to how to send all our things to Uganda, and then went home, while our friend Mr. Millar went to the dentist.

After he had returned we got ready to go and stop with Sir T. Fowell Buxton, and drove to Liverpool Street station and got into the train. At the end of our journey we found a carriage, and another kind of vehicle called a motor-car, which was driven by gas that comes off from some chemical, and was a very clever thing; however, we refused to go in it as it made so much dust, and so we got into the carriage, and arrived safely to find our friend awaiting us and tea ready. After tea he took us round his garden and over a new church which had just been built, but which was not quite finished and was a very nice one. He also took us over his stables, which were very fine indeed. It is hard to tell Baganda about England, because those who do not understand call all that one says absolute lies.[63] If you tell the Baganda that in Uganda there is not a single nice house, even including those of the chiefs and of the Europeans – such as they live in at the present time, though perhaps in a great many years there may be a house as good as those in which a rich Englishman would keep his horses – those who hear you think you are telling lies. Those who think thus are not only the

---

[63] Again, Mukasa foregrounds the difficulties of representing the alien and different to his Bugandan audience, but this time the focus is on the ideological problem of representing a privileged other. People do not always doubt because they disbelieve, but because ideal Englishness appears so immeasurable and perhaps unachievable.

common people – even the clever people and some of the chiefs think this also; doubt and stupidity are not seen on the outside of a man like poverty and deformity, but are perceived in the words which express his thoughts, so that good words may come from a common man or a countryman, while a chief may appear to be a very fine man, but his words may be very bad indeed; and he himself may not understand how very foolish his words are, and how they are not worthy of his position. Long ago, in the year 1894, Archdeacon Walker said to us, 'You have not yet got in Uganda a house as good as those in which we in England keep our animals', and we all laughed, not because we disbelieved him, but because we saw how backward we were, though perhaps some may have laughed because they did not believe him. When I reached England, I remembered this, and saw far more than I had been told.

After dinner Sir Fowell Buxton showed us some of the things that had belonged to his ancestors, and Lady Buxton also showed us some other things, and the presents which the Queen had given her mother – a bag for books and a lock of her hair, which is now treasured up. Lady Victoria Buxton's mother used to wait on Queen Victoria just after she was married, and Queen Victoria had been Lady Buxton's god-mother at her baptism, as she was the daughter of her beloved lady-in-waiting. The following were the presents which she had given her – a fine cap, a silk bag which the Queen had worked with her own hands, a picture of the Prince Consort, and many other things. Lady Buxton had a glass box in which she kept all these things, and in which we saw them; but she took them out and showed them to us because she was so kind, though she does not show them thus to other people. After this we went to our rooms. This house was as large as a castle, though it is all one building. The ancestors of Sir T. Fowell Buxton brought in a law to free the people in all lands from slavery; therefore they should be always remembered, since they freed us all from slavery.

The next morning, Sunday, August 3rd, we all went to church to a place about three miles off – that is, as far as from Nakasero to Kabowa. Apolo Katikiro, Sir Fowell Buxton, and the Rev. E. Millar went in one carriage, and eight of us went in another; we found a great many people at the church who had come to look at us and our clothing, which was of a kind they had not seen. The church was eight hundred years old, and thus it was a very old one. On the way home we got out of the carriage, and Sir Fowell Buxton took us through the park to see the trees, and we stayed in the courtyard some time and looked at a thing the children play on (a see-saw). After lunch we went to see our host's eldest son, who does not live with his father, but has his own house very near, and has four children. He took us all over his estate and showed us the stables, in which he had nine fine horses, and we had tea with him and then went to church at five o'clock, where Mr. Millar preached.

After dinner we talked about a great many things, and the Katikiro asked Sir Fowell Buxton how many members there were in the House of Commons, and he told him there were 646; and we asked if even young people could sit there, and he said that they could do so if their fathers were dead and they had come into the property, and they sat there to hear what was debated, so that they could take their share in the work when they had grown up.*

The next morning, August 4th, we said good-bye to Sir Fowell Buxton and drove to the railway station, a distance of three and a half miles, and took the train to London; we left at 10.35 and reached London at 11.35, a distance about as great as from Mengo to Kinakulya (fifty miles) though it only took us an hour. After we reached our hotel old Mr. Walker and Dr. Walker came to say good-bye to us; they were going away to a part of the country called Wales, as at this time of the year in England all the people on the first Monday in August go off into the country, and all the shops are shut and do not sell anything; only the very small shops are open.

The next morning, August 5th, we again went out shopping. On our return we were asked to go and see the Earl of Rosebery – he is the man who settled to make the British Protectorate over Uganda; and our friend Sir Harry Johnston came round himself to ask us to go and see him, as he wished to see us. Sir Harry Johnston told us how Lord Rosebery, when he was Foreign Minister, settled to make the Uganda Protectorate, and what a nice man he was, and how some day he might be Prime Minister again.

After lunch we went to see Lord Rosebery, and he took us all through two rooms in his house, and made us sit down in the third, and asked us how things were going on in Uganda, and how many soldiers were guarding the country. He asked the Katikiro if he was the tallest man in Uganda, and he told him that he was taller than many others, but that there were others taller than he was. He asked this question because he had read in some book written by an Englishman that there were no tall men in Uganda except the Katikiro, though this is not true at all; those who do not travel about the country have many falsehoods told them about the country, and perhaps the man who wrote this described the short men whom he had first come across, and never saw any others.

Lord Rosebery also asked us how old our King was, and we told him that he was six years old; he asked if he would be a wise man, and we said that

---

* The author has confused this with what had been told him by Sir Benjamin Stone about the House of Lords.

he would. The Katikiro told him how the King was trying to learn English, and knew all the English salutations. He asked also if our King would be crowned like the King of England, and the Katikiro said that he would be crowned when he reached the age of eighteen.[64] He also asked us what most astonished us in England, and we told him that it was the number of the people, and the large houses, and fine streets, and the speed of the railway trains. After this he took us all over his house, which was very beautiful and very large, and when we saw this house we understood that the great men of England and the rich men do not want kingdoms such as the kingdoms in our countries, because many kings have none of the comfort which these men have. After we had been all round the house, Lord Rosebery asked his daughter to come and see us, and we then went home and rested a little while.

In the evening we went to dine with the soldiers who guard the palace of the King; the officer who asked us to dine with them was Captain Hobart, D.S.O., who had been in Budu, Uganda, and whom the people called Pati. We drove there in Captain Hobart's carriage, which he sent for us, and found a great many men in their fine Guards' uniforms, and during dinner they told us about the coronation. After dinner we waited a short time, and then went home to the Westminster Palace Hotel.

The next morning, August 6th, we went to see the soldiers who guard the King changing places with others, who took their turn on guard. First of all one set of soldiers came and drilled a little, and then some others came; there were also eight men on horses and a two-horse carriage (these had come from Buckingham Palace to get used to the soldiers in readiness for the coronation); the soldiers blew twenty-two bugles, and played on ten flutes and nine drums and four cymbals, and all played one tune together which had a good swing to it. Captain Hobart called the captain of the guard who was to relieve him, and introduced him to us; he was a very tall man, taller than the Katikiro. After the band had played four tunes the two guards said good-bye to one another, and those who were relieved went home as their turn was over, and Captain Hobart said good-bye to us and went away too, and we went home, and rested.

After a short while we went to see Sir Clement Hill, whom we found in his room in the Foreign Office of Africa, and talked to him about many things, and told him what was going on in Uganda; and he told us what we ought to do to help forward our country, and asked us what astonished us

---

[64] The discussion here points to some of the ways in which the colonised were appropriating invented British traditions, notably the whole idea of regency and the crowning of the Kabaka in the manner and style of the British monarch.

in England, and we told him the speed of the trains, and the numbers of the people, and the high houses that were like mountains and the precipices which are on mountains. He said to us, 'Work hard at cultivation and at learning everything that brings money to your country'; he also said, 'Although our country is a very fine one and you praise it very much, and it is a very rich country, yet it was not so at first; we were like you are once, or even worse off, and you too if you work hard will be like we are now. It is no good being in too much of a hurry to learn, do not be in too great a hurry'; he said also, 'The book which you are going to write telling about your travels, should be put into English, as a great many people will want to hear about all you have seen; the Baganda and a great many English people, too, will be glad to read it'; and we agreed to do as he had suggested. He also introduced us to some other officials of the government – the chief of the Treasury Department, and the chief of the Legal Department of the Foreign Office. He also told the Katikiro that the rifle which he was going to buy, and the printing-press, would be given to him as a present from the Government.[65] We were very pleased indeed to hear this, and went away to look at some rifles to see what sort of one we should buy; and when we had chosen one we sent the bill to him, and went home. He told us also that we two, Apolo Katikiro and Ham Mukasa, were going to see the King on August 8th, and we were filled with joy, for it is a great thing with all people to see the King of the country face to face and talk with him.

[65] The presentation of a rifle and a printing press would be welcome for Sir Apolo, who had come to power as a warrior and a writer.

Chapter XIII

The next day, August 7th, we went to Windsor to see what the King's other palace was like. We started from the station called Waterloo, and reached Windsor and went to the house of the teacher who is called Dean, and reads prayers for the King when he is at Windsor. We found he was still in church, but his daughter and her brother received us and welcomed us, and kept us occupied until their father came. When he arrived we talked to him for a short time, and he then handed us over to some one to show us all we wished to see. We first went into the great courtyard in front of the house, in which there is a little hill with a cannon on the top, and then entered the hall, where there were a large number of suits of the old armour men used to wear when they went to war – iron coats, and old guns and flint-lock muskets; we saw one gun which had seven barrels and only one trigger. These are the first kind of guns they made when they began to invent new ones – breech-loading rifles came afterwards.[66]

We next went into a room in which were pictures of all the kings, and princes, and princesses, and great men; there were also the skins of wild animals called bears that had been brought from other lands. This room was wonderfully fine; everything in it was of gold – gold chairs, and lamps of gold and precious stones. We saw there, too, a great many pictures – the Queen being married to the Prince Consort, King Edward being baptised when he was a little child, etc. – and many places where the King sits, and the chair upon which the Queen (Victoria) used to like to sit after dinner, which is in a long passage; near it is a very small and beautiful table. We saw there also a table six hundred years old, the maker of which is unknown; it

---

[66] Guns and old armour fascinate the African travellers because they remind them of a recent past in which they had been involved in the Religious Wars in Buganda; indeed, beneath the mask of civility which the prose seeks to sustain lie the writer's and his companion's violent pasts.

was very fine and very cleverly made, and had a great many drawers in it, and the wood of it was like the wood we have in our country which we call 'mutogo'; it was quite as good as many of the tables that are made at the present time, though it was made in 1303 A.D.

We saw also a very old book which had come from Abyssinia, the country which in old days was called Ethiopia, from whence came the eunuch whom Philip baptised, as we read in the Acts; and also many other books which Queen Victoria read and which had been given to her by her friends.[67] We saw also a most marvellous clock, which told the years and months and days of the week and seasons of the year, and the stars and the sun and moon in their courses; there was also a picture of all the earth, and all the changes which the earth goes through were gone through by this clock. We saw also in this place the finest road in the country, for it was three miles long and did not twist at all; there is no such other road in all the earth like this, and though I have not been all over the world, yet this is what I think. At the end of it there is a small house, which is opposite to the King's palace of Windsor Castle, and when one looks down the road from Windsor it is a very fine sight. We saw too a picture of the present King Edward and another prince on horseback going along, and a picture of his mother, Queen Victoria, at one side of it.

Windsor is the finest town in England, because there is no noise there, and it is on a hill. It is raised up like a pulpit, and there is a very good view from it in all directions; there are some beautiful trees which are very fine to look at, and the grass also is beautiful. The hill which has the cannon on it is very high, and is in the courtyard of the King's palace; there are policemen guarding the place very carefully, as their custom is to look after everything.

Ras Makonnen, the Abyssinian chief, who is prime minister of his country, met us at Windsor, as he too was going round the castle.[68] He had with him about ten companions, and an English guide who was taking him round, and we greeted one another as we met. After this we went to see where they bury all the English kings, and entered the church in which they bury them, and saw their graves, about sixty in number. We saw also the

---

[67] The author's basic ideas about the world beyond Buganda had been shaped by the colonial library and in this sentence we can see the three branches of this institution – the ethnographic text ('the old book'), the biblical text and the central documents of Englishness (represented here by Queen Victoria's private collection).

[68] Ras Makonnen was prime minister of a country (Ethiopia) which had a double meaning for other Africans: on one hand, it was the modern symbol of ancient African Christianity represented by Abyssinia in the Bible; on the other hand, by defeating the Italians at the Battle of Adowa (1896), Ethiopia represented the possibility of African autonomy in the age of imperialism.

graves of great chiefs and brave men who have conquered other countries, and the graves of princes, and also many banners that told about each person.

We saw too the grave of the King's eldest son – he is buried in a very valuable stone, which had been hollowed out; but we did not see where the Queen (Victoria) was buried, for they do not yet allow people to go there; she is buried in the same place as her husband. After seeing all this we went back to the Deanery for lunch, and then went to see the sister of Captain Speke (who discovered Uganda), at the town called Wokingham. We found there a great many people, both ladies and gentlemen, though the ladies were more in number than the gentlemen. Sir H. H. Johnston was also there, and our friend Bishop Tucker. There was a great deal of talking, and we enjoyed our visit very much; our hostess gave the Katikiro half-a-dozen china coffee-cups, and after we had had tea our photographs were taken, and we then drove to the railway station and went back to London, where we arrived at 8.35 p.m.

The following day, August 8th, was the greatest day of our whole journey, because on it we saw the King. At half-past eight we saw a letter from Sir Clement Hill, which said

'Dear Mr. Millar, –

'I tell you that the Katikiro and Ham Mukasa will see the King at one o'clock, but you yourself cannot go; Captain Hobart will take them.'

When we heard this we were very joyful indeed, and got ready, because we had thought that we should only see the coronation, and should not see the King in his palace because he had been so ill, and nearly died, but God in His kindness heard the prayers of all the nation and healed him. We were therefore very glad – for his sake, that he had not died, and for our own sakes, that we were going to see him.

When the time arrived, Captain Hobart brought us a very fine carriage in which to drive to the palace, and we both got in, and drove to the great open space in front of the palace; when we left this we went in by the main entrance to the King's courtyard, and into the inner court, which is in front of the palace and extends on each side of it. When we left this we arrived at the palace itself, and got out of our carriage at the door.

We stepped right out of our carriage into the building, and the keepers of the door showed us in, and we walked through many passages and rooms, each room with a passage leading to it, and door-keepers to it, who stopped us at every door, asking us to wait while they announced us to the next door-keeper, and so we went on, each door-keeper announcing us to the next. Each room we entered we thought would be the one in which the King would see us, though it was not so; we found they took us on somewhere else. The building was most splendid; each room was finer than the last, and everywhere we went was most wonderful. There was one room in which they kept us waiting about ten minutes, and then they called us and took us along a very long passage into another room, through which we passed, and entered a very large room in which the King receives his ministers of state. We there met three great men, chiefs of the soldiers who guard the King's palace, and also Lord Lansdowne, who, after he had greeted us, went to announce us to the King, and then returned to take us in to the King's audience chamber, which was quite close to where we were.

There was a very large door, which was covered with gold; – the whole palace was very magnificent, all the walls being covered with gold and mirrors, the space not filled by a mirror being covered with gold, except in the rooms which we had first entered – the inner rooms were wonderfully fine. On one side of this great door was a looking-glass about 10 ft. high and 5 ft. wide, and we passed through it, Lord Lansdowne going first, and then the Katikiro and myself, and then Captain Hobart. When we passed through the door we saw the 'Father of the Nation' sitting upon his throne, dressed in magnificent kingly raiment; he bowed his head three times, and we did the same and bowed three times, and he then told the Katikiro to sit down, and he sat down on a golden chair, while I and Captain Hobart stood up.[69]

The King asked the Katikiro, 'Do you like this country very much?' and he replied, 'It is a very fine country, and the work which is done in this country of yours is most wonderful. I am amazed at the houses and streets, and the people like locusts in numbers, and the railway trains which go marvellously fast; a three months' journey on foot is done in eight hours by train.' The King answered, 'Yes, that is true, these things are wonderful.' The King then said, 'I read about what is going on in your country, and hear about it, because a great many of the English people who have been there have written about it, and I have read what they have written about your country and what it is like.'

The Katikiro then thanked him for sending government officials to protect our country, and said how sorry he was that the King had been so ill. The King then said, 'Come with me, and I will show you the presents

---

[69] This representation of the king is a unique moment of cultural translation in the text. The whole paragraph is intended to capture the magnificence of the occasion, but it is notable that the terms and objects that make the palace magnificent – gold and mirrors – are those which the author's native culture (and his biblical readings) have valorised as signs of glory. Similarly, the representation of the king as the 'Father of the Nation' has more resonance for the Bugandan readers than their British counterparts; in the former culture, perhaps more than the latter, the paternal nature of the monarch tends to be underscored.

which all the different nationalities have given me, and the things from Uganda which you yourself have given me.' He then went out of the room, and the Katikiro followed him, and I and Captain Hobart followed, and we went into a small room where we found the things that had come from Ras Makonnen, the Prime Minister of Abyssinia, a sword and a helmet, and bracelets and a mat, and a belt and a golden cross, and many other things which he had given him.

The King thought our things were there also, and praised up everything, saying, 'This is very fine', and 'This is very fine', and took the different articles up in his hands to show them to us, though the things the Katikiro had given him were not there at all. As he was showing us these things Lord Lansdowne said to him, 'Sire, bid farewell to your visitors, you will get tired, and to-morrow is the coronation'; and the King listened to him, because in the court there are some people who can speak to the King.

The King then stood up very straight – when he stands up you would think he had not a joint in his body, because he straightens himself so nicely – and we said good-bye to one another with our heads; he bowed his head, and we all bowed our heads, and went out walking backwards, because one cannot turn one's back on the King, though when one has passed the doorway one can turn round and walk forwards.

Let me tell you all about our interview. The following were present: The King, 1; Lord Lansdowne, 2; Apolo Katikiro, 3; an officer, 4; Captain Hobart, 5; Ham Mukasa, 6; a door-keeper who stood at the door, 7. Seven people in all were there when we saw King Edward VII. He had on a coat trimmed with ornaments of gold only, and a fine long sword, glittering shoes with spurs, short trousers of gold only, and a belt of gold; he had nothing on his head; his eyes were large and very fine. When he is amongst other men, there is no need to ask, 'Which is the prince?' he can be seen at once to be of royal blood. He has a magnificent chest, which he throws out like a lion; his voice rolls from it like that of a lion, as is the custom with princes. He has a very fine beard which is nearly white, and which adds to the majesty of his appearance; his baldness also makes him look the finer, as baldness is becoming to large men, and is therefore very becoming to him.

This is how we saw the King of England, Edward VII, an extremely kind man, very kind to all his visitors.

When we left his presence we went out through another door, which we had not passed before, and there we found the King's secretary, who wished us to write our names in the book of the King's guests. Captain Hobart said, 'Go on, I will write your names.' We did not like this at all, but we kept silence knowingly, and let the man who was in charge of us do as he wished, and he himself wrote down our names.

We then got into our carriage and went back, and in front of the palace found a great many people who had come to see what we were like, as they had read in the newspaper that the Baganda would have an audience with the King at one o'clock, and therefore a large number, perhaps as many as forty thousand, had come together. We soon reached home, as the distance was only as great as from the gate of the King's palace in Mengo to the market-place, and when we arrived we told our friend Mr. Millar all we had seen, and how we had seen the King himself, and how he had made us very happy.

After a short rest we went to see the Archbishop, who is over all the bishops in England, and is called the Archbishop of Canterbury. There were four of us who went – Bishop A. R. Tucker, Apolo Katikiro, Rev. E. Millar, and Ham Mukasa – and we reached the palace, which was a very large one; the door-keeper announced us and the Archbishop sent his secretary to bring us in, and we found him and his wife sitting down; he could not get up to greet us, as he was a very old man, but he welcomed us very warmly. There were five other bishops there also, and we all had tea together, and our bishop told him all about Uganda.

After tea we went over the building, which was very old; the secretary, who showed us over it, was a very nice man indeed, and explained everything to us very kindly. We saw a room in which were the portraits of all the archbishops from the earliest times; we saw also the library, which contained books of all kinds, and the chapel, which is about eight hundred years old; we saw too the chapel of Cranmer, a great and wise Christian man about whom you read in church history. We saw too the church in which all the bishops are consecrated, and in which are their portraits, and among them that of a black bishop. There are also many very ancient books, including a New Testament which was translated from the German, and was forty years old, and the Koran, the book of the Muhammadans.

After seeing all this we said good-bye and went back to our hotel, and after a short while the Katikiro went to dine with Sir Clement Hill; we others went in there after dinner, and found the guests examining the skins and horns of many animals which he had collected. We there met Major Ternan, who had been the Acting Commissioner in our country, and many other people, and stayed a long time, and drank coffee standing up. After this we went home, Sir Clement Hill escorting us as far as the door of his house, and thus ended the greatest day of all – the day on which we saw the King, and the day also on which we saw the Archbishop of Canterbury; both these were great people, and I therefore call it the greatest day of all, as it was like seeing the sun and the moon.

The next morning was the great day of the coronation, and at eight o'clock we got ready to go to the church which is called 'Abbey', where they were to crown the King. Our party consisted of Bishop Tucker, Apolo Katikiro, Rev. E. Millar, and Ham Mukasa, and we reached the church, each with his letter to show his place, and went in, and each one showed his letter that they might see the number of his seat; the bishop left us at once and went to his place, but Mr. Millar went with us and gave us over to a policeman to show us to our places. They made us go up a staircase in the scaffolding which they had put up, with seats on it so that people could see everything, and there we found Captain Hobart, who took us to our places. Apolo's number was 197 and I was in seat No. 198, and we sat there and waited for the King to arrive.

We waited two whole hours, which brought us to ten o'clock, and meanwhile all those who were invited came and sat in their places. A large crowd of singers came in, both boys, and men with deep voices, and went up into the gallery which is across the building, and under which was the road by which the King was to pass. There was also a large organ, and the choir brought their instruments, which are played with a stick held in the hands, like those of the Swahili coast men. The bishops and clergy came and got ready the Communion table, and then carried down the three crowns of honour, and the four golden sceptres, and a golden cross on a staff, and about four other staves of gold, and went with them to fetch in the King.

The chiefs of counties then came in (peers) with their wives, but when they got into the centre the ladies went to the left and the men to the right. After this came a princess in great state with her ladies of distinction, all wearing dresses with long trains which rustled greatly, and were carried by others behind who held them up; these trains were about twelve feet long, and glistened very much. Those who bore the trains were magnificently dressed also; the trains were carried some by two people, some by four, and those of the ladies who were not so distinguished by only one person.

After this some great soldiers arrived with ermine caps, and the Lord Mayor of London and many other distinguished people came, all walking very slowly. The choir sang very nicely some most beautiful hymns, accompanied by the organ and violins and flutes and cymbals, and the band, all playing and singing together, so that one beat time with one's head and foot because the music was so lovely. The pages then came with the coronets they were carrying, and so we understood that the King was about to arrive.

The Queen then entered; they brought her in great state – her train was carried by eight pages, four on each side, and they sang a hymn to welcome her, and all the men and women cheered and clapped their hands and bent down their heads to greet her, as is the way to greet kings. When she reached her chair she sat down, right in the centre, the King's chair being beside her.

After this there entered the lords of great honour, who are like kings (Kings of Arms?), the Lord Mayor of Ireland, and the Lord Mayor of Scotland, and the Marshal of London, England (Earl Marshal), also came, and then after a short interval the King between two bishops, one on his right, that of Canterbury, and one on his left, that of York, and the King between them, and they all walked very slowly indeed; the King's train was carried by eight pages, four on each side. When he reached the centre we all who were in the building cheered very much, and they played on all the instruments, the singers sang, the flutes were blown, they played the violins, and beat all the drums, and clapped the cymbals, and the people clapped their hands, and the whole building boiled over, and resounded, and vibrated, and he who had but one eye would have liked two, and he who had two would have liked four, that he might see better than he could with two, though of course you cannot add any part to the body that you have not got.

When the King had sat on his chair he first prayed to God to give him strength in this great ceremony of taking possession of his country. After he had again sat down the work of the bishops began, and the Archbishop of Canterbury prayed; after he had prayed he read the questions asking the King if he would rule aright, and the King replied as is the custom, and they brought a book for him to swear on, and the Archbishop made him swear, as all kings swear, and they brought him a pen to sign his name, and he did all these things. He then left the chair in which he had been sitting and went to that in which he was to be crowned and anointed with oil. This throne had a magnificent back to it, and ornaments of gold like doves.

After they had sung a hymn he sat down and they anointed him, and the Archbishop prayed a short prayer; they then brought the crown on a silken cushion, and the Archbishop took it in his hands and lifted it up, and asked saying, 'This is the man whom we wish to crown as the King of this realm; if any man has anything to say against it, let him speak'; and when no one spoke he put the crown on the King's head. When he did this it was a wonderful sight, for each of the peers took his coronet in his hands and lifted it up, and when the crown rested on the head of the King they all put on their coronets, and cheered with a loud voice, and the electric lights were turned up all over the building and flashed out, and the organ, and violins, and flutes, and bugles, and drums all sounded, and the singers sang, and it was a marvellous thing, and one's hair stood on end on account of the exceeding great glory!

In the evening they lit lamps all over the city, and it was like daylight, and after dinner we went a journey of about two miles and a half. We first went in the railway that goes underground, and leaves the city above, and goes under the River Thames, leaving it above. There were an enormous number of people underground, like locusts in numbers, and they had there electric lamps burning day and night, but when we got above ground again (Cannon Street) and on to the roads, we were amazed at the number of people.

You can understand the numbers when I tell you that the crowd nearly lifted the Katikiro off his feet, it was so thick and squeezed so hard. Mr. Charles Millar, the brother of the Rev. E. Millar, wanted to lift me up on to his shoulders, for fear they should kill me, and told me how his wife had once been carried a long distance without touching the ground, and this was the reason he pitied me, and offered to carry me, but I refused. We reached home at 11 p.m., having been away three hours looking at the sights. The people were singing for joy as they went along, and playing about and shouting to one another, both great and small. They stopped all carriages along the roads and only allowed foot-passengers, because where carriages are allowed the people cannot walk comfortably.

Chapter XIV

Westminster Abbey – St. Paul's – Farewell to England – Lord Salisbury – Across France vâ *the Mount Cenis – Rome – Naples – S.S.* König *– 'German kindness' – Mediterranean Sea – Portuguese rule and English impartiality*

The next day, August 10th, was Sunday, and we went to the church called 'Abbey', which is next to the church in which the King was crowned, but just as we were about to arrive we met people coming away, who said to us, 'Do not go there, there is not room for a single person', and so we went to another church.

When we came out it was raining heavily, and I and Sir John Kennaway (who was staying in the same hotel, and was with us) took refuge in the door of a shop; but the Katikiro and Mr. Millar went right on, and when they got to the hotel Mr. Millar very kindly started back with two macintoshes for us, but he met us just as we had reached the hotel, and so he took them back. We had lunch with Sir John Kennaway, who all the time was asking the Katikiro about affairs in Uganda, and the Katikiro told him all about everything. After lunch Sir John Kennaway said, 'Let us pray to God together', and so we prayed to God in two languages, English and Luganda; Sir John Kennaway first prayed in English, Mr. Millar interpreting it for us, and then the Katikiro prayed in Luganda, Mr. Millar interpreting it into English. After this Sir John Kennaway went away to his room in another part of the hotel – as this hotel was very large and had about three hundred rooms in it. We then prepared for our journey, as there were only two days left before we were to leave London.

The next day we went with Sir John Kennaway to see round the church in which the King had been crowned, because on the coronation day we were unable to see it properly. We saw everything, from the road by which the King entered right up to the thrones on which he and his consort sat; we saw there a great many things, and we also met Bishop Welldon, who had been Bishop of Calcutta. We also met a man who knew about everything in the building (Canon Wilberforce), and he showed us all there was to be seen everywhere – the doorways and the reasons for having them, and the tombs of the kings and the statues of those who were buried there, and the throne on which the King sits on great days – the one he sits on first, and the one used afterwards when he is crowned. We saw also the golden dishes and spoons and cups and flagons and sceptres, and the cross which Ras Makonnen of Abyssinia gave the King – the whole stem was of gold, as was the cross itself, and this was carried before him when he came into the Abbey. All these things were of gold and of great price. We saw also a new door made for the King to escape in case of any danger, and then returned home, having seen everything well; for on the coronation day we were unable to take in the glory of everything, because it would have been impossible for any one to have done so.

After a short rest and lunch we went to St. Paul's Cathedral, and climbed up it. After we had gone up three hundred and sixty steps our friends said to us, 'Go over there and listen – you will hear what we say'; and we went with one of our companions, and they spoke against the wall on one side of the dome and the voice went round and we heard it on the other side, just as one hears in a telephone. After this we went on up very high indeed, to the very top, and from thence we saw over the whole city. The houses looked like lumps of stone, and did not seem at all high; the horses looked like fowls, and the people like mice; we tried to see where the city ended but could not do so, even though we had gone up to such a height – for this city is like a country; there are no hills that prevent one from getting a view, there is only the smoke from all the work that is being carried on. All the towns of the English are covered with smoke, owing to all the work that is being carried on in them. London is a town of low hills, like Busega and Natete; there are no high hills in it, and the breadth of it is about twenty miles – in some parts more and in some less.

If it were not for the smoke in England, one would be able to see the country very well, both the houses and all the land, but the smoke hinders one from getting a good view. The Katikiro tried to get on to the roof (the ball), but the wind and giddiness drove him down again, and Mr. Millar tried, but did not stay long; and then I tried and got to the top, and sat on the end of the ladder, but the wind deafened me and made my eyes smart, and so I came down to my friends, and we all went to the bottom, and got into our carriage and went off.

Mr. Millar left us in the carriage while he went to see about our places in the train that was to take us to France; but when he came back he told us he could not get us places to sleep in, but only seats to sit in, and we were unhappy at the thought of getting no sleep for four whole days.

We then went back to the Westminster Palace Hotel, and Sir Clement Hill came and had dinner with us, and asked us about our country, and we told him what we could. After dinner he stayed a short time, and then went away after giving us some presents; the Katikiro he gave a golden spoon like the one used for anointing the King, me he gave a very beautiful glass inkstand, and our King he gave a beautiful spoon with a picture of King Edward on it. The mother of Mr. Kitching, who teaches in Toro, also came to see us on that day, and brought her daughter with her.

The next morning, August 12th, we did up our things and left at ten o'clock, and went to Victoria Station, and got into our railway carriage, and our great friend Sir Clement Hill found us there when he came to bid us farewell. You all know how very kind he is and how he came with Captain Hobart to greet us on our arrival. He gave us some maps of Uganda, and we waited a long while in the train, and then the engine whistled to say it was going off, and our friend said good-bye to us very kindly and left us, and the train started.

As we went we were filled with amazement at seeing what London was like on that side, and how large it was. If in all the world there is another city larger than London they do not call it a city, but the gathering-place of the whole earth – but there is no such city. Well, when we reached the end of it we came to a place where a man had built an enormous house (Temple of Jezreel, near Chatham), and said that the saints of God were to remain in this house to await their Lord's return to this earth; but before he had finished it he died, because he had tried to do a thing which should not be talked about in that way. After we had seen this we went on, looking at the various towns we passed on our way; we kept passing one after another; there were a great many of them.

We passed Canterbury, the seat of the Archbishop who is over all the Church, and they pointed out the Cathedral and his house, which are both together; it was a very old building, perhaps eight hundred years old. After leaving Canterbury we reached Dover, the port for France, and it was at this port that I saw the Katikiro of England, Lord Salisbury, as he was on his way to Germany.[70] He is a very large man, and extremely tall, taller than a great many tall men (he was standing on the footboard of the carriage, but the author did not perceive this); he is very old, perhaps eighty-two years of age, more or less. When his mother looks at him she must be very pleased, because he is a man of very great honour, and very wise – every one praises his wisdom and his kindness; and to him has been given all these gifts – size,

---

[70] The description of the British prime minister as 'the Katikiro of England' is another example of the reciprocity of cultural translation. When the British occupied Buganda they translated the name and function of the head chief (the Katikiro) into 'prime minister'; here Mukasa reverses the cultural grammar and renames Lord Salisbury the head chief of the British!

height, wisdom, and kindness. Well, are not all these things difficult to obtain in this world, and therefore I say that when his parents look at him they must be very pleased indeed.

We got out of the train with all our things, and went on to a steamer which had a paddle on each side, and the Katikiro soon got unwell, because the sea was very unkind indeed to him, and so he would not eat any lunch, and Mr. Millar and I had it by ourselves. We soon reached Calais, the French landing-place. The sea is twenty-five miles across, and the journey takes a little over an hour, because the boats go very fast indeed.

We left Calais at four o'clock, and got into the train for Paris, the capital of France, and as we went we looked at their country, which is a very nice one; there is no smoke like there is in England. We arrived at Paris at eight o'clock, and saw all the lamps and the wide streets, which are nicer than those of England; but they are not crowded like the English streets, where the people are like locusts in numbers – if you went no farther than Paris you would not think there was any larger town, though really there is London.

We met there our friend Mr. Charles Millar, who knows French very well, and helped us to get carriages, and to get food, and to get into the train again. After dinner, at about ten o'clock, our train came in, and we got into our sleeping-car and our friend Mr. Charles Millar said good-bye to us in the train, after he had helped us in every way he could. We travelled all that night, and the next morning the train was still going. We did not pass Marseilles, but went more to the north, and went by land past Rome; when dawn came we were at a place called Chambery.

When day broke on August 13th we went along looking at the country to see what France was like. When you cross their boundary you get into Italy, the country of the Romans; but on this side the country has some very high hills in it, and is stony, and not so nice as the country round Paris and Calais. We passed through a hill called Mount Cenis, through which they have made a hole to get to the other side. It is a wonderful piece of work, and makes one marvel at the cleverness of the Europeans. We were thirty-five minutes inside this hill, right underground. You know how fast a train goes, a mile every minute; but here the train went slowly, perhaps a mile in two minutes; and although we went like this, still it is a marvellous thing to tunnel hills in this way.

After we had come out of the hill we reached a town of the Romans called Turin, which is a very large town, and has three hills in it; the houses are built as we build in Uganda, at some distance apart, and not close together as in other towns. After this we passed through many other places, and at night reached a town called Genoa.

Daybreak on August 14th found us nearing the city of Rome, where the King himself lives, who used to be known to all men in the whole world and called Cæsar; but now he has long since lost his great distinction, and has not the strength of old times, but rules over his own land, because the European nations have so arranged it. If it were not so, one of the more powerful nations, the English, or the French, or the Germans, would rule over him; but he rules because they have arranged that every king should rule over his own land.

At eight o'clock in the morning we reached Rome, and wondered at the ancient things we saw – the old walls, the ancient roads, and the forts on the hills. The town of Rome is on flat ground; though there are hills on each side, yet it is flat between them. We waited two hours, and got out of the train and had breakfast; we also saw some soldiers wearing an old-fashioned dress such as you see always in pictures – helmets of iron and swords, and coats with trimming down the back like those of servants in England or France. After breakfast we left the city, and as we went along we saw many ancient things – the forts on the hills, the ancient gateways, and a very ancient aqueduct which is still standing; it looks like a bridge, but is extremely long.

We saw also the King's palace, and the Pope's cathedral and his house. We did not go into these places, but only saw them from a distance, for they are seen clearly because there are no hills, and as we were on high ground we could see everything very well. The city stretches out to some distance on each side, and reaches up on to the hills. In Italy there are many mountains with snow on the top, but there are none in France or England. We were very much surprised, too, to see the way the high hills had been tunnelled, and passed through many of them – the one mentioned above, that took us thirty-five minutes, and others which took us ten, six, five, four, three, two and a half minutes, and so on, every hill with a tunnel for the train to pass through, right up to Naples, which is on the sea coast, and near to which is the town that was destroyed by fire that came out of the mountain.

When we reached Naples we left the train and went to have lunch in a traveller's house where they sold food. We saw there a very large man, who was like a young hippopotamus; in all respects he was like the child of a hippopotamus.

After lunch we went out in a carriage and bought the things we needed, and then went to the landing-place, and they brought us a steamer, and we went on board to go to the ship which was to take us home. It was called the *König*, Hamburg. They showed us where we were to sleep, and we sat down on deck, and slept on board.

The next morning, August 15th, we left Naples, and on that day we understood the difference between the customs of different races of Europeans.[71] In all European countries there is no race nearly so kind as the English, because of all the English from Uganda onwards I only saw one who was not kind to us, and where he was there was another man who acted up to their good repute, although his companion did not try to help us, and was perhaps an Englishman in body but not in heart. Well, from Uganda to Mombasa we met with kindness only, and from Mombasa on the sea in the ship *Nevasa*, Glasgow, we met with only kindness as far as Aden; then from Aden onwards in the ship *Manora*, Glasgow, the captain took us safely to Marseilles, and we met with kindness only, and in England all the gentlemen and common people, and men, women, and children, right up to the King himself, were always kind to us.

But on the day we entered the German steamer we saw the enormous difference there was.[72] Well, let me tell you about it; when we entered the German ship they showed their disgust in every way, and treated us like dogs, and tormented us; they refused to allow us to eat at the same table, because we were black men; they refused to clean my boots, and to give me water to wash my face; they refused to give me tea in the morning; they refused to show me where the bathroom was; they made me sleep in the hospital – but there was a good reason for this, as my cabin was occupied by a married couple. If we asked them to do anything for us they did not reply; in all these things we found the English kind, and saw they made no difference on account of our despised race, and we praised the kindness of the English to every man. I pray earnestly to God for them that their kindness may spread over all the lands which they rule, as the light of the sun shines over the whole world, and together with the rain brings the fruits of the earth to perfection; and also, that in their government they may never depart from God, who supplies what is lacking.[73]

I also prayed that God would make the Germans who were on the boat kind, so that they should not be nasty to us; and to make some of them

---

[71] The discovery of the 'different races of Europeans' is a key moment in the travellers' education. It brings them head to head with a central paradox of the culture of colonialism which represented Europeans, to the colonised, as unified by a common Christian culture and civilisation even as their rivalry in Africa exposed their differences.

[72] As already noted (note 37), the Germans were considered the antithesis of the British. What is notable here are the terms in which 'racial' difference is represented: the Germans lack the values that make the British the most civil and civilised people in the world – kindness, charity and comity.

[73] Having long accepted the reality of colonial conquest and rule, the author's prayer is that the colonial mission continues to be one of enlightenment ('the light of the sun') and Christian morality.

friendly with us, so that they could help us in our ignorance; and that though we were foolish in their sight, they might help us on account of our ignorance; and that because we had paid the money for our passage, and were not given a free passage, they should see that it was not right to refuse to give us the food we needed, when we had paid for it. All this I refused to tell Mr. Millar, because I did not want to be always troubling him.

One day they only gave the Katikiro a very little food, although he was very hungry, and on this day we saw the chief man of the boat, Captain Zemlin, and talked a little to him because he knew English well, but he did not stop long with us. The Germans paid no attention at all to Mr. Millar, their fellow white man. I myself tried very hard to be friendly with the stewards, that they might wait on me kindly, but they would not be friendly, and looked downwards when they saw me. Seeing this I gave up the attempt.

The next day the sea was quite calm, and we entered the Mediterranean Sea, which St. Paul was taken through on his way to Rome. The Katikiro was not ill, as there was no wind and so we had calm weather, and I managed to persuade two German boys, who knew English, to make friends with me, and we talked a long time to them every day. The way the Germans get drunk is terrible; they were always quarrelling with one another. I saw also there a Swede, who talked to us of most disgusting and unspeakable things, and I begged him to leave off talking in such a disgusting way; I never saw any European who could talk in such a way, and even a black man would have been ashamed of himself. On this ship there were men of many nations – English, French, Portuguese, Greeks, Italians, Boers, Baganda and Nyasaland people, nine languages in all, and the whole number of passengers was about eighty.

The next day, August 17th, we reached Crete – an island known to St. Paul and where he left Titus – and saw what it was like, and how very large it was. We reached it at midday and left it behind at 9 p.m.; well, when you wonder at hearing that our steamer would only take a day from Entebbe to Kisumu, you can imagine how large the island was when it took us nine hours to pass it. We went close to it and saw the villages on the side nearest us, but they were only small, the largest ones being on the other side; the hills are all bare, and are like the hills at Aden; perhaps there is grass inland, but we could not see any, we could only see some things like creepers at the bottom of the hills.

After passing Crete we entered the Sea of Cyprus, which reaches to Port Said, the port in Egypt at the entrance to the Suez Canal, and the sea was rough for a short time, but soon quieted down again; but the waves came into the ship, and even though these ships are very strong and large, yet the sea is stronger, and we were amazed at its strength, for our ship was a very large one of seven stories from the keel to the top. Our Uganda canoes on this sea would look like plantain stems, and be as weak, for one cannot see any islands on these open seas, and the whole way from Mombasa to Aden, a journey of seven days, one sees no island at all except Cape Guardafui, the cape on the Somali coast, which you see on the sixth day.

The following morning, August 18th, found us in the Sea of Cyprus, where the wind was fairly strong, but soon quieted down, and I came across a black boy from Mozambique, on the River Zambezi, who was on his way back from England, with an Englishman called Mr. D. Macdonald, who had taken him there. Mr. Macdonald was a very nice man, and we thought him very kind to have taken this boy to England and paid his passage for him. I made great friends with the boy, and asked him a great many questions about his country, and he told me a great many things about it and the way they dressed, and built their houses, and cultivated their land, and the kind of food they ate in their country. He also told me that they had had a king who used to smoke bhang (Indian hemp) and get drunk, and made friends with other bhang smokers, and wanted to fight against the Europeans, though he could not really do so. However, he was afterwards turned out, and a wise man was chosen instead.

He told me also how his people were governed, and said that the English were very kind and ruled very well, but other Europeans called Portuguese ruled very badly and put to death people who were not deserving of death, and beat and imprisoned others without any trial, and sold people, just as if they were not a European nation. The English, however, were very kind, and settled every matter very carefully; when he said this I saw he was speaking the truth. He told me too that the Portuguese wanted him to work for them because he knew their language, but he refused, even though they offered him high wages, and said he would always serve the English. I was pleased at this, because the English are careful in all they do, and have no favouritism in judging cases, but judge all men alike; chiefs and common people, kings and princes, rich and poor, great and small, men and women, are all judged fairly and uprightly, and the judges take care to make no mistakes, and therefore all we black peoples like the English. I asked this boy his name, and he told me it was Muchekdon, of Mozambique, on the River Zambezi, and I told him that my name was Ham Mukasa.

I also made friends with an English boy called Norman Reid, who was born at the Cape in a town called Ladysmith, where the English fought with the Boers. He had been to England on a visit with his father, who was a Scotchman, and I talked to him a little; but he was an unruly boy, and not like English children, who are brought up carefully; he would not obey his father or his mother, and was not afraid of any one, and soon took a dislike to me because I told him he ought to obey his parents; so I made friends with another boy called Gerald Arnold, who had been born in Natal, in South Africa.

Chapter XV

The next morning, August 19th, we were in the Mediterranean Sea, which reaches to Port Said, at which place we arrived at half-past seven, and stayed there some time while they were taking coal on board, because we had used up our supply. When we saw that we should stop there for some time we left the ship, and went on shore to see what the town was like. The houses are like European houses, and there were carriages, both large and small, but nothing like the enormous number of them which there are in Europe, because the European carriages are like locusts, in London and in Paris.

We walked about the town, which is quite flat; if an earthquake were to shake the earth with great force, perhaps the sea would destroy it, for it would be shaken up by the earthquake, and so would overflow the town. The sea is on both sides, and the ground between is quite flat like a table.

We went back on board at half-past eleven, and the Egyptian boatman caught hold of Mr. Millar and demanded more pay, although he had already paid him for the boat which had brought us off from the shore. Still, he wanted more than his rightful fare, and Mr. Millar refused to give it him, and so he seized him by the leg as he was going up the ladder on to the ship, and tried to throw him into the water; and we were very much surprised to see the insolence of the Egyptians in not respecting Europeans.

We saw also two clever men; one of them conjured with a great many things. He swallowed a whole egg and brought it out of his forehead, and pulled a chicken in pieces and it came to life again, and also put a chicken and some eggs into a glass thing and made them pass into a man, and then took them out again; and we could not see how he did all these things so cleverly. The other man dived for coins which people threw into the water, and brought them up from the bottom.

At twelve o'clock we left Port Said, and entered the channel called the Suez Canal, which has been cut out, and through which ships pass very slowly, so as not to bring down the sand from the banks and lessen the depth of the canal. This sand gives a great deal of trouble; they are always digging it out. I cannot tell you about the machines that dig out the sand – they are very clever indeed. In the canal a ship takes about six minutes and a half in travelling a distance of one mile. We passed a large ship called *Oriental*, Greenock, which had perhaps come from India, as there were many Indians on board; we passed it when we had gone a distance of about forty-seven miles, and there were still forty more to do, since the canal is eighty-seven miles long. We got out of the way of it and tied our ship to the bank till it had got past, as it is the custom when ships meet in the canal.

We spent all night in the canal, and got to Suez at about six o'clock in the morning, and stopped there for nearly an hour and took on some passengers and their goods; and then entered the Red Sea which the Israelites crossed, and came to the place where Pharaoh and his host perished, and got a view of the wells and a great many palm-trees on the Arabian shore, where the Israelites encamped after they had crossed.

The sea is very narrow here, about as wide as from Gaba to Kisinsi, and you are about sixteen hours before you lose sight of the land on both sides; we also saw Mount Sinai in the clouds, and how large a mountain it is. All the hills on the shores of the Red Sea are bare of grass and seem to be only rocks, though they are really covered with earth.

I saw here how the Germans and the Portuguese get drunk. They have a band, with four bugles and five flutes and two drums and five violins, and all these together play one tune; and the dancers dance, and the singers sing, and the man who sells drink collects tumblers of drink and takes them round on a large plate, and goes in and out among the people. They sell the drink and do not give it away, and those who want to buy it go on doing so all night and do not go to sleep; if a fool who drinks goes on board a German boat he comes off it without a single farthing, because they go on buying drink and drinking it all night. A ship, you remember, is like a town, and has streets and passages, and all that you would require in a town you can get on board ship; both good things and bad things are there, and also the most evil amusements.

In English ships, however, I never saw anything at all like this. These ships have large rooms in them, each containing from seventy-five to a hundred seats; is it not an amazing thing for a ship to be like a house? All the ships of the Europeans are like this, and none of us can despise a European, though they despise one another; and the chief nation of them all – the head of all in ships – is the English nation.

The next morning, August 21st, found us in the middle of the Red Sea and out of sight of land, and there was no wind; but the heat is as bad as a wind, for it often kills Europeans, and at night they all sleep on deck without any covering over them. When you sweat, you sweat like a man being baked in an oven, your sweat is so great. Some Europeans played a game which consisted in tying their legs in pairs and running round the houses in the centre of the boat, while others sat reading their books, each one the book he wished, whether it was the Word of God or a book of travels like this one, as a traveller is always anxious to hear what other lands are like, so that if he go there he will know all about it. If he be a preacher of the Gospel he wants to hear what is being done, and if he be a trader he wants to hear if the things he wants are in the country.

The heat of this sea begins at Naples and comes along with you gradually as far as Egypt, and goes on through the Red Sea to Aden, and then to Mombasa and Zanzibar; but its birthplace at Aden in Arabia is too awful for words!

The next day, August 22nd, found us still in the Red Sea. I tell you, my friends, England is a hard place to go to, day after day on the sea. We passed five ships during the day. The stewards fought among themselves when they were very drunk indeed, because the Germans are not quiet people – they are most lawless, and I never saw on an English vessel the disgraceful and outrageous behaviour which goes on on German vessels. If ever any of you want to go to Europe, you had better go on an English vessel, but one cannot always get one. When you are fording a bad stream you may have to catch hold of thorns for want of anything else; the Germans are the thorns, and the bad stream is the time of your journey corresponding with the time of departure of a German steamer. I saw two English ships, the *Nevasa*, Glasgow, and the *Manora*, Glasgow, and their officers and servants were all excellent.

In this sea the Katikiro slept on deck, but I slept below in my room. I used to pour a great deal of water on the floor, which was made of stone and very firm, but in five hours it would all have dried up, and I would have to put down more. I used to cover up the window and the door, and put out of the window the thing that brought in the air, and slept like this, because I did not want to have disputes with the people who were walking about on deck.

The following morning, August 23rd, we were still on that very great sea; when the sun sets on this sea all the clouds become red, and so does the mist; perhaps this is the reason it is called the Red Sea. We passed some ships going homewards. All our passengers were drowsy, and slept most of the day, owing to the heat; none of them walked about – they were too tired, and very weak, and I saw how much the heat was to be feared. Soon after three o'clock we began to see signs of land, and at about six o'clock saw an island, the first thing one sees on the way out from England, and passed it after dark.

On August 24th we were still in the Red Sea, and at eleven o'clock we passed the island of Perim, which is near Aden and is strongly fortified by the English. The island is like Aden in having no grass on it, and the food for the people on it has to be brought from India, and Egypt, and Europe. We were told that we should reach Aden at eight o'clock in the evening; we first caught sight of it at half-past seven, and saw the lights shining like the stars in the Great Bear.

Aden is a large place, about six or seven miles long, and runs along the sea-shore, and on the tops of the hills are the forts of the soldiers, and the cannon that protect all the sea. When we got near Aden our band began to play, and we were very pleased with ourselves for having such a good band. They began playing a long way off, and played until we reached the harbour; we passed a ship on the way, and when the band was quiet its passengers clapped their hands to applaud the music. When we reached our anchorage the band played three tunes, and then the anchor was let down, and a great many Somali boats came all round the ship on both sides, to sell food and other things, and to take off any passengers who wanted to go ashore. These Somalis were not at all afraid of Europeans, but came on board the ship, and even though the Germans struck them and kicked them, they paid no attention to them, and I was amazed to see that the Somalis were regardless of all authority, and had hearts as obstinate as mules.

At nine o'clock we went ashore to look for our friend Mr. Hattersley, because we had heard in England that he had been very ill at Aden and at death's door, and so we wanted to find him. After searching for a while, we reached the hospital in which he had been, and the doctor told us that he had been so ill for a week that he was not expected to recover, but that he had left for England ten days before. We were very pleased to hear this, and thanked God very much for restoring our friend to health, because he had taught our country to do arithmetic, and to send the children to school to be taught reading, writing, and arithmetic.

When we left the hospital the Somalis brought us carriages to ride in, and begged us to get in, but we preferred to walk, because we had been a long time on the boat, where we could not walk about; but the Somalis followed us, begging us to get into their carriages.

On reaching the landing-place we got into a boat, and went back on board covered with perspiration; all the Katikiro's clothes were soaking wet. At night all the Europeans slept in their chairs on account of the great heat of Aden, and the Katikiro slept in his chair; but I slept in my cabin, and poured water over the floor, and opened the port-hole and put out the windsail, and so I got cool and slept well. We had some lemonade on shore and on the boat, and it was as sweet to us as its mother's milk is to an infant.

Aden and the islands in the middle of the Red Sea are like a door of iron, because the Gulf of Aden is like the main gate of all Europe. I think that if there is a great war in Europe between the different European powers, when the English who are in the fort of Aden close the door no other European will get through. The commander of Aden is like the king of the earth, for he is the door-keeper of all Europe, and when he closes the door many will cry out, because the road past Aden is blocked, and that is the reason I say he is like a king.

We left Aden at eight o'clock on August 25th, the band playing all the time we were in the harbour, and entered the Sea of Guardafui – the cape at the corner of Somaliland; and at night it was very windy and extremely hot, so that none of the passengers could sleep in their cabins, but all came on deck. I brought up the Katikiro's bedding and arranged it for him, and left him asleep, and then went to my cabin; and soon after the sea became quiet by the kindness of God.

At night I noticed the poverty of the Somalis; they all slept in their clothes just as they were, both old and young, and had nothing to cover themselves with.[74]

On the morning of August 26th we reached Cape Guardafui at eleven o'clock, and in the afternoon the sea became very rough, and the waves came on board, and I was very frightened at the size of them, and their power, which enabled them to get on board a ship as large as an island, and to toss it about just as our canoes are tossed about on our lake.

A great sea requires large boats, and a small sea small boats. I saw that a great many people could not eat anything, and were constantly sea-sick through the motion of the boat. I myself looked for some place to sit in, but could not find one; they brought me food, but I refused to eat it, as I was afraid of being ill, and I hoped to be able to eat something the next morning. This continued till night.

The next morning, August 27th, found us still in the Indian Ocean, and the bad weather continued all day and all night, and a great many of the passengers were sea-sick, and were just like people who were very ill indeed.

[74] One of the most obvious examples of the influence of Englishness on the colonised is the way conduct is privileged as a sign of cultural enrichment. In practical terms, the Somali sailors may earn more than Mukasa, but their poverty is apparent in the absence of bed covers. It never occurs to the author that the Somalis may prefer to sleep without covers given the high humidity in the region!

After breakfast I went to see the Katikiro, who told me how he had slept and how ill he had been, and that he could not eat anything. The storm was very severe and some of the supports of the awning were broken, and a great many of the passengers did not leave their cabins; at last all the awnings were taken down, and this showed us how bad the storm was. I was very glad that I was not always sea-sick myself, when I saw how ill most of the passengers were.

The next morning, August 28th, at nine o'clock, they brought me a little food, and some meat that smelt very strong, and two soft-boiled eggs, and I forced myself to eat a little, but soon afterwards the sea conquered me and I was sea-sick; and this was the only time I was sea-sick during the whole journey. When I told the Katikiro that I had been ill, he said that he was glad that I had been sick, because now he had a companion in misery. He himself was ill three times and could not keep anything down, and many of the passengers could not eat anything; Mr. Millar himself was very nearly sick, but he is a very good sailor.

There were many good sailors on board, who played at games, and ran races, and had pillow-fights. They took a pole and tied it up crossways, and two men sat on it as one would on a cow; each man had a pillow with which he struck at his friend, and these pillows were very soft so that they did not hurt one another. The man who could keep his balance and knock his friend over was the conqueror.

On this day all the pipes on the steamer were examined, and water was pumped into it (fire drill), and we saw how the sailors, who do not fear the sea, prepare for any great danger. We saw too how they get all the boats ready.

We watched the waves breaking over the ship, and were afraid that they would break it, and called upon God continually to take care of us.

The following day, August 29th, the sea was rougher than ever, and we were continually eating a little food; but the food of the Germans is very bad indeed – some of it smells very nasty; all their meat smells, and is not at all nice to eat. One should never go by a German boat if he can get an English one; they are to be avoided. At five o'clock they had some sports. They put up some nets in two places, and ran and climbed over them, and then ran round all the houses in the centre of the boat, and came to a tank which had in it water up to the waist, and all ran through this, and the first man to arrive at the winning-post was the conqueror. The sailors raced first, and then the Somalis and some Europeans.

They next tied some people up so that their hands and feet came together; they tied them to sticks and then they fought with their feet while their hands were tied (cock-fighting), and the one who turned the other over was the winner. Mr. Millar entered for this, but was beaten, and we were very sorry.

In these sports we saw the ruffianism of the Germans; they played just like children, and quarrelled with one another all the time.[75] Some of them abused the English in the games, and I was amazed to see the abusiveness of the Germans; the men were abusive, and the women were abusive, and no one rebuked another. We were very much surprised to see that no one tried to stop this abuse, but that they were all like children; we were afraid of them, because they were quarrelling every day among themselves. We ourselves were just like prisoners in our fear of being struck by them: we saw one German who three times wanted to strike the Katikiro for no reason whatever; he found me standing to one side, and pushed me out of the way, though I was a long way away from him, and altogether showed himself to be like a ruffian.

We were afraid of telling Mr. Millar all these things, for we did not want to trouble him daily and hourly; as while he was in England he had worked very hard indeed in making everything nice for us with every one.

The rain came down very heavily during the day, and we hoped that it would quiet the sea a little. The Katikiro was continually asking me how many more days we had on the sea, and I told him, as the sailors had told us when we would arrive.

On August 30th the rain came down very heavily at eleven o'clock, and the sea became calm, and we got some peace. They went on with the games, having races round the houses in the centre of the boat, and taking oranges out of the hands of ladies, and running back to the starting-point, the one who got back first being the winner. At six o'clock they gave out that at seven there would be a gathering for pleasure, and we saw that it was going to be a great one, because they hung up numbers of flags and electric lamps, and got out a great many seats, and all dressed themselves very well.

After dinner the band began to call together those who wanted to amuse themselves, and a great many people collected – about three hundred in all – and they began their amusement, the men and women taking hold of one another in pairs, a man and a woman, and going round together, jumping up and down, a most strange thing. I saw a man who had got himself up in every way like a woman, both in the way he talked and in the way he was dressed, and he had on flaxen hair which looked just like a

---

[75] Another instance of conduct as a standard of cultural judgement. The 'ruffianism of the Germans' is reflected in their verbal conduct; what Mukasa calls quarrelling is really the absence of restraint which, as late Victorians, the African travellers consider to be paramount in communication and even play.

woman's hair, and thus they amused themselves. I thought it was very wrong for a man and woman to hold on to one another and dance together; these dances are like the bait which is on a fish-hook. However, each nation has its own customs, but I do not think every one approves of this custom.

After this they read out the names of those who had won prizes in the games. The prizes were as follows: knives, cups, ostrich feathers, nice sticks, looking glasses, spoons, pens, and things of all kinds; every one gave what he had as his tribute to the games.

The next morning, August 31st, I went to see the Katikiro at 8 a.m., but found him still asleep, and so I did not wake him, as he is usually a bad sleeper. I myself had a slight attack of fever. We were very glad to hear that they hoped to arrive the next morning at Tanga, a city of the Germans on the coast, like Entebbe is in our country. I asked how far it was from Aden to Zanzibar, and they told me it was 1,770 miles. It was rather chilly, and so the Katikiro moved his chair to the other side of the deck; but I was afraid to go there, because it was not our usual place, and I was afraid of the Germans, who are not kind to any one who has not yet learned their customs, and do not tell them their mistakes quietly like the English, who, when they find any one in the wrong, tell him his mistake quietly. The Germans are very savage.

On September 1st we reached Tanga at about eight o'clock in the morning, and saw what it was like. An arm of the sea goes a long way inland, and the heavy seas cannot come there, since the channel is narrow, and not deep like the sea. When we got into the harbour we saw the houses of the Europeans, which were very fine and were close to the sea. They had planted a great many mango-trees, which from a distance looked like our cherry-trees, owing to their dark leaves; there were also many cocoanut-trees, which looked like a forest of palms. When the ship had anchored, they brought a number of small boats alongside, and we went ashore to see what their town was like. We landed at a wooden pier which is at the end of the railway which the Germans began (to the Victoria Nyanza) but could not finish; they have only done about forty miles of it.

We passed the custom-house and went straight on, looking at the rows of houses which had been built and the nice trees which had been planted along the sides of the road. The native houses are very bad; the Europeans and Indians have nice houses, but the Arabs and Swahilis have very bad ones. We saw what the market was like; they sell in it all kinds of meat – beef and goat mutton, and fish, and fowls – and all kinds of vegetables – plantains and sweet potatoes, bananas, Indian corn, oranges, mangoes, and cocoanuts, and many other things for which we have no name in our language. There was a very deep well there, from which the water was drawn with a rope, which was wound up by a windlass.

We then went back on board to go to Zanzibar, but the ship was late in starting, owing to the numbers of Europeans who had come on board to see their friends. We started off at one o'clock, and looked at the various islands which we passed – Pemba, which is a smaller island then Zanzibar, and other small islands near it, one of which was called Marukubi, and had on it some houses which used to belong to the Arabs, but Said Barghash had plundered them of all their goods for some reason which I was not told.

Chapter XVI

We reached Zanzibar in the evening – a journey of six hours from Tanga – and saw the lights of the town, like stars in number; and all the electric lights in the palace of Said Ali, the Sultan, which were very brilliant.[76] We were just about to have dinner when Mr. Kestell-Cornish, who had been sent for us by the Consul, came to tell us that we would have dinner on shore; so we collected our things and got into a boat, and were taken to the Consul's landing-stage, as the sea reaches right up to the Consulate.

When we reached the Consul's house we found he had gone out, and so we went to our hotel, which was called the Africa Hotel, and were shown our rooms. When we were ready they summoned us to dinner, and we were given a table to ourselves – Apolo Katikiro, Mr. Millar, and Ham Mukasa; there were a good many other Europeans at another table by themselves.

The next morning, September 2nd, after breakfast, we went to see the Consul, Mr. Basil Cave – the representative of the Consul-General, who was away. Mr. Cave is a very kind man indeed, and asked us about our visit to England, and how we saw the King; and we told him about all that we saw, because he was a very nice man, like all the English, and a true-born Englishman in his nature, and not one to be disowned, and his ways and his words were those of a true gentleman; a very clever man, who speaks slowly and asks questions worth asking. He spoke to us in Swahili, because he knows it very well indeed, and will know it still better. We asked him a great deal about Zanzibar, and he answered all our questions very nicely and kindly; and we then went home, after he had promised to lend us a carriage to take us over the island of Zanzibar.

The carriage came round at three o'clock, and we got into it with Mr.

---

[76] Zanzibar was at this time the political and cultural centre of British territories in East Africa, and although primarily Muslim, it was also the headquarters of the Church Missionary Society in the region.

Venables, who had been asked by Mr. Cave to show us round the island; the horses were very fine ones and very strong, and the driver had on the Sultan's livery, which was very fine; we drove out about six miles, and saw the way the Swahilis cultivated, and the kind of food they ate, and what their houses and roads were like. The people are very poverty-stricken and live in wretched houses, which they thatch with palm-leaves, and have not much food, as many of them do not know how to cultivate. Their cultivation is like that of the people of the Sese Islands, in our country of Uganda, and the various kinds of trees which they have take the place of their fields (in providing them with food); but this is not the case with all the people. The fruit of the greater number of trees has already been pledged and sold to the Indians, for an Indian in a country of foolish people soon finishes it up and gets possession of it all, buying it slowly bit by bit.

The houses of the Zanzibar peasants are like the houses of the Uganda goats; and that is the reason I pity them so much, for they long ago saw the cleverness of the Europeans, but could not learn it for themselves, because they trusted in their own wisdom, though it was of no profit to them, since they never applied themselves to cultivation of the land and the building of houses, but were like strangers to the country; and that is the reason I pity them, as their houses and their streets all smell very badly.[77]

Well, if Europeans have been so many years in their country, and they have not yet learned any better, when will they learn to build and cultivate their land properly? They will be a very long time indeed in learning, because in their foolishness they think that their own wisdom is profitable to them, and despise that of the Europeans, which would be of real use. The streets in the town itself are very narrow and smell very badly, and are just like ours were nine years ago, though now our streets are clean and wide. I think that in about fifteen years we shall have in Uganda a town which will be larger and finer in every way than Zanzibar, because I think the Baganda want to leave behind the old things, and go after the new in everything which they learn, and they can pick out what will be useful. I myself am a Muganda, and I speak about what I know will take place. At Zanzibar, when one is on the water and looks at the town, it appears very fine indeed; but when you get into it, the streets and the inside of all the Arabs' houses smell abominably, and the only houses that are nice inside and out are those

---

[77] The author's pity for the Zanzibaris contains insights into – and indeed a rationale for – his own acceptance of colonial authority, for he pities them not so much because of their poverty but because they had opportunities to learn from 'the cleverness of the Europeans' (since they were the first to be colonised on the East African coast), but they chose to stick to their old ways ('they trusted in their own wisdom'); in the process they have missed out on the most rudimentary aspects of civilisation ('cultivation of the land and the building of houses').

of the Europeans and of the Sultan. The Sultan's palace is very fine indeed, just like an English country-house, and is the finest house in Zanzibar; there is no other that nearly comes up to it, not even the house of the Consul-General, for that was originally only an Arab house.

On our way home we went to see a lion and a tiger in cages, in a place called Victoria Gardens.

Alidina Vissramu (the chief Indian trader in Uganda) paid us a visit in the morning, and offered to lend us his carriage to drive about in; but we told him that the Sultan was going to lend us one of his royal carriages.[78]

On September 3rd, at noon, we went to lunch with the Consul; we walked to his house, and found him waiting for us. He made us sit down in a room which looked out over the sea, and which had in it many beautiful things from all parts of the world, and also a large and very nice piano. The floor was covered with English mats, of the kind which we in our language call mattresses (carpets), and on the verandah which looked out over the sea there was a screen of palm-leaves, beautifully made.

We met there Mrs. Cave, the wife of the Consul, and also another important European, General Rogers, who is Regent to Said Ali, the Sultan. The Consul introduced them to us as is the custom in Europe, and they greeted us very warmly. Another man, Dr. Mackinnon, also came with his wife, and after we had greeted them we waited a short while, and then they told the ladies to go to the dining-table. We followed, and sat down to lunch, and as we ate we talked to them in Swahili and English. I talked to Mrs. Mackinnon, who did not know Swahili; she asked me all about England, and what we saw and what most astonished us. If you know a little of their language, the English ladies are very pleased indeed if you will talk with them.

After lunch the Consul told the ladies to go away, and we men only remained and talked a little, and then the Consul said he would send us a carriage to take us out to Mbweni and Kiungani, and we went home to our hotel.

At four o'clock our carriage arrived, and we drove out along the road called 'Mnazi moja', which is praised very much as the finest road in the town, though it is not nearly as good as our road in Uganda, which goes to Munyonyo from the back of the King's palace, and which is very much finer. We reached Mbweni, and found there a lady called Miss Ward, who

---

[78] Alidina Vissramu was a pioneer Indian trader with numerous businesses in the East African countries and, as this example illustrates, a man who often mediated between Africans and the colonial authorities, through both his businesses and charitable work, most notably the rebuilding of Namirembe Cathedral after it was destroyed in a storm in 1894.

had come from Hampstead, the place where Mr. Millar and Drs. A. R. and J. H. Cook were born, and the place which we chose as our resting-place from the noise and rush of England. It is a very pretty place, and the people who are born there are very kind indeed, and many missionaries have gone out from there, and I praise it because its sons are so kind, and very clever indeed at everything.

This lady, Miss Ward, showed us the church and the schools, and we met some ladies and English children in the courtyard – amongst them the wife of the Gabunga (chief of the canoes, *i.e.* port officer) of Zanzibar.

We next went to Kiungani, where our friend the Rev. Henry Wright Duta (chief native pastor in Uganda, and co-translator of the Luganda Bible) was trained. We found there a very kind European, who showed us the church, and schools and dormitories for the boys, and the dining-room. We also saw a number of the boys who had come there to be taught; they came up to look at us, though they did not greet us – perhaps it is not their custom. We were told that there were in all about sixty boys who had come there to be trained as teachers.

The next morning we went out shopping, and then went to the judge to accuse a Swahili who had cheated the Katikiro (a year or more previously) of a thousand rupees. The judge asked us to describe the man, and we did so, and he said he would search for him, and we left Alidina Vissramu, our friend the Indian trader, to be the Katikiro's representative in the matter.

After a short rest we went out to lunch with General Rogers, whose house was only about three minutes' walk from our hotel. We there met Major and Mrs. Raikes and Mr. Childe, and they all welcomed us, and after we had sat for a short time dinner was announced, and we went in, and had dinner, talking to one another in Swahili and English. General Rogers had dressed up his servants in very fine liveries, coats all covered with gold and beautifully white clothes, and we thought he was very kind indeed to dress his servants up thus in our honour. He is a very nice man, and knows Swahili very well, having come to Zanzibar in 1890; he has travelled a great deal up and down the coast, and knows it all well; just now he is acting as guardian to the Sultan of Zanzibar. His house is so full of beautiful things from all lands, spears and horns and old swords and guns, that one cannot keep one's eyes away from looking at them. I was very sorry for him because he could not speak in comfort, as his arm was very painful, and he had to wear it in a sling, and the pain prevented him from speaking properly; but his joy for our sakes was like a second arm to him, so that he was not in such pain as usual.

We were amazed at seeing how all the English everywhere were alike in their habits, and I therefore think when I see any one of them who is not kind that he is not a true-born Englishman in his nature. There are two marks of the English nation, and when I see any one who has not these, I am in doubt whether or not he is a true Englishman; these two things are kindness and bravery, and when I see any one who has not both these, I consider him one who would be disowned in England. Kindness is the mother and bravery is the father of their nation, and between these two is great wisdom, worthy of being sought after. If all nations were like the English, all the world would be at peace. I speak what is absolutely true, there is no particle of untruth in what I say; I have no doubt at all of what I say about that nation.

A short time after we had got home our carriage came round; it had two horses in it, like those in which we travelled in England, and we went along the Sultan's road to the palace of Said Barghash at Chueni. It is a very fine building, and is built beyond an arm of the sea which is crossed by a bridge guarded by policemen. After we had seen all over it we returned home, looking about as we drove to see what the place was like, and what sort of houses there were, and how the people cultivated, and how they dressed and everything else. We went home by a different road from the one along which we had come.

The inhabitants of Zanzibar praise it too much, and say it is the finest place on earth.

In the evening we went to dinner with Captain Agnew, R.N.R., the Gabunga (port officer) of all the ships. We passed on the way the Sultan's palace, the electric lights in which were like suns, and on our arrival we were met by Captain Agnew and his wife and two children. Mrs. Agnew played to us on the piano, and the children sang and danced, and then both went to bed, and shortly afterwards we went in to dinner. The party consisted of Captain and Mrs. Agnew, Mr. J. A. Bailey, Rev. E. Millar, Apolo Katikiro, and Ham Mukasa, and after dinner Mrs. Agnew showed us some photographs, amongst others one of her brother who was drowned at sea with about four hundred others.

After we had talked together for some time we went home, and on the way we examined the machinery that made the electric light in the Sultan's palace. Mr. Bailey very kindly went with us as far as the hotel; he is a kind man, and very pleasant to talk to.

At nine o'clock the next morning, September 5th, the Consul came to take us to see the Sultan, Said Ali, and we all drove to the palace, although it was raining very heavily indeed. When we arrived in front of the palace the carriage stopped, and the soldiers played the tune which is played to welcome great men, and all saluted, and we then entered the Sultan's palace and went upstairs. In the first room at the top of the stairs we were met by the Sultan and two of his attendants; he was standing a little way apart from them, and first greeted the Consul, who then introduced us all to him, Apolo Katikiro, Rev. E. Millar, and Ham Mukasa, and he took each of us by the hand and then took us into the council chamber, in which he had left his councillors, and where we found many Arabs and Indians and Banyans and the head of each clan in Zanzibar, all of whom had come together to greet the Sultan's visitors. They were all beautifully dressed, each one in the dress of his own nation; the Arabs had on their burnouses, and large turbans of fine coloured cloth, and daggers in their waist-belts as is their custom.

We sat down, and the Sultan asked the Katikiro how things were going on in Uganda; and he told him that he had been a month without receiving any letters, and so he did not know what was going on at the present time. The Sultan told us that he wished to come to Uganda, and we were very pleased, and told him what our country was like, and how we had very bad houses, only made of grass, and how we had not yet got our roads into order; while they in Zanzibar had houses built of earth and fine buildings of stone. After we had stayed for about a quarter of an hour we said good-bye, and he accompanied us as far as the top of the stairs, and then went back, whilst we went downstairs, followed by the Arabs.

The Sultan's palace is very fine and like the country-house of a rich Englishman. All the things in it were like the things one finds in an English house; the chair of the Sultan, and that of the Commissioner, and that of the Regent, General Rogers, were all of gold.

When we reached the courtyard in which were the soldiers, they played a tune to bid us farewell; and we then got into our carriage and drove home.

After a short time we went to visit an Arab who has a shop in our country, and whose house was near to our hotel. He welcomed us very kindly, and told us that the English were very much better than all the other European nations, and were much richer than all other nations, and governed all their colonies very well.

His house was just like that of a European inside, and had large windows and things spread over the floor, and was quite clean, and had in it chairs and tables and easy chairs, just like a European house. He said, 'I have travelled in a great many places, and see that keeping one's house clean and neat makes one live longer, and keeps one from being constantly ill; and I therefore keep my house like that of a European, since the Arabs are not clean at all and are therefore always unwell.' He gave us some coffee and sherbet, and a kind of flour mixed with butter, which the Katikiro would not eat; but I took a little so as not to vex our host.

If it were not for the prayer-mats you would not know that this man was an Arab, as all the furniture would lead you to think he was a European; he has chairs and carpets, and pavements worked in designs, and tables and clocks, and in everything has tried to make his house like that of a European; and were it not for the Muhammadan prayer-books and praying-mats you would not know he was an Arab.

After a short rest at the hotel we drove to see the Cathedral at Mkunazini, which is the Cathedral of Zanzibar, just as the Cathedral at Namirembe (Uganda) is the Mengo Cathedral. The site on which it is built is the site of the old slave-market; when Said Barghash was told to abolish slavery he did away with this market, and gave the site to the (Universities') Mission, and they built the Cathedral on it. The first bishop of Zanzibar was Bishop Tozer, who came out in 1864, but Bishop Steere built the Cathedral; he began it on June 6th, 1873, and finished it in 1879.

When we reached the Cathedral we found two ladies, Archdeacon Evans, and the storekeeper of the mission, and they took us all over the building, both inside and out. We climbed up on to the roof and got a view over the whole town, for the building is very high and far above all the other houses.

We went over the hospital and nurses' house, both of which were very nice. In the hospital were many different kinds of people – Swahilis, Arabs, Indians, Banyans, Somalis, etc. We bought some books which we wanted and then drove towards Chwaka, but turned back before we arrived there.

The next day, September 6th, we went again to the law courts about the matter of the Swahili who had cheated the Katikiro out of a thousand rupees, and obtained a warrant against him and gave it to our friend Alidina Vissramu. We next went to see the printing office where all the books in Zanzibar are printed, and which is called the 'Gazette Office'; we then went to say good-bye to the Consul, and came back to the hotel for lunch.

After lunch we packed up to go away, and they took all our things down to the sea-shore, and we followed them down to a place where there was a very large market, quite close to the Sultan's courtyard and to the prison. Our things were put into a boat, and we went off to the ship which was to take us to Mombasa, and which was called *British India*, B.I. They took on board all our goods and those of other passengers, and we sat and looked at the town of Zanzibar, which you can see very well from the sea, and which is a very fine town to look at. We saw a ship which had been sunk when the Arabs fought against the English (1896) in Zanzibar; only the masts are now visible, because the ship is at the bottom of the sea; the Government are going to clear it away, as it prevents ships coming into the harbour properly; it will perhaps cost £5,000 to do this.

We waited a long time while they were still taking in cargo, and amused ourselves with some Somali divers, who dived after money thrown into the water; the Katikiro threw in ten pice and I threw in three, and they went down after them and found them, to our great surprise. A good many European passengers also threw in money for them.

Captain Agnew, the port officer, came on board with Mr. Bailey and said good-bye to us, and then went ashore, and we remained with Mr. Bailey looking at Zanzibar through our glasses. Eight priests also came on board, under the leadership of Père Bulesu, who had brought them out from Europe. He knows Luganda and English very well, and we stayed a long time talking to him and to Mr. Bailey, both of whom are kind men; and even though one of them is a Frenchman, still he is very kind to the Baganda, and likes them very much. We left Zanzibar at about five o'clock in the evening, and it became dark as we were nearing Pemba Island.

Chapter XVII

The following morning, September 7th, we reached Mombasa at about eight o'clock, and our vessel blew its whistle to tell the people of Mombasa of its arrival, and we entered the narrow harbour where all the ships anchor.

Our friend Mr. D. J. Wilson, who had met us first at Mombasa Station on our arrival when we were going to England, came to take us off the ship, and brought us a boat to take us on shore, and when we landed we got on to trollies. Apolo Katikiro got on to one with Mr. Gilkison (Vice-Consul) and Mr. Millar, Mr. D. J. Wilson, and I, Ham Mukasa, got on to another, and we were pushed up to the house called the Grand Hotel, which is a very large house as African houses go, but would be a very inferior one in England. When we reached the hotel they showed us our rooms, and we then had breakfast.

At four o'clock in the afternoon we went to see Mr. F. J. Jackson, the Deputy Commissioner of Mombasa, a very old friend of ours who is well known in Uganda, and a very brave man in war.

We walked to his house, which was the official residence of all the commissioners, a very fine stone house, roofed with corrugated iron and three stories high. It is built in an excellent situation, and has a view of all the ships that come to the harbour, whether by day or night, as it has near it a tower with a light on it which can be seen from a great distance. The house is very well furnished, with carpets, and tables, and chairs, and many other things to look at, such as all European houses have in them; but although it is called the Commissioner's residence, yet it is only like an English country-house.

When we arrived Mr. Jackson himself got up and met us at the door, and welcomed us and made us sit down, and introduced his secretary and his nephew to us, and also introduced us to the wife of Mr. Gedge, who came to Uganda a long time ago together with Mr. Jackson. This lady asked the Katikiro all about England, and he told her a great deal about all he had seen, and she was very pleased, and asked him, 'What did you think of the sea?' and he shook his head and said, 'It was terrible', because he was very much afraid of the sea, not from mere fright, but because it made him very ill and sea-sick. After this we went to church, as it was Sunday, and then went home.

We received a large number of letters from Uganda and read them: some brought good news, and some bad; a great many people had died of sleeping-sickness, and many were very ill. We heard that the Government were going to turn about a hundred chiefs and peasants out of their estates, which were in the neighbourhood of Kampala, and that a chief called Kikojo was going to be turned out of his estates near Entebbe; and we were very much afraid, because a promise had been made that some of these people should not be turned out, and they were being turned out after all! This frightened us very much, as we thought that perhaps other treaties would be in the same way broken; but after all everything ended satisfactorily, for when they saw that a great many people were angry, and that both great and small, chiefs and peasants, were very much troubled about it, the English did as they always do when they think they have done wrong, and the Commissioner, Colonel Sadler, refused to allow the arrangement, and it came to nothing.[79]

On September 8th, the following day, at eleven o'clock, we went to lunch with Mr. Jackson, the Deputy Commissioner, and found him with Mr. Hollins and Mr. Archer, and another man called Mr. Lorimer, and also Mrs. Gedge; and we sat and talked for a while and then went in to lunch. We had some turtle soup, and the Katikiro did not know what it was and drank it; and then Mr. Millar asked him if the soup was nice, and he said it was very nice indeed; and Mr. Millar laughed and told him it was turtle soup, and he replied, 'When one is on the war-path, one does not refuse anything.'* After lunch we had some coffee, and talked about what we had seen in England, and about what was going on in Uganda, and what news

---

* The author has confused this lunch with the one we had with the Lord Provost of Glasgow, at which we had turtle soup. At Mr. Marsden's, two days later, we had lobster salad; hence the mistake. Turtles are not eaten by the Baganda.

[79] As a Protectorate rather than a Crown Colony, Buganda's relationship with Britain was determined by a treaty (the [B]Uganda Agreement) signed in 1899. The treaty established the boundaries of the kingdom, affirmed the principle of indirect colonial rule (through the Kabaka and chiefs), and allowed land to be held in freehold. The educated African elite considered the treaty to be the guarantor of Buganda's (and their own) privileges within the colony, hence the anxiety expressed by Mukasa here.

our letters had brought us, and Mr. Jackson said he was sorry to hear we had not good news.

After this we went back and explored the island of Mombasa. It is a small island and flat, like our island of Lulamba, but about as large as the island of Buvu, or a little smaller.

In the evening we went to dinner with Mr. J. A. Bailey, and after dinner played a game called 'Pingpon', which is played on a table with small round india-rubber balls, about the size of a fowl's egg; we played two or three games and then went home. It was a very wet day, and Mr. Millar had a slight attack of fever.

The next day, September 9th, at eleven o'clock, we went to see what Kilindini was like. We were pushed across the island in trollies, and went down to the railway bridge between Mombasa and the mainland, and then went on to see where they store kerosene oil. They have two very large barrels of iron, into which they pump the oil and store it up there till they require to draw it out. One of these barrels holds two hundred and fifty tons of the oil, and the other a hundred tons. We saw also a damaged steamer which they were mending, and then came home very tired. I was just like a sick person, and my boots were making my feet burn, as they were too tight for me. The Katikiro was not tired, and we were both very glad to have seen what the island was like; because a traveller ought to look round every place, so that he can tell his friends what other countries are like.

After lunch we were taken to see the old Portuguese fort, which is very old, having been built by them in the year 1400 A.D.[80] It is a very large place, and there are many ancient things in it – cannon, and cannon-balls for these old cannon, which are like the stems of trees; the cannon-balls are like stones in number, and are all thrown out in the courtyard as they are of no further use; the fort has now been made into a prison by the English, and is a very strong place, and has many houses in it.

We saw there a great many prisoners – three of whom were Europeans and were engaged in caning chairs, while the others were doing other work. The prisoners are well looked after, and have good food and nice houses to sleep in. We saw also a very old well made by the Portuguese, which is in a house; and when it rains the rain-water is collected in it, and so the people in the fort get a supply of good water which lasts a long time.

After this we wrote our names in the visitors' book, and then were shown photographs of the prisoners, which were very well taken. They register the prisoners very cleverly; they first take photographs of them, and then write

---

[80] This is a reference to Fort Jesus, the symbol of Portuguese domination of the East African coast in the age of discovery.

down the height of each man, and the size of his chest, and his colour, and his offence, and the length of his imprisonment, and the place he comes from, and his name and religion. All this they do to remind themselves about each man, so that when he commits another offence it is always known what he is like in every respect.

I thoroughly approved of this, because it teaches us a spiritual lesson. If we men have the wisdom to mark criminals who offend against our human laws, how will it be with the Creator of heaven and earth? Let us then take care that we have no marks of evil put on us, but only marks of good, because as we judge others we ourselves shall be judged. I put this in to remind the hearts of all of us who know God, and although this is a book about earthly matters, still this matter should be put into it, as it is like what we know; it is not as if this book were written for those who knew nothing of God, but it is to be read by all of you who know God.

Well, to continue our story. After leaving the fort we went to have tea with Boustead Ridley (Mr. R. N. Boustead), and then went to see the Roman Catholic priests, and after that returned home, and Mr. Ishmael Semler, the pastor of the Frere Town Church, and the father-in-law of Mika Sematimba, came with his daughter to see us.

The next day, September 10th, we began getting ready for our journey to Uganda, as we hoped soon to be starting, and at twelve o'clock the Vice-Consul, Mr. Marsden, came with his trolley to fetch us to lunch with him; the Liwali (chief judge) of Mombasa was also with him, and we went to his house and had lunch, and they asked us about England, and we told them of all we had seen. All Europeans are anxious to hear something new from every part of their land and other lands.

The son of the Liwali of Mombasa was also there; he knew English very well, because his father had sent him to England, and he had remained there for a year or two; he can also write very well, and is now at work in the Mombasa Government offices. He in his turn has sent his son to England to be taught, and is going to leave him there eleven years, so that he may get very well educated.

After lunch Mr. Marsden brought out his singing machine, which the English call a phonograph, but which we call a 'talking machine', and it made us laugh very much, because you hear its voice, which is just like the voice of a real man, as you know yourselves if you have heard the phonograph which Mr. Millar brought to Uganda. After this we went home, because Mr. Marsden had a great deal of work to do, as he was the Vice-Consul, and we did not want to waste his time by sitting there talking.

After this Mr. Millar and I went to see our friends at Frere Town, in accordance with a promise we had made, but Apolo Katikiro did not come as he was afraid of being sea-sick when crossing the harbour, and also he wished to get ready to go to Uganda.

When we arrived at Frere Town we went to see the Rev. H. K. Binns and another missionary, and then went to the Rev. Ishmael Semler, the father-in-law of Mika Sematimba, and afterwards visited the ladies of the mission, and then returned home.

In the evening we went to Mr. Bailey's house, and there found twenty-five English people, who had come to hear about England and Uganda; there were also four native Christians from Mombasa. The Katikiro told then a great deal about England, and they were very pleased indeed, and laughed with joy. We then had prayers and went home. It was raining very heavily indeed, but Mr. Bailey very kindly saw us home to the Grand Hotel, as he is a very kind man, like all true Englishmen.

The next morning we fastened up all our things, as the train which was to take us was on the way to fetch us, and arrived at twelve o'clock. We sent our things to the station, and Mr. Millar went with them to get them put into the train and then came back, and we had lunch. At one o'clock we went to the station; we hoped soon to get to the end of our journey, and to arrive in Uganda in a few days – three days in the train and two on the steamer, five in all, or perhaps six if there was any breakdown on the way.

A great many of our friends, both English and Swahili, came to see us off, and when we got into the train we were very pleased indeed, just as if we could see Uganda with our eyes. I saw how very pleased Mr. Millar was; he was nearly out of his senses with delight at being in the train that was to take us to Uganda. Though he had fever, yet the fever left him at once, and he sang some English songs we could not understand, and slapped his knees and my knees, and hit me on the scar of my wounded leg in his joy, and I was not vexed with him for doing so, because I was so pleased to see how happy he was. I, too, was very pleased, but my joy was very small compared to his. My joy was like that of a man who has discovered a silver mine, while Mr. Millar's was like that of a man who has discovered gold, and silver, and pearls, and precious stones.

Among all the Europeans who go back to Europe I never saw any who were as pleased as this at going home to see their parents, and their beautiful country, and their relations; and I was therefore very much surprised at seeing Mr. Millar as glad to get back to our country as if he had been born there; perhaps, though, there may have been some other reason which I did not know of. I think, however, that this was the true reason, as Mr. Millar is very fond indeed of the Baganda, and we were amazed at his not stopping in England to rest; he was only there a few months with us, and came back again without having had any rest, or having seen his own relations and friends properly, as he was always busy over our business; and therefore this that he did for us ought always to be remembered.

As we went along in the train we looked at the coast scenery. They have put iron telegraph posts by the side of the line, and on these are iron plates, having on them the number of miles they are from the coast; we thought this a very good idea, because you can see how far on the journey you have got, and how much remains to be travelled. The whole length of the railway is 580 miles.

Night fell as we passed Maungu, and we went to sleep; and the train went on all the while we were asleep. The things of the English are very nice; it is pleasant to go to sleep in a boat that travels over land while those who are not engaged in working it can go to sleep.

The next day, September 12th, we were in the train all day. We saw the magnificent bridges that had been made near the Kedong escarpment – over the large rivers that had cut ravines out of the hillsides. Formerly they had a machine there that let the carriages up and down the hill by a rope made of iron, but they did away with it as every one was so frightened of it.

The next morning, September 13th, near Lumbwa, we saw a train that had left the rails and had fallen into the valley; there were no people in it, but only the bodies of two horses and three donkeys belonging to an Indian trader, and these smelt very badly indeed. At first we thought that there had been some people in the train; but they told us that it was only some animals that had been killed. When we reached Fort Ternan we met a great many Baganda, and talked to them about England until ten o'clock at night, as they did not want us to leave off.

The following morning, September 14th, after leaving Fort Ternan, we passed another train which had left the rails. The rain had been very heavy, and that is the reason the line got so much out of order and these accidents occurred; and although it gets out of order, yet it is kept in good repair, because the engineers are very clever. To people who bridge seas and cut through mountains and go under lakes, is it a difficult matter to keep the line in repair? There is no doubt that it will be made all right and sound.

We arrived at Port Florence at two o'clock, and on arrival found there was no house in which we could sleep; so the Katikiro and I slept in the railway carriage, and had our meals in a small hotel. A great many Baganda collected together to hear about England, and we told them a great deal about it. Paulo Kawawulo, the chief man of the Baganda at Kisumu, gave us a present of a large goat, and we ate it. We saw too how they had begun to build a town at the terminus of the railway on Ugowe Bay (Kavirondo Bay).

The next day, September 15th, after breakfast, we got ready our things, and they were taken down to the steamer *William Mackinnon*, and were put in charge of Mr. Brown, who used to be at Nakasero (Mengo), and he sent them on board; but we ourselves stayed some time talking to our friends, and telling them about all we had seen in England, and when everybody else had gone on board we joined them. The passengers consisted of eight Europeans, about forty Indian soldiers, and four Goanese clerks. We were very much pleased with the kindness of the English, because the Consul-General at Zanzibar had telegraphed to Colonel Sadler, the Consul-General in Uganda, to tell him we were there, and to ask him to send the steamer for us; and they sent it over quickly for our sakes, and we were very pleased to find it all ready for us when we reached Kisumu.

We therefore praise the kindness of the English, because it is like the sun that ripens fruit; they make a fool into a wise man, and do not like any one to do ill to his neighbour, but want peace everywhere. They are like the father of the nations of the earth in teaching habits of kindness, and were the first to abolish slavery in all lands, and the other European nations learned this from them; though some have not yet given it up, such as the Portuguese. I say this because I saw a black boy with an Englishman, who had redeemed him for twenty pounds from the Portuguese, who were going to sell him. Well, see what the kindness of the English is like![81] This man is now teaching the boy all kinds of things, so that when he has learned them all he can go anywhere in peace, and make his own living. Is not this man just like his real father in teaching him all these things?

What I myself think is this. Before the end of the world has come a great many people will leave the country of their birth and go to the lands ruled over by the English, because a great many other European nations rule very badly indeed, killing people for nothing, beating them before they have been tried, and confiscating their goods without cause. Other Europeans, seeing a man who should be rebuked only, beat him, and kill those who only deserve a beating. Is this not a terrible thing? They say, 'Killing a black man is nothing'; but though they speak thus, their boasting is vain, and leads to destruction. A king who rules over a land should show his kindness to all men, as God does to every man; but a rule that does not follow the example set by God endures but a short time. A kind king rules for many years, but a cruel king reigns but a short time.

Look at God, the King of kings. He does not distinguish between those over whom He rules, but gives to every kind of man happiness and peace and those things he requires – wisdom, and the understanding of difficult

---

[81] That the English had, during their colonial mission in East Africa, committed similar acts is a fact to which the author is impervious. He was committed to an ideal portrait of Englishness without which his own conversion would be hard to justify.

matters. If God made a distinction between races, and chose one race and gave it all the things He now distributes to all races, who then on all the earth would have been wise, in the way that we now find wise men in all nations? No, there would have been no wise nation on the earth except the Jews, who are called the chosen people; but God, not despising any man and being kind to all nations, enables them to obtain wisdom of all kinds, and above all to know the Words of Life, which some call foolishness, and trust in their own wisdom and make it their god, trusting in it more than they trust in God who gave it to them.

Men like that, whether white or black, who trust their own wisdom, are like a man who trusts a rotten tooth; but the energy of the English race gives wisdom to many nations, which before were foolish, and have now become wise; and I therefore say that the English are greatly blessed for their kindness, for they work hard in teaching all men the fear of God, and such wisdom as is suitable for them and is not evil, but helps men of every kind and of every nation, whether white or black. If you see a man who rules badly, such a man is not a true Englishman, even though he were born of English parents; his evil habits show him to be of a different race.

In our country of Uganda we have a saying that is said to insolent men, 'Are you a German?' meaning, 'Are you a ruffian like a German?' Because after the Germans had killed Romwa, the King of Buzinja, and also King Lukonge, and had killed a great many common people in their country who were not worthy of death, it began to be said to any vicious or drunken man, 'Are you a German that you do this?' since people do not think that the Germans are a Christian nation; they say that in the German nation there is not a single Christian, but that it is an entirely heathen nation, although this is not really true.[82] However, I have never yet heard any one say, 'Are you a ruffian like an Englishman?' No, never have I heard this; no one ever says such a thing. The English are held in esteem in all things that are sold in our land, and every peasant going to buy anything in a shop asks, 'Is this English?' meaning, 'Was this made by the English?' and if they say yes, he is willing to buy it, because there are different qualities of things. There is English fine cotton sheeting, and English grey calico, and English gunpowder, and English guns; and of all the things which I have mentioned, calling them English means that they were made by the English; for all men in our country, be they chiefs or peasants, great or small, all buy English goods.

[82] Another instance of how colonial rivalries had over-determined the image of the Germans in the British colonies! The reports about Germany which Mukasa was reading in the colonial press painted it as a 'heathen nation', an image confirmed by World War I. Against the force of colonial representations, it would be difficult to convince anyone that Germany was the 'natural home' of Protestantism.

If, however, you call the thing German, he just goes away home and will not buy it. Well, you see how every article tells about its maker, whether it is good or bad; a thing made by a good man tells of the goodness of its maker, and the thing of a bad man tells of the badness of its maker.

In the old days we did not look closely at the habits of the different Europeans, but their goods told about them, and what they were like, whether English or Germans. The habits of a good man are heard about far off, and those of a bad man likewise. We at first saw as in a mist, not seeing the people themselves; but afterwards we reached their land and saw all that we had heard of, and more too, for the love they had for us was wonderful, and therefore I give my verdict that the English are the kindest nation on earth.

Listen to this story. Once upon a time there were two men, and each of them obtained a fowl, and each looked after his fowl as he thought fit. The first thought about what he could best do for it, and said, 'I do not want to eat all the eggs that my fowl lays; I will eat just a few of them, and leave the others so as not to annoy it; and I shall not eat all the chickens which it will rear, but will eat a few, so that the number of my fowls will soon be very great.'

The other, however, said, 'What is the use of a bird if it does not feed you?' and so he ate up all its eggs, and only occasionally left a few, and then when the fowl reared chickens he ate them all up. When this fowl saw that the other had a great many young ones, because it was properly looked after by its master, it was very sorrowful, and made plans, and when it saw it was about to lay an egg, it jumped over to the house of the man who looked properly after his fowl. Now there was a law known to all in the town and throughout the land, that a fowl that left one man and went to another was not to be brought back by its original owner. Now when the owner of the fowl which had run away hunted for it, and found it at his friend's house, he asked for it, saying, 'I wish to take back my fowl'; but his friend replied, 'I cannot give you the fowl, because there is a law known to all in the town and throughout the land, that the fowl of any man may not be fetched back, if it goes away to some one else.' When the owner saw that he could not resist the law, he went back home sorrowing over his fowl; but after a few months that fowl had a very large number of chickens, and was extremely happy.

Well, the meaning of this story is this. The fowls are the inhabitants of the lands ruled over by European nations, and the owners of the fowls are the various European nations; well, a great many people will leave the countries ruled over by other European nations, on account of their bad government, and go to the English and to the countries ruled over by them, in order that they may have peace.

In the lands ruled by the English, both men, and animals, and birds, all have peace; with the exception of wild beasts, and evil men who do not want peace in the land; such men are hostile to the English, and when they see the lands of the English, if they wish to do wrong, they do not remain in them, because the English wish all lands to increase in all useful knowledge which is good, and not evil.

Then, again, where there is peace everything increases well; both men, and cattle, and goats, and fowls, if they are at rest, increase well, and the land is quiet and settled. How can a ruler of a country like this fail to be pleased? And how can the inhabitants also fail to be happy? Thus all the rulers of the countries of the English are happy, and those who are ruled are happy also.

I therefore pray that God's blessing may rest on the English, so that their land may protect other lands. I compare the rule of the English to the sun, and that of other European nations to the moon; and as the light and glory of the moon are not equal to those of the sun, so the ruling and the power of other nations are not equal to that of those English.

If any man could stand in the track of a railway train and stop it from passing him, or if he could run his head against a mountain and pass through it, such a man might check the power and glory of the English; but such a thing is absolutely impossible.

If the English were to boast of their power, their King would be worthy of being called Cæsar, but they are gentle in all their dealings.

At half-past six we anchored in the part of the lake called by us Magali (Kavirondo Bay), near Bunyoma. We had left Kisumu at half-past one, and so had been a voyage of five hours.

Chapter XVIII

On the lake – Arrival at Munyonyo – A great reception – A triumphal progress – Thanksgiving service in the Cathedral – Reception at Kampala by the Deputy Commissioner – Telling the story of our travels

The next day, September 6th, at half-past five in the morning, the captain ordered the anchor to be weighed, and we entered the part of the lake we called 'Bwengula', which reaches as far as the island of Kama, and we had, by the blessing of God, a smooth journey without any storms; had it been rough the Katikiro would have been very sea-sick. We passed Kama at half-past ten o'clock – a journey of nine hours for our canoes from Magali; an hour and a half later we passed Dolwe – a journey of four and a half hours by canoe – and at last reached Bugaya at a quarter past three in the afternoon – a journey of nine or ten hours by our canoes, but only four hours in the steamer.

See how hard it is to tell of the wonders of the English! The journey from Magali to Bugaya that took us nine and a half hours in the steamer, takes our canoes four days. One is, therefore, very much astonished at the work of the English; what used to be a long journey they make a short one, and what used to be difficult they make easy. You see how their industry goes hand-in-hand with their wisdom, and every year they invent wonderful new things; were they lazy people, how could they do such wonders year by year? No; their cleverness and industry and inventive power year by year increase more and more as time goes on; but industry is not their's alone, for in all countries every industrious man will not fail to find what he searches for, but a lazy man is always wanting things and never obtaining what he wants.

When we reached Bugaya we were met by Luka Miyamba, the chief of the canoes at Munyonyo, who had been sent by the King to welcome us, and had also brought us our letters from Uganda, which we were very glad indeed to read. We also found there Nova Jumba Mbubi, and Muzito, the chief of Bugaya, who greeted us warmly. We inquired about the sleeping-sickness, and they told us that an enormous number of people had died from it on the islands; and we were very sorry indeed.

After this I told Jumba about what we had seen in England, and how we travelled through the country, and about all we saw there; but more especially I told him about how we saw the great King, and what his palace and his attendants were like. All the Baganda who were present, hearing this, shook their heads with amazement at what they heard.

Later on some Indian soldiers, who had borrowed a canoe to go ashore, were returning on board, when one of them, as he was trying to get back, seized a rope near the stern, and the Bavuma paddlers took away the canoe, and he remained hanging because he had seized a rope at a place where he could not get on board. He shrieked very much, but in spite of his cries the Bavuma would not bring back the canoe to take him off, and he was nearly leaving go of the rope, when I went up and seized him to drag him on board. He said, 'Leave me alone, I am a dead man; I cannot get on board.' I called for help, and the Katikiro and an English passenger came to help me; the Katikiro seized me by my bad leg and pulled me by it, and I pulled at the Indian – though I was nearly letting him go as my leg was so painful. However, I gained strength from the Katikiro's help, and persevered, and pulled very hard, and with the help of the English passenger we got the Indian on board; and he thanked us very much, as did the other soldiers, because he was nearly lost; perhaps he did not know how to swim – he shrieked a great deal in his fright.

After this Jumba went ashore for the night, the Katikiro helping him into his canoe as the lake was very rough, and it was tossing about.

The next morning we left Bugaya at half-past five, and I pointed out to the Katikiro some islands which he did not know in the Buvuma group, and also pointed out the hills of Uganda on the Bukunja coast, and showed Mr. Millar my estates of Kyazi and Lulagwe on the Koja peninsula. We were all very happy at the thought of reaching Mengo that day, and when we got near the island of Damba the Katikiro said, 'Let us put on our best clothes to arrive in, as we are near the end of our journey'; and we did so, and sat in our chairs, looking at the hills which we knew so well. We were perhaps like an Englishman who is happy when arriving at Dover, or a Frenchman who is very happy as he approaches Marseilles; thus we were, and we saw in the distance a large number of people at the landing-place at Munyonyo, and the horses of the chiefs who had come to meet us and welcome us. We saw also our own horses, which had come to fetch us, and we heard Silasi Mugwanya's drum on the mainland, where he was himself.

When our steamer was midway between Munyonyo and Bulinguge it stopped, and they brought out canoes to take us on shore; but the chief of the steamer, Captain May, said he would send us ashore in his own boat. They brought it round and we both got in with the man who was to row us on shore, and said good-bye to all our English friends on the steamer, and were rowed ashore to the pier for sailing-boats, where we met Silasi Mugwanya and his drummer and boys. When we got ashore he greeted us most joyfully, and his servant Kiza helped us out of the boat. He then took us to the rest-house where there was a table spread with many kinds of eatables, and we found there a very great number of people standing like soldiers in two lines, all dressed in beautifully white clothes. When we got to the middle of the line they all began cheering and clapping their hands for joy at seeing us arrive safely.

We entered the rest-house and found a great many chiefs waiting for us, who all welcomed us joyfully. We found there also biscuits and tea and lemonade, and after they had welcomed us we had tea, and told them about all we had seen in England, the vast numbers of the English and their cleverness, and their beautiful houses, and streets, and bridges, and boats, and about all that they do in their land, and how their land is so peaceful, and how much kinder they are than we are. We told them all this as we sat at the table; there were there a great many people who had come to meet us, both English and Baganda.

After a rest we started for the capital, and on the road met enormous numbers of people, perhaps about three thousand. We went in two groups: the Katikiro went with a number of people whom he was telling about England, and I followed with another crowd of people telling them about all we had seen. As we went along we met numbers of people, and the women came out of their houses by the side of the road as we passed, and knelt down and clapped their hands and cried for joy, and congratulated us on our journey.

When we got near the King's palace he sent messengers to greet us. He himself sat at the principal gate, with many of the chiefs, Zakariya Kizito and Samwili Mukasa Kangawo, Yosuwa Mugema, and others. When we reached the road from Rubaga my father Zakariya Sensalire met us; he first welcomed the Katikiro, and then the Katikiro brought him to me, and I got off my horse, and the Katikiro said, 'Well, Zakariya, do you see your son has got back safely?' and he said, 'Yes, I see him, and I congratulate you very much on your journey.'

When we reached the front of the palace we found it crowded with people; perhaps there were five thousand people there, and we went up to greet the King. Apolo Katikiro fell on his neck and embraced him; I merely greeted him, and then Mr. Borup took a photograph of the Katikiro embracing the King. The Katikiro told the King a little about what he had seen, and then Zakariya Kisingire said, 'There will be a meeting of the

Parliament to-morrow; we must not tire out our friends, but let them go home, because we have welcomed them back, and now they had better go and rest.'

The King then went away, and we went to the Katikiro's place, and in the courtyard met his wife and many other people, both men and women, who crowded round us so much that we could not get through them, because every one wanted to get near him. They were so pleased to see him that they could not think of his tiredness or of his dignity, they were all so pleased to see him back again. We sat in the courtyard a little time waiting for the people to settle down, and then went to the inner court, where we found a table set for us with all manner of things to eat and drink, which Samwili Mukasa, the Kangawo, had got ready for us; there was tea, and biscuits, and lemonade, and lime juice. He had also strewed grass all along the roadway, and had put up bananas and flowers and palms to gladden our eyes.

When we reached the inner court I said to the Katikiro's wife, Samali, 'Do you see how I have brought back your husband safely?' and she said, 'Yes, I see him; you have looked after him very well indeed.' After this I went off to my own house with my two friends Teofiro Musalosalo and Yosiya Kasozi Kweba. When I got home I found my wife Hana Mukasa and a great many other people waiting for me, and after I had greeted her we went into the house, but found that all the people could not get in, as there were so many, so I went out into the courtyard and sat on a chair, and they all sat looking at me, and I told them about all the wonders of England and what the country was like, and what a fine land it was.

I also told them how great was the population of England, and how they tamed elephants and all kinds of animals. Some of my hearers thought I was merely telling stories when I told them how an elephant fired a gun, and beat a drum, and lit a candle, and how a hippopotamus was called, and came just like a dog in other lands that they knew of. They were very much astonished to hear of a hippopotamus leaving the water when it was called, and going back again when it was told. Some did not understand that I was speaking the truth, while others, who knew that we would not tell them what was false, did not hesitate to believe it.[83] I sat there from half-past six in the evening until one o'clock in the morning.

The next day, September 18th, we went to the Cathedral to thank God for bringing us back safely. The Rev. H. W. Duta preached the sermon, and praised the wisdom of the Katikiro, telling how he was the first to write a

---

[83] Mukasa's fears that his representation of Britain could be met with incredulity are finally confirmed. It is interesting that his eyewitness accounts are reduced to stories (a better translation is fairy tales) the very opposite of the truth he sought to capture in his narrative.

book to tell about our land. He called him the 'key to the wisdom of Uganda'.[84]

After this we went to the Parliament Hall at Kampala, which Mr. G. Wilson had built of brick, and which was a very fine building.[85] In the courtyard we saw Mr. Deane and the Soudanese and Baganda soldiers, who played a salute when we arrived, and when we entered the hall all who were in it stood up to give the Katikiro honour. We then sat down on our chairs, both together, so that we could remind one another about what we had seen. The King and chiefs and a great many Europeans were there. Mr. Wilson was the representative of the Commissioner, who was away visiting Unyoro, and read us a speech congratulating us on the completion of our journey, and thanking those to whom the Katikiro had entrusted his work, and saying that he hoped now that the Katikiro had seen England and English ways, he would work at getting Uganda into order. All this was said in English, and Archdeacon Walker turned it into Luganda.

After this the Katikiro related some of his experiences in England, which made the Europeans laugh very much; Archdeacon Walker translated his speech into English for the Government officials who did not know Luganda.

The Katikiro told them a great many things: how the ladies dressed, and how they greeted one another, and how they gave feasts to us, and what the houses and roads were like, and what vast numbers of people there were, and how the men dressed very well, and how kind they were, and how kind the King was, and what his palace was like; what the trains and the carriages were like, and what large ships they had, and how large the sea was, and what the waves were like, and how large the English cities were, and many other things which I have not written down. After this the session was over, and the King went away, and so did all the Europeans, very pleased with what they had heard about their country.

All the time from September 17th to October 31st we had no rest by day or night; some people went to the Katikiro, others came to me, all wanting very much to hear all about England; and I showed them the things we had

---

[84] The notion of wisdom, clearly the basis of Sir Apolo's political and moral authority in Buganda, has at least two meanings or connotations: first, Sir Apolo is considered wise because of his mastery of writing which makes him a mediator of colonial relationships (between the natives and the British); second, he is wise – in a biblical sense – because of his judiciousness.

[85] Both the colonial government and Bugandan Christians were determined to reproduce British institutions in the colonised space and parliament was one of them; in praising the building, instead of the political institution, Mukasa is unwittingly calling attention to the lack of representative government in the Protectorate.

got from the various factories of all kinds, and showed them too the photographs which had been taken of us while we were in England, and the pictures of the King's coronation – a great many of these had been printed and sent all over the world, that all might understand how it went off.

On October 14th Colonel Sadler, the Commissioner, came back, and we all went to see him – Apolo Katikiro, Mr. Millar, and I, Ham Mukasa – and we told him about England, and he was very pleased, and told us about what he had heard in our absence.

Well, my friends, you should read this book very carefully and attentively, that you may understand what other and wiser lands are like; and though we call these lands wise, you should remember that wisdom does not come to a lazy and weak man, but to one who works hard and thinks daily about his work.[86] Thought and perseverance thus increase a man's wisdom every year and every month. 'He who goes slowly goes far'; 'a crackling sound is not a fire', and a great city is not built in one year. Let us then go ahead slowly and surely; perhaps our grandchildren will be much wiser than we are, but we should encourage our children daily to learn all they can, that they may teach their children after we have gone, and so they may go on increasing in wisdom both in the mind and in handicrafts.

Well, this is the story of the journey of Apolo Katikiro, Ham Mukasa, and the Rev. Ernest Millar.

---

[86] 'Wisdom' is used here, in a biblical sense, as a synonym for enlightenment, but it is worth considering how certain values of Englishness – notably hard work – are represented as the enabling conditions for the knowledge that makes a culture whole.

Glossary

Baganda	The people of the kingdom of Buganda
Buganda	The name of a kingdom in East Africa on the shores of Lake Victoria
Kabaka	The monarch or king of Buganda
Katikiro	The chief (prime) minister of Buganda
Luganda	The language of the Baganda people
Mengo	The Royal Capital of Buganda
Uganda	The Protectorate established by the British colonial government in 1900 including the kingdom of Buganda; also the name of the postcolonial state that succeeded the Protectorate

Bibliography

Abeele, Georges Van Den (1992) *Travel as Metaphor: From Montaigne to Rousseau*, University of Minnesota Press: Minneapolis

Adorno, Rolena (1996) 'Cultures in Contact: Mesoamerica, the Andes, and the European Written Tradition', *The Cambridge History of Latin American Literature*, ed. Roberto Gonzalez Echevarria and Enrique Pupo-Walker, Cambridge University Press: Cambridge

Bhabha, Homi (1994) *The Location of Culture*, Routledge: New York and London

Burton, Richard Francis (1860) *The Lake Regions of Central Africa: A Picture of Exploration*, Longman: London

Chambers, Ross (1991) *Room for Maneuver: Reading Oppositional Narrative*, University of Chicago Press: Chicago

Certeau, Michel de (1984) *The Practice of Everyday Life*, University of California Press: Berkeley

Dawson, Graham (1994) *Soldier Heroes: British Adventure, Empire, and the Imagining of Masculinities*, Routledge: New York and London

Deleuze, Gilles and Felix Guattari (1986) *Kafka: Toward a Minor Literature*, University of Minnesota Press: Minneapolis

Dirks, Nicholas B. (1992) 'Introduction: Colonialism and Culture', *Colonialism and Culture*, ed. Nicholas B. Dirks, University of Michigan Press: Ann Arbor, MI

Gikandi, Simon (1996) *Maps of Englishness: Writing Identity in the Culture of Colonialism*, Columbia University Press: New York

Greenblatt, Stephen (1991) *Marvelous Possessions: The Wonder of the New World*, University of Chicago Press: Chicago

Guha, Ranajit and Gayatri Chakravorty Spivak (1988) *Selected Subaltern Studies*, Oxford University Press: Oxford

Kiwanuka, M. S. M. (1971) *A History of Buganda: From the Foundation of the Kingdom to 1900*, Longman: London

Lo Liyong, Taban (1975) 'Introduction', Ham Mukasa, *Sir Apolo Kagwa Discovers Britain*, Heinemann: London

Low, D. A., ed. (1971) *The Mind of Buganda: Documents of the Modern History of an African Kingdom*, Heinemann: London

Lowe, Lisa (1991) *Critical Terrains: French and British Orientalisms*, Cornell University Press: Ithaca, NY

Melman, Billie (1992) *Women's Orients: English Women and the Middle East, 1718–1918: Sexuality, Religion and Work*, University of Michigan Press: Ann Arbor, MI

Mills, Sara (1991) *Discourses of Difference: An Analysis of Women's Travel Writing and Colonialism*, Routledge: London and New York

Mills, Sara (1994) 'Knowledge, Gender, and Empire', *Writing Women and Space: Colonial and Postcolonial Geographies*, Guilford: New York

Mudimbe, V. Y. (1988) *The Invention of Africa*, Indiana University Press: Bloomington

Mukasa, Ham (1904) *Uganda's Katikiro in England: Being the Official Account of His Visit to the Coronation of His Majesty King Edward VII*, Hutchinson: London

Phillips, Richard (1997) *Mapping Men and Empire: A Geography of Adventure*, Routledge: London and New York

Pirouet, Louise (1995) *Historical Dictionary of Uganda*, Scarecrow Press: Metuchen, NJ

Pratt, Mary Louise (1992) *Travel Writing and Transculturation*, Routledge: London and New York

Rafael, Vincente L. (1993) *Contracting Colonialism: Translation and Christian Conversion in Tagalog Society Under Early Spanish Rule*, Duke University Press: Durham, NC

Ranger, Terence (1983) *The Invention of Tradition*, ed. Eric Hobsbawn and Terence Ranger, Cambridge University Press: Cambridge

Ray, Benjamin C. (1991) *Myth, Ritual, and Kingship in Buganda*, Oxford University Press: New York and Oxford

Richards, David (1994) *Masks of Difference: Cultural Representations in Literature, Anthropology and Art*, Cambridge University Press: Cambridge and New York

Roberts, Andrew (1990) *The Colonial Moment in Africa: Essays on the Movements of Mind and Materials, 1900–1940*, Cambridge University Press: Cambridge

Roscoe, John (1911) *The Baganda: An Account of their Native Customs and Beliefs*, Macmillan: London

Sinha, Mrinalini (1995) *Colonial Masculinity: The 'Manly Englishman' and the 'Effiminate Bengali' in the Late Nineteenth Century*, Manchester University Press: Manchester

Speke, John Hanning (1864) *Journal of the Discovery of the Source of the Nile*, second edition, Blackwood and Sons: Edinburgh

Standard Swahili–English Dictionary (1939) Inter-Territorial Language Committee, Oxford University Press: Oxford

Stanley, Henry M. (1890) *In Darkest Africa,* Scribner's Sons: New York

Twaddle, Michael (1993) *Kakungulu and the Creation of Uganda, 1868– 1928,* Ohio University Press: Athens, OH

Wrigley, Christopher (1996) *Kinship and State: The Buganda Dynasty,* Cambridge University Press: Cambridge

Youngs, Tim (1994) *Travellers in Africa: British Travelogues, 1850–1900,* Manchester University Press: Manchester

Index